Praise for *Catalysts for Change*

"*Catalysts for Change* is for everyone who cares about making a difference, and about effective ways to bring about long-term, sustainable positive change."

– Jeffrey Hollender, co-founder and former CEO,
Seventh Generation (from the Preface)

"This book is filled with inspiring gems. It tells true stories of transformative change in Vermont — the kind of thing that can happen when strategic philanthropy meets good people with vision and a willingness to roll up their sleeves. (If today's news has you down, this book is for you!)"

– Paul Burns, Executive Director,
Vermont Public Interest Research Group

"The intelligence and courage with which these organizations confront complex and weighty problems is an antidote to despair. Through hands-on engagement, the activist Lintilhac Foundation builds authentic, long-term relationships with Vermont nonprofits to drive change forward — and this inspiring book testifies to the power of their approach."

– Barbara Floersch, author of *You Have a Hammer:
Building Grant Proposals for Social Change*

"What a delight to read a book ostensibly about foundation giving and discover it is about all aspects of Vermont's recent history: full of inspirational stories about people with vision and passion to create a better world, about the evolution of health care, conservation, cultural institutions, environmental work and education, along with a broad understanding of the way work gets done in this special place. This is a wonderfully readable book that reflects on the philanthropic imagination of the Lintilhac family and should serve as a road map for others who are motivated toward positive change."

– Christine Graham, consultant to nonprofits

"*Catalysts for Change* is a compelling tale of civic leadership and the important role that philanthropies and nonprofits can play in giving citizens a stronger voice. An engaging writer, Wilhelm tells the remarkable stories of how Vermont became a national leader in maternal care, clean energy and online journalism, tackled the challenges of Lake Champlain cleanup, and protected its working landscape."

> – George Hamilton, co-founder and former President,
> Institute for Sustainable Communities

"The great theme of *Catalysts for Change* is health — health of the individual, of the environment and of the democracy. Doug Wilhelm's book ranges over the wide landscape of good works promoted by an active and engaged foundation, which channels its resources toward dedicated people working on everything from maternal health to water quality to independent journalism. It's heartening to see so many people doing so much good and to gain an insight into the mechanisms of philanthropy that help it happen."

> – David Moats, author of *Civil Wars* and winner of
> the Pulitzer Prize for editorial writing

"*Catalysts for Change* is a deeply compelling history of the Lintilhac family's three generations of philanthropy. It begins with the story of Claire Malcolm Lintilhac, born to a Canadian medical missionary in China. Claire's empathy and vision become the guidestar for her son Phil, his wife Crea, and, later, their three children, Paul, Will and Louise, as they support and invest in midwives, mothers, newborns, gender equity, independent journalism, renewable energy, and the air, soil, and waterways on which our lives depend. This extraordinary story charts a path for philanthropy that enhances humanity."

> – Bill Schubart, author of *The Lamoille Stories* and other books

"A great history of Vermont pioneers and innovators connecting the dots and working effectively for a sustainable future based on renewable electricity. We are in a time of dramatic change and this book inspires us to do the hard work required."

> – David Blittersdorf, founder of NRG Systems and CEO,
> AllEarth Renewables

Catalysts
for Change

How Nonprofits and a Foundation
Are Helping Shape Vermont's Future

Catalysts
for Change

How Nonprofits and a Foundation
Are Helping Shape Vermont's Future

Doug Wilhelm

Preface by Jeffrey Hollender
Co-founder, Seventh Generation

Introduction by Crea Lintilhac
Executive Director, the Lintilhac Foundation

Rootstock Publishing

Montpelier, VT

Hardcover ISBN: 978-1-57869-082-4
Paperback ISBN: 978-1-57869-063-3
eBook ISBN: 978-1-57869-083-1
Library of Congress Control Number: 2021918618

Published by Rootstock Publishing
www.rootstockpublishing.com
An imprint of Multicultural Media, Inc.
info@rootstockpublishing.com

Cover design by Mason Singer, Laughing Bear Associates
Book design by Kimberley Quinlan, KO Designs
Cover: Photo illustration, Shelburne, Vermont, vermontalm/Shutterstock

Printed in the USA

This book is dedicated to all the people, past and present,
who have worked so hard for nonprofit organizations,
to make Vermont's democratic engagement stronger and
the state a healthier, kinder, more sustainable place.

Top left: Xander Landen of *VTDigger*, left, at the State House with Attorney General T.J. Donovan. Top right: helping to build the Philadelphia II, a replica Revolutionary War gunboat, at the Lake Champlain Maritime Museum. Above: staff members and volunteers with the Vermont Public Interest Research Group make calls before the Vermont State Senate voted not to renew the operating license of the Vermont Yankee nuclear power plant in February 2010.

Contents

———— ⁄ ————

Preface

by Jeffrey Hollender

Co-founder and former CEO, Seventh Generation
Co-founder and CEO, American Sustainable Business Council

———— ⸜⸝ ————

When we moved to Vermont from New York City in 1992, our first acquaintances were the Lintilhac family. Their three children, Louise, Will and Paul, mirrored our own Meika, Alex and Chiara. We ate together, skied together and generally romped across this beautiful and special state. Today they remain at the center of our community and our closest and dearest friends. Despite the pandemic, you might find us huddled outside in near zero weather sharing a meal or a drink, undeterred by the climate, which in Vermont has yet to get balmy with the changes brought by global warming.

As co-founder and the former CEO of Seventh Generation, a 30-year-old Vermont company committed to using business as a force for social and environmental good, I share many of the same aspirations as the Lintilhac Foundation, and recognize the critical role that their community-oriented foundation plays as a partner in ensuring a healthy future for the state.

We have been privileged to have ringside seats to watch the amazing work of the Lintilhac Foundation's vision for the future of Vermont unfold. For all who love Vermont, this book is an essential read.

Catalysts for Change is also for everyone who cares about making a difference, and about effective ways to bring about long-term, sustainable positive change. Each chapter tells the story of how, on a complex and challenging issue, Vermonters at dedicated nonprofit organizations have worked with this activist, engaged funder to achieve real and lasting progress — in health care, informed public discourse, environmental science, water quality and clean energy.

Finally, this is a brilliant working model for the world of community-based philanthropy. Around the country today, foundations that operate close to their communities are searching for ways to play a more engaged role, to work in partnership with organizations and change-makers rather than simply issuing grants. The Lintilhac Foundation has been doing just this, in its own pioneering way, for almost half a century.

Change is never easy. It requires vision, patience, deep commitment and endless innovation. The challenges we face are both relentless and stress our human and natural systems. The Lintilhac Foundation has truly changed the arc of history by aligning precious funding with activist intervention. I'm not quite sure where the state would be without them.

We're so very lucky to have the Lintilhacs in Vermont. Their story provides inspiration and valuable lessons for community foundations and activists across the nation, to follow in their footsteps to make the world a better, healthier and more just place.

Introduction

by Crea Lintilhac

———— ⚡ ————

The Lintilhac Foundation has been operating in Vermont for many years, and it is our hope that this book can highlight the valued relationships we've developed with the nonprofit organizations that have been our grantees. In *Catalysts for Change* we tell stories of the expertise, strategic accomplishments, persistence and dedication of these organizations, which have worked to ensure access to health and welfare for all Vermonters.

As executive director of the foundation, I have worked in a realm where I personally know the advocates, legislators, businesses, state agency staff and politics. As we move into a new generation of family leadership, our trustees will continue to work knowing that what we do here in collaboration with Vermont nonprofits can resonate across the country. Our grantees are key drivers in defending clean water, promoting renewable energy alternatives to fossil fuels and nuclear power, improving maternal and child health, protecting land for people and wildlife, and keeping local news alive.

In this work, we're all trying to understand the underlying risks and the downstream effects of the behaviors that we believe should guide environmental and other public policies. Our priorities include expanding the networks for businesses, organizations and individuals involved in Vermont's media landscape and in our state's renewable energy and clean water economies. It's this network of collaboration that we feel requires the foundation's trustees to join nonprofit boards of directors, attend legislative committee meetings at the State House, and generally be active members of the Vermont community.

This firsthand experience has opened our eyes to the work and concerns of our grantees and their staff members. In meetings, we hear their debates. In arranging field trips, our trustees acquire a broader view of the challenges we face in the protection and restoration of land, water and wildlife. We are firmly committed to protecting and promoting public access to nature.

While change may originate in the field, in the lab or on the State House floor, we have come to believe that public awareness of local issues is a major part of building strong and informed communities. That is why the foundation has supported nonpartisan investigative reporting at a time when the culture and economics of the internet challenge both practices. The gradual disappearance of local news outlets is the most troubling media story of our time, and a slow-moving disaster for our democracy.

Litigation has also played an important role in our philanthropy, especially in our environmental work, and it can be unpleasant, expensive and time-consuming. Getting a regulation enacted or winning a lawsuit does not ensure that the outcomes will be implemented. It's important that we work closely with the environmental nonprofit groups the foundation supports. They play an important role, not just in shaping policies but in ensuring their implementation. Among the nonprofits we also support are the news sources that inform the public about potentially harmful decisions and activities in their own communities, and the conservancies committed to protect Vermont's ecosystems.

There's another factor that comes into play with environmental nonprofits and university academics. Vermont has one of the smallest legislative staffs in the country. Within the State House, legislative counsel and the Joint Fiscal Office provide legal drafting support and financial research services for the Legislature. However, without a large staff, lawmakers must often rely on the nonprofit sector to help them with the policy research needed to construct verifiable, evidence-based policy as they address, for instance, environmental concerns with water quality, energy and land conservation.

I have been asked, "What have you learned in your years at the helm of the Lintilhac Foundation?" What leaps to mind is the importance of showing up to the State House, where meetings are sometimes tedious but it's always important to show interest, to learn about the issues while listening to testimony in committees and having lunch in the cafeteria with lobbyists and legislators. This has been important whether following the mission of the foundation or getting exposure to other issues of public interest.

One specific encounter was with Beth Robinson in the State House cafeteria. Beth, who is now Judge Robinson on the Vermont Supreme court, was lobbying everyone she could before an important vote on same-sex marriage. She wanted to sit with me for a moment to explain how the arguments against gay marriage mirrored, literally mirrored, the arguments against interracial marriage in the Loving v. Virginia case of 1967.

She had an ability to move the issue with one of the most convincing arguments I had encountered. That was fuel for moving forward with convincing arguments for legislators, and for the public and the governor, to pass the legislation that created civil unions in 2000, and later same sex marriage in 2009, without being required to do so by a court decision.

When my mother-in-law, Claire Lintilhac, created the foundation in 1975, her goal was to create and support nurse-midwifery at what is now the University of Vermont Medical Center. That program, now 45 years old, continues to promote perinatal and birthing care in Vermont. For us, this priority area of concern has grown to include funding for women's mental and emotional health before and after childbirth, and for a support network and resource base that will help to prevent and address family mental health issues in the future.

Shortly after Claire died in 1984, my husband Phil and I proposed that the foundation should be administered as a family enterprise. We have worked together over the ensuing years to run the foundation out of a home office, with myself acting as executive director and with the invaluable help of our long-time administrative assistant Nancy Brink.

In an earlier life I was a working scientist. As a graduate student at the University of Vermont, I worked with Allen Hunt in the 1970s on the research vessel Melosira I. We cored the sediments of Lake Champlain, and I had the job of identifying one-celled fossils called foraminifera that once lived in a marine environment. This process allowed Dr. Hunt and his students to map the extent of the prehistoric Champlain Sea. The experience was the beginning of my life-long interest in water quality and lake studies. I went on to work in oceanography for Sandia National Laboratories, in a position funded by the U.S. Department of Energy. My role was to find the most quiescent, stable areas of the Pacific Ocean floor that might be suitable for the disposal of high-level radioactive waste. Participating in that research project was my introduction to the nuclear industry and energy policy in general.

I am a proponent of renewable energy and carbon pricing. My work experience helped give me the confidence I needed as the foundation's focus moved into the energy sector. My longtime participation on the Board of Directors of the Vermont Public Interest Research Group has introduced me to legislative committee work on energy issues, and has educated me in the shaping of policy through dedicated advocacy work.

One of my greatest pleasures in working with the foundation through these many years has been the relationships we have built with many of the environmental groups in Vermont, and with the faculty, staff and boards of advisors at the University of Vermont's Rubenstein School and Geology Department, the Lake Champlain Sea Grant, and the Water Resources and Lake Studies Center. We have a long-standing appreciation also for Pat and Tom Manley, faculty members at Middlebury College who have engineered important advances in the body of knowledge of Lake Champlain, including a first-time comprehensive mapping of the lake floor that revealed new information about sediment, hydrodynamics and how material travels throughout the lake. Another great pleasure has been holding events at our home to build the social capital needed for environmental nonprofits, many of whose staff spend endless days in committee rooms at the State House to influence and support legislators and effect change.

One of the attributes of being a woman in philanthropy has been the sensitivity to women's tendency to be uncomfortable with leadership and power, and a continual refrain of "I don't know enough" to launch into one or another project outside of a comfort zone. I remember Hub Vogelmann, a UVM botanist and conservation leader whose pioneering research focused the nation's attention on the threat of acid rain, telling me about a friend of his who ran one of the largest conservation organizations in the country and had conserved more land than anyone else he knew. "And this guy," Hub said, "couldn't tell the difference between a squirrel and a chipmunk!" But he had skill sets that included good communication and negotiating expertise.

From Hub I learned that it is important to push forward to see the world in a new way, even when it becomes difficult and confusing and takes far longer than is comfortable. Gradually, with persistence and steadfast attention, we have seen our grantees achieve significant results in combating environmental degradation, fighting the loss of local news outlets, and strengthening our nurse-midwifery programs to improve maternal and infant health outcomes. Together, these organizations represent the patient, steady work and sustained focus that is required for genuine, long-lasting progress.

The Vermont State House. *Photo by Tim Newcomb.*

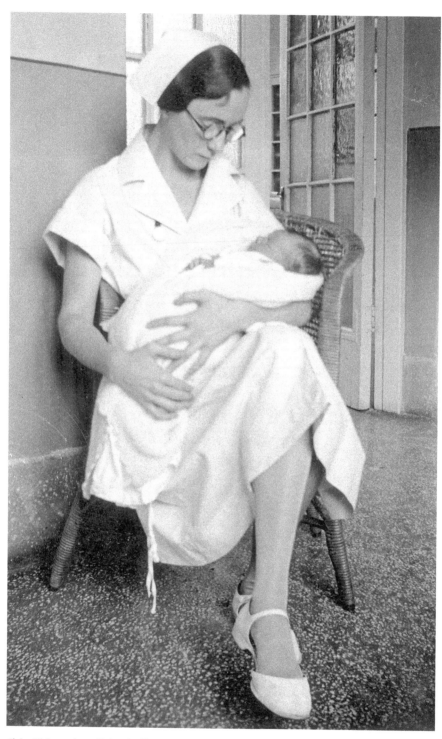

Claire Malcom, later Claire Lintilhac, discovered her passion for maternity care as a nurse in China during the 1920s and early '30s.

1

Claire, the First Catalyst

A former nurse in China helps to change maternity care in Vermont

———— ⚘ ————

Claire Malcolm was 22 years old in spring 1922, fresh from her nurse's training at the British Municipal Hospital in Shanghai, China, when she had an experience that she would remember in vivid detail for the rest of her life.

Claire had been born in Hsinchen, a small mission station in the interior of Henan province in North China, on December 20, 1899. Her father, William Malcolm, was a Canadian medical missionary who spent nearly all his career in China. Claire was the second of the four children that Dr. Malcolm and his wife, Eliza Pringle Malcolm, raised there.

Dr. Malcolm was a strong influence on his daughter. Learning to speak Chinese as he did, Claire grew up observing her father's medical work. She absorbed his commitment to the Chinese people, and as a teenager she occasionally helped out in the clinics he ran at various postings in the country's interior, and in ports along the coast of the East China Sea.

Claire began her nursing education in 1918, at "the end of the First World War and the tail end of the Victorian Era in England," as she later wrote. When she had completed her training at the close of 1921, she came home to Chefoo (now called Yantai in English), a port city in North China where her father had served as community medical officer since the outbreak of World War I.

Claire was energetic and sociable, friendly and compassionate — and, for her day, quite independent-minded. Freed from the rigid routines of her Shanghai training, she plunged into the social life of the international community in Chefoo, where U.S. Navy destroyers were often stationed in the years between the world wars.

One night in that spring of 1922, her nursing career began in a way she had not expected. As Claire later wrote the story:

> I think it was sometime in March. I had come in late from a party and was beginning to undress when I heard a man's voice calling me from downstairs outside my window.
>
> I opened the louvres of the shutters just enough to peek through. In the circle of light cast by a lantern, I could make out a pair of feet. When I asked who was calling, the voice said he was the man from the coal yard down by the jetty. He went on to explain that his wife was in labor and was in trouble, and would I please come quickly.
>
> Coming down to earth with a thud, I asked the man to wait a minute. I didn't own so much as a pair of scissors, much less equipment to cope with some complicated delivery. I decided that I had better ask my father. Tiptoeing into his room, I apologetically wakened him. Explaining the circumstances, I asked him what I should do.
>
> "Go," he said.
>
> "But I don't have anything to work with," I pleaded.
>
> Practical as always, Father told me where I could find the few things I might need down in his office. But he cautioned me not to bite off more than I could chew, adding that if I needed any help, I had better send for him. I knew he had enough to do, though, caring for his regular practice and all the ships that came in.
>
> I went back to my room and, calling to the man to wait, I got out of my party dress and into something more practical. I went down to Father's office and collected what I needed — then I went out into the night.
>
> I could see only a bare outline of the man and his bulkily clad feet. I followed him down the narrow, steep path that led from our garden, a shortcut to the jetty. All I could see in the lantern's dim light was a pair of receding heels. Down, down we went and along the waterfront. Finally we arrived at a gate in the high brick wall that enclosed the coal yard. At the far end of the yard was a little hut.
>
> In the dim light of a little oil lamp, I could make out three little children standing quietly by, and I heard the cry of a newborn baby. The mother was moaning. She said the pains had got worse just after her husband left. Suddenly the baby's head had come down, but not the body. With one desperate effort, she had managed to deliver the baby herself.
>
> Urging the mother to relax and rest a little, I examined the baby. I found that in her frantic effort to deliver the baby, the mother, in

clutching at the head, had gouged out its eyes.

Withholding comment for the moment, I prepared to deliver the afterbirth. First tying off the cord, I started to cut it with my sterile scissors. But the husband, holding back my hand, picked up a rice bowl and cracked it on the edge of the *k'ang*, or brick bed. He handed me one of the broken pieces, the sharp edge of which he asked me to use to cut the cord, explaining that it was bad luck to use scissors.

Chinese people knew from experience that to cut a cord with scissors was indeed "bad luck" — but they didn't know that the bad luck came from dirty scissors. I realized that under the circumstances, it was as well to do as the husband asked. If I used my scissors and if the baby died, I knew my scissors would be blamed.

After getting the mother settled, I examined the baby again, then handed her to the father. He looked at her closely.

"Do you think she will live?" he asked.

I told him that if he took her to the mission hospital up on Temple Hill on the far side of the city, then maybe, *maybe* they could save the baby's life.

"Can they save the baby's eyes?" he asked.

"Nobody can save the baby's eyes," I said. He nodded.

After a moment, the father said calmly that it was out of the question for him to leave his wife and children for the doubtful advantage of having a blind baby live. He handed the little bundle to the mother.

I came down frequently to visit her. She recovered well, but the baby lived only a few days. There would be more babies. The mother knew, and I knew too, that for a blind baby in such a poor home, life would have been grim indeed.

When Claire wrote that account more than five decades later, in her late seventies, she recalled everything about that tragic night. All her life after that experience she was passionately devoted to the cause of women's health — especially to her conviction that every pregnant woman deserves expert, safe, caring assistance, and that she should have that help during her pregnancy, while she gives birth, and in the weeks that follow.

From 1922 until the early 1930s, Claire gave her considerable energies to working as a private-duty nurse traveling up and down the Chinese coast. She was the only Western nurse providing that service among the international settlements of the treaty ports, where her patients were primarily British, American, European and Japanese residents and their families. She also helped Chinese people in need whenever she could:

In my spare time I had many calls on my modest efforts to help, but often conditions were so extreme that it was too late to do much. Even so, I did what I could for rickshaw drivers, servants and their families, and for friends who had no one else to turn to for any kind of help.

But my full-time nursing was, of course, among Westerners. In the summers I was kept busy right in Chefoo, looking after the families of American naval officers. In the winters I would be called to small ports along the China coast, where there were never any other nurses, and on occasion no hospital or doctor.

Whenever I was called on a case, it was to a very sick patient. I was never needed for convalescent nursing, for there was no shortage of help in the homes. At the same time, there was never another nurse to share the work with me, with the result that once on a case I could never leave my patient.

During those busy years Claire deepened her passion for maternity care. "My first choice of nursing had always been maternity," she wrote in her memoir, published posthumously as *China in Another Time: A Personal Story* (Rootstock Publishing, 2019).

In 1932 she accepted a full-time position at a maternity hospital at the Wellington Nursing Home, a birthing center within the British settlement in Tientsin, now Tianjin, on the northern coast. "I doubt if any nurse anywhere has ever been happier than I was for the next four years," Claire said.

That job ended in 1936, along with her active nursing career, when Claire married Francis "Lin" Lintilhac, a British businessman in Shanghai. Lin's father and grandfather, French in family origin, had spent their careers as silk traders in China; Lin was an executive with Imperial Chemical Industries (ICI), a firm founded in 1926 that for many years was Britain's largest manufacturer.

In March 1940, having moved to Shanghai and taken over the complex running of Lin's household, Claire delivered Philip, her only child. By then Shanghai was occupied by the Japanese. Early in March 1941, when Philip was a year old, "the British Consulate suddenly announced that all women and children were to be evacuated as soon as possible," Claire recalled.

From her Chinese cook she quickly learned how to prepare a few simple dishes, before Claire and Philip traveled to the United States on the Yawata Maru, a Japanese ocean liner. Claire noticed, on board, that the ship's decks seemed unusually broad. After Japan's December 7, 1941 attack on Pearl Harbor, she read in the *New York Times* that the Yawata Maru had been quickly converted into an aircraft carrier, the purpose for which it had really been built.

A devastating loss, and a new community

Claire and Philip spent the war years in a home in Brewster, New York that was owned by her younger sister Mary and Cornelius Vander Starr, Mary's husband. "Neil" Starr was an American entrepreneur who had built a fast-growing insurance business in China. Lin stayed on in Shanghai, and for the rest of the war years he and his father were interned by the Japanese in a camp for noncombatants. (After he was released, Lin confessed to his wife that he had secretly been working as a British intelligence agent, which the Japanese never discovered.)

Claire, Lin and Philip returned after the war to their home in Shanghai. Lin went back to working for ICI, while China's Nationalist and Communist parties struggled violently for control of their nation. Claire and Lin witnessed firsthand Shanghai's largely peaceful takeover by Communist troops in 1949. When it became clear that foreign-owned businesses would no longer be welcome in Communist China, in 1950 the Lintilhacs slipped out of the country, on a freighter sailing from Tientsin to Hong Kong.

The family settled in New York City, and Lin took a new job with Neil Starr's firm, American International Underwriters (AIU), which had moved its headquarters there from Shanghai. Lin's experience and expertise were valuable as the company expanded into Japan, Hong Kong, the Philippines and Singapore, along with other parts of the world.

Claire sometimes accompanied Lin on his travels through Asia. On vacations and holidays the family also spent time in Stowe, Vermont, a ski town where, in 1949, AIU had purchased the Stowe Mountain Resort.

In September 1957, Lin, then 49 years old, entered a New York City medical center for hip replacement surgery. The operation went well, but three weeks later, still in the hospital in the very early morning of October 16, Lin had a a blood clot in his lung, a pulmonary thrombosis. He died before a nurse could reach his room.

Devastated by Lin's passing, Claire and Philip decided they would rather

Francis "Lin" Lintilhac and Phil in North China, in late 1946.

live in Vermont than in Manhattan, and in June 1958 they moved to Stowe. Although her means were now relatively limited, Claire did have a number of shares in AIU that Lin had left her. Over the coming years, as she got involved in the Stowe community and made many deep friendships in Vermont, AIU grew into a giant corporation with agents and offices in more than 75 countries. In 1967, it was reorganized as the American International Group (AIG), for years the largest insurance firm in the world.

As Claire's AIG holdings exploded in value, she began to make private donations to a project that engaged her passion: helping to bring hospital-based nurse-midwifery into the U.S. system of health care.

"Midwives ... treat childbearing as a normal process"

D uring the early decades of the 20th century, midwifery as a profession moved in opposite directions in the United Kingdom and the United States. In the U.K. it became central to maternity care, while in the U.S. it was almost wiped out.

"By 1900, midwives were attending about three-fourths of all births in England," wrote Judith Pence Rooks in her book *Midwifery and Childbirth in America* (Temple University Press, 1997). England's first Midwives Act, approved in 1902 despite strong physician opposition, created a board that regulated midwifery and required that providers be licensed. By 1970, nearly all births in England had a midwife in attendance. That year, more than 18,000 midwives, 80 percent of whom were also nurses, were practicing in England and Wales.

But in this country, a determined campaign by top obstetricians and other physicians pushed midwifery to the extreme margins. When the 20th century began, most American births still took place in the mother's home — and doctors often blamed midwives, who at that time tended to lack formal training and mostly worked in poor, immigrant and minority communities, for the nation's high rates of infant and maternal mortality.

During the so-called midwifery debate from 1910 to 1935, leaders in U.S. obstetrics called for midwifery to be abolished. They argued, Rooks wrote, "that pregnancy is a dangerous condition requiring complicated care available only from highly trained specialists." From 1900 to 1935, the portion of U.S. births attended by midwives fell from about 50 percent to 12.5 percent.

But in those same years, maternal deaths in childbirth rose dramatically. The numbers began to decline only after antibiotics became available in the mid-1930s. In other industrialized countries where antibiotics came into wide use, similar declines in maternal mortality also occurred — no matter whether babies were delivered by midwives, general practitioners or obstetricians.

In the 1950s, American public opinion around childbirth began, slowly but gradually, to change. A pioneering book by an English obstetrician, *Childbirth Without Fear: The Principles and Practices of Natural Childbirth*, published in the U.S. in 1944, sparked the first stirrings of interest in childbirth without medical intervention. In 1956, seven Chicago-area women founded the International La Leche League to promote breast feeding, which then was often discouraged by doctors.

In her 1959 book *Thank You, Dr. Lamaze*, a young mother from New York named Marjorie Karmel described how she had given birth without pain by working with the French obstetrician Ferdinand Lamaze, who taught breathing, relaxation and movement techniques. Karmel's book became widely read and brought new energy to what, by the early 1960s, was starting to become a natural childbirth movement.

Already in the early 20th century there had been indications that nurse-midwives — professionals who were trained, certified and regulated in a system similar to England's — could play an important role in American mainstream maternity care. In rural Leslie County, Kentucky, the country's first health-care service that employed nurse-midwives was created in 1925 as the Frontier Nursing Service, and that county quickly saw a steep drop in its once-high rate of maternal and infant deaths.

In 1931, the country's first nurse-midwifery school opened in New York City, and was soon followed by four more. But those schools all focused on training nurse-midwives to work on the margins, in areas where poverty, isolation and other barriers cut many pregnant women off from access to physician care.

In the U.S. mainstream, by midcentury the delivery of babies had become a largely mechanized process. In 1960, almost all U.S. mothers were delivering in a hospital. Almost all obstetricians were male, forceps were often used in delivery, and women were routinely anesthetized and wheeled into delivery rooms, to wake up later with no memory of the birth. Wrote Rooks, in *Midwifery and Childbirth in America*:

> The main focus of medical education, training, knowledge, skills and role is pathology — the diagnosis and treatment of disease and trauma. ... Focusing on pathology leads to certain perceptions: Women's bodies are very imperfect at giving birth; medicine can and should improve on nature.
>
> In contrast to medicine, the midwife's education, training, knowledge, skills and role focus on protecting, supporting and enhancing *normal* childbearing and family formation. Midwives ... understand that there are risks and constantly observe for signs of abnormality, but treat childbearing as a normal physiological process that has profound meaning for many people.

By 1963, only 535 nurse-midwives were working in the U.S., but there were pressures for change. Opening a 1968 national conference on midwifery, an official of the U.S. Department of Health, Education and Welfare (later renamed the Department of Health and Human Services) noted that even though this country had invested hugely in maternal and child health programs, the infant mortality rate in the U.S. was double that of Sweden.

Medicaid became U.S. law in 1965, greatly increasing access to health care among low-income Americans. But, noted Rooks, "Neither the federal government nor the states were willing to pay enough to attract large numbers of obstetricians to participate in Medicaid." There was a growing need for professional providers who could reliably, competently fill that gap.

At the same time across the country, obstetricians often found themselves stretched thin as they sought to meet their pregnant patients' changing needs and desires. More and more mothers-to-be were asking for prenatal education, emotional support and alternative approaches to delivery — all areas in which obstetricians tended to have no training, little or no experience, and often little interest.

Into this situation stepped a Vermont obstetrician with an idea.

John Van Sicklen Maeck was the highly regarded chair of the Department of Obstetrics and Gynecology at both the University of Vermont (UVM) College of Medicine, in Burlington, and the adjacent Medical Center Hospital of Vermont. He believed that if nurse-midwives could be accepted as part of the hospital's team for prenatal care and delivery, they could supply what both pregnant women and their obstetricians needed.

Dr. Maeck had found a close ally and supporter for his idea in a patient who had become a friend — a Stowe resident named Claire Lintilhac.

"The leadership power and the passion"

I remember John said one day that he was going up to Stowe at the end of the day to see this very nice lady who said she wanted to talk to him. She was persistent, and he said, 'All right,'" recalled Doris Maeck, Dr. Maeck's widow, in a 1994 interview. "He was just thrilled with her, and immediately they became friends. I remember he said, 'Oh, you'll love her. She's little and feisty and knows what she wants.'"

Dr. Maeck knew what he wanted, too. He and Claire seem to have met in about 1968, when she went to see him for gynecological care. They found they shared a strong interest in introducing nurse-midwives into U.S. hospitals, and they quickly became a team in creating and funding one of the nation's first hospital-based nurse-midwifery programs. That program, at the Burlington medical center, soon grew into a state and national model.

"The object," Claire wrote, "was to demonstrate the need for the nurse-midwife: a service by qualified, technically trained women in the care of expectant mothers before, during and after delivery. An area of care in which the service of a woman is uniquely appropriate."

"What Claire and John did was revolutionary," recalled Kathy Keleher, a certified nurse-midwife (CNM) who joined the nurse-midwifery service in 1979 and served as its director from 1985 to 1995. "John had the leadership power, and Claire had the passion. I always thought of it as yin and yang — they brought together the assets that they needed. From 1968 to the mid-70s, what they really accomplished was laying down the infrastructure, the foundation to make this service successful."

Dr. Maeck had long been interested in both midwifery and nurse practitioners. In 1968, he and his wife were traveling to Sri Lanka so he could do some work with the hospital ship SS Hope. On the way they stopped in London, where through a physician friend Dr. Maeck arranged to meet with Marjorie Bayes, executive secretary of the London-based International Confederation of Midwives.

The year before, Bayes had attended a conference in the United States at which she presented a paper on the training and responsibilities of the British midwife. In London, she and Dr. Maeck had lunch at the headquarters of the Royal Society of Medicine. That led to the agreement by a British midwife, Josephine Morgan, to come join the OB-Gyn Department at the Burlington medical center.

After Morgan arrived, "John kind of eased her in," Kathy Keleher said, "doing nonthreatening things like talking about midwives, who they were, starting to have her see normal, low-risk women in the clinic, not doing births right away at all. Very slow and gradual, which was very wise."

"At the beginning," Claire wrote, "the chief obstacle to the program was the resistance to it by the medical profession." Dr. Maeck set about making the case to his colleagues, in Vermont and across the country, that accepting nurse-midwives had strong benefits for them, even when it meant sharing their fees and patient load.

In a 1971 article titled "Obstetrician-Midwife Partnership in Obstetric Care" in the journal *Obstetrics and Gynecology*, he lamented that "45 percent of women in low-income families receive no prenatal care" in the U.S. "The rapidly diminishing number of generalists who in the past cared for the pregnant woman, as well as the increasing number of patients, have added to the obstetrician's burden," he wrote. "It is time that the profession takes a

Dr. John Maeck

hard look at how it spends its time."

What the profession needed to do, Dr. Maeck argued, was to reduce the rate of infant deaths, "provide improved prenatal and postpartum counseling for all women," and provide those services affordably and effectively — which it simply could not do by itself. "It is my belief," he wrote, "that such ancillary help can best be obtained by involving the midwife as a partner with the obstetrician-gynecologist in the delivery of health care to women."

And although "the term 'midwife' carries an unfavorable connotation," Dr. Maeck added, "... in present context, she is a highly intelligent, broadly educated, sympathetic person with a depth of knowledge in the biology of reproduction and the psychology of women. ... Her qualifications permit her to share obstetric care with the obstetrician, who could then afford to devote more of his effort to the patient at risk."

"... A model of total maternal care based on this thesis is being developed at our Medical Center," Dr. Maeck's article announced. In that model, nurse-midwives take most responsibility for prenatal education; they conduct follow-up exams after the obstetrician has first seen the patient; and they take part, Dr. Maeck wrote, "in the conduct of labor and delivery of the uncomplicated pregnancy."

"I didn't know Dr. Maeck, but I could see him embracing midwifery for just this reason — that it allowed the men to be the leaders, and they didn't need to waste their time with quote 'normal' OB," said Dr. Eleanor Capeless, who later served as medical director of the hospital's nurse-midwifery service. "That's really kind of true, and it was part of his pitch: This was an advantage to the docs, these are physician extenders. But it's also what women want."

"To give women what they wanted"

When I first came, women didn't want to see men anymore," said Dr. Capeless, who joined the medical center staff in 1981. "They had gotten to the point where they were saying, 'No, I want to be cared for by women.' So the nurse-midwifery practice was huge, and very, very popular — and the docs that backed them up were very appreciative of that, because it was a way to give women what they wanted."

Claire Lintilhac wrote the checks that paid the salaries of that first midwife, Josephine Morgan, and of a second British midwife, Virginia Rodwick, who came to the Burlington hospital in 1970. At that point, along with their work in clinic and office-based care, the Burlington nurse-midwives began to help train students who came to the hospital from the nurse-midwifery program at Yale University, and soon after from other programs around the country.

Dr. Maeck and the hospital's first nurse-midwives also worked on the state level, advocating for professional standards and credentialing for nurse-midwives, which Vermont enacted when it expanded its Nurse Practice Act in 1974 to cover both nurse-midwives and nurse practitioners. By then, the first two British midwives had left the Burlington service, but the medical center decided to affirm its commitment to the new program. Its third midwife, the Wisconsin native and Yale School of Nursing graduate Mary Lee Mantz, was then providing about half of the service's office-based care to pregnant women, and had begun working with one physician on labor and delivery.

"The whole model that Claire and John Maeck built this on was physicians and nurse-midwives working together," Kathy Keleher recalled. "That partnership. John did it in a way that didn't instill a lot of fear or trepidation, and he set the model for the whole state. Claire was very generous in supporting the project. That's really what got things started."

At about this time, Claire decided to do more than write personal checks and provide personal support. Primarily to support the nurse-midwifery program, she would, she decided, create a new family foundation.

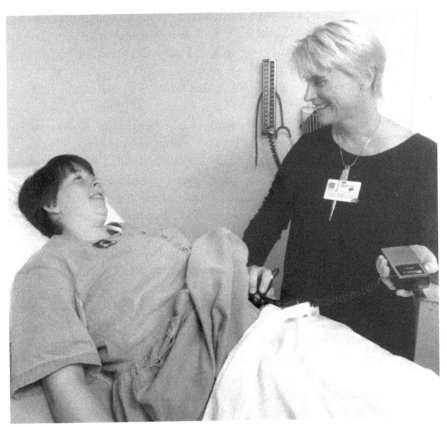

Kathy Keleher, CNM, joined the Burlington hospital's nurse-midwifery service in 1979, and was its director from 1985 to 1995.

ᘃ

The inaugural meeting of the first trustees of the Lintilhac Foundation convened on June 27, 1975, at Claire's home in Stowe. Claire was elected president. The board also included attorney Francis Mulderig of Stowe, attorney Thomas Amidon of Stowe, who became secretary, and George Sharrow of Charlotte, Vt., a vice president at the Burlington-based Howard Bank who became treasurer. Also named a trustee was Philip Lintilhac, who had graduated from UVM and earned a PhD in plant biology from the University of California at Berkeley, and who the next year would join the UVM faculty.

The board first discussed a proposal for creating a new walking and bicycling path in Stowe [see chapter 7, page 163], an idea of Claire's that the foundation would go on to support. It also made small grants of between $1,000 and $5,000 to UVM, the Medical Center Hospital of Vermont (MCHV), the local fire department and rescue squad, and Vermont Educational Television.

Then, say the first minutes, "Trustee Claire Lintilhac indicated her desire to continue to assist the midwifery program at the MCHV in Burlington."

The board considered a proposal that it fund a chair in midwifery at UVM. But in September, the trustees decided to support the midwifery service more directly: They approved a five-year grant to the nurse-midwifery service at $60,000 per year, "plus $10,000 toward hiring at least one more nurse midwife."

By March 1978, Dr. Maeck had retired. That year, with the foundation's support, the nurse-midwifery service brought on three more nurse-midwives and became a full-time program, serving women twenty-four hours a day, seven days a week.

The Burlington medical center added a labor lounge and adopted more flexible labor and delivery policies for low-risk, uncomplicated births. MCHV converted several small, single-patient rooms into birthing rooms, where expectant mothers in low-risk situations could go through labor and delivery in a more relaxed setting, with partners and family members present as desired, and with any equipment that might be needed either in the room or right nearby. The midwives also saw patients for annual exams, contraception and minor gynecological issues.

In 1979, pregnant women were offered a three-option system: they could see a physician only, a physician alternating with a nurse-midwife, or the four nurse-midwives. The system has since evolved so that all patients see a physician at least once during their pregnancy.

Since 1979, nurse-midwives have delivered about 16 percent of total births at the medical center, an average of 400 per year, and have performed almost all the first prenatal visits with mothers-to-be. They have also provided most of the hospital's obstetric and gynecological care for teenagers.

In 1980, the foundation renewed its commitment to the nurse-midwifery service with another five-year grant. Reviewing the impacts of the program for the foundation, Dr. Leon Mann, who then headed the OB-Gyn Department, noted:

"The Vermont Health Department recently released statistical information that ranks the State of Vermont #1 in the United States in terms of infant mortality rate.

"While there are many variables that have resulted in Vermont being 'the safest place in the United States to have a baby,' a major factor has been the introduction of nurse-midwives to the care of obstetrical patients," Dr. Mann declared. "The program developed by our Department with the support of the Lintilhac Foundation has led to similar physician/nurse-midwife health care teams in other parts of this state, so that the overall well-being of obstetrical patients has been greatly improved."

From the start of 1980 to the end of 1985, the number of pregnant women who chose the nurse-midwife option at the Burlington medical center almost doubled, until certified CNMs were attending about 16 percent of all births at Vermont's only tertiary care and teaching hospital. Those numbers were reported in autumn 1986 by the *Journal of Obstetric, Gynecological & Neonatal Nursing*, in the article "Nurse-Midwifery Care in an Academic Health Center," by Kathy Keleher and Leon Mann.

Among the 2,126 patients who chose to work with nurse-midwives in that period, the journal said, 84 percent had spontaneous vaginal deliveries, 60 percent delivered vaginally in labor or birthing rooms, and 67 percent didn't require anesthesia. The rate for primary, or first-time, cesarean section among nurse-midwife patients was 10.4 percent — "somewhat less than the rate of 15 percent for the Medical Center Hospital of Vermont obstetric service."

Overall, the article concluded, "the added skills of the CNM in childbirth education, counseling, and labor support were recognized as assets for comprehensive obstetrical care."

"She was just so committed"

A t the end of the 1970s, Claire began asking to meet with the nurse-midwives for informal, friendly luncheons at her home.

"Yes, with a whole spread — and she made it all herself," Keleher recalled. "She was really interested in what we were doing day to day. She was very inquisitive, and always asked, 'Well, what else can you do? Where are you going with this now?' She was always very encouraging, to keep pushing the goals of the service. It was so invigorating and so encouraging to have that support, to have someone who was an advocate for what you were doing. Those were some of my favorite times."

"I remember Claire having us to her home, talking to us about her life in China as a missionary's daughter," said Mary Gibson, CNM, who joined the service in '79. "She was just so committed to the idea of women being with women during labor, it was such an important thing to her. There was something radiant about her. She just emanated compassion and kindness."

In 1979, the medical center was considering whether to move the nurse-midwifery service to a separate area or clinic outside the hospital, to provide care for what it termed normal deliveries. Now almost 80, Claire wrote a letter that made the case for keeping the nurse-midwives and obstetricians in the same setting:

> Physicians are now recognizing and accepting the Nurse Midwife. And expectant mothers are more and more welcoming, with enthusiasm and confidence, the expert and very special touch of the Nurse Midwife.
>
> ... An expectant mother in labor is not sick but she is anxious and nervous and even apprehensive at times. So, to provide a homey atmosphere in the hospital, a Labor Lounge was set up right within the Birthing Area. This, I understand, is a success. Here, a mother in the early stages of labor can wait and relax with the comfort of knowing that the Birthing Room is nearby. Here too her husband can be with her at all times and also be free to come and go.
>
> The Birthing Rooms (five) are fully equipped for normal deliveries, yet without the clinical appearance of the large Delivery Rooms. ... At the same time, in the event of an emergency, the large Delivery Room is immediately available.
>
> The more I think about it the more I question the need for

After leaving China in 1950, and following her husband Lin's death in 1957, Claire M. Lintilhac lived in Stowe, Vermont from 1959 until her own passing in 1984.

(and the expense of) setting up another similar, but separate area, for more or less the same purpose, outside the hospital (or even within the hospital building). It seems to me that this arrangement would tend to polarize the Nurse Midwives and the Physicians and thus gradually set the Nurse Midwifery Program right back to the beginning. ... The Nurse Midwife Program has come a long way I know, but it still has a long way to go. I would be sorry to see it suffer a setback now.

The hospital decided to keep the service on-site, within its OB-Gyn Department.

"Another concern of mine," Claire's letter added, "is the continuity of care for the normal young mother, especially one with her first baby, for the business of having a baby doesn't begin and end with delivery." The new mother, she noted, "needs to learn as much as she can, before her baby arrives. ... She is too busy afterwards."

Soon after delivery, Claire also observed, the mother "may go through a very definite period of depression." She was describing here a need that the nurse-midwifery service and the Lintilhac Foundation, working together in years to come, would do much to meet.

"She was always full of stories"

In July 1983, Claire's son Philip married Crea Sopher, who would soon become a major figure in the foundation's development. Like her husband, Crea is a scientist. She earned a master's degree in teaching in geology from UVM, and did postgraduate studies and research at the Marine Science Institute in Connecticut, the Graduate School of Oceanography at the University of Rhode Island, and the Geophysics Department at the University of Edinburgh in Scotland.

By mid-1983, Claire's health was failing. Then her faith in the Vermonters she had come to love was badly wounded when it was discovered that George Sharrow, the treasurer, had embezzled almost half a million dollars from the Lintilhac Foundation. At an emergency meeting, the board made Phil Lintilhac the foundation's new treasurer; it removed Sharrow, who would plead guilty to the embezzlement charge, in January 1984, and go to prison.

"I think her trust was absolutely devastated," Doris Maeck observed. But the foundation continued its work, and would soon again renew its support for the nurse-midwifery service.

The last time Claire met with the nurse-midwives, "she was kind of on her deathbed — but she wanted to see all the midwives," remembered Audrey Linn, CNM. "She just told stories and stories, about her life. She was always full of stories. It was wonderful to see her, and to have her want to see us."

Claire kept a journal throughout 1983, the last full year of her life, noting visits with friends, family news, and her own struggles with her health. At the close of December, she wrote her final entry:

The big happy event of this year [was] Phil and Crea's being married. Now I can die happy.

In early 1984, Phil and Crea revealed that Crea was pregnant. Claire wanted very much to see her first grandchild, but the closest she came was to learn that the baby would be a girl.

On August 15, 1984, Claire Lintilhac passed away at her home in Stowe.

"Of all the places I lived, Stowe feels like home and I've been the happiest here," Claire said in a quote that was included in an obituary tribute to her by *The Stowe Reporter*, her adopted community's weekly paper.

"In her continuing deep concern for infants and mothers, Mrs. Lintilhac was instrumental in introducing a nurse-midwife program at the Medical Center Hospital in Burlington, Vermont," the *Reporter* wrote. "Mrs. Lintilhac has funded the refurbishing of the Medical Center Hospital of Vermont's Lintilhac Labor Lounge and Birthing Center. Her efforts, inspiration and financial support have also made possible the existence of the nurse midwife program."

The first of Claire's three grandchildren, Louise Lintilhac, was born at the Burlington medical center on September 10, 1984.

In 2004, a newly constructed birthing center at the hospital — designed in large part to provide a homelike, supportive atmosphere for labor and delivery, and built with the help of a $500,000 foundation grant — was dedicated as the Claire M. Lintilhac Birthing Center.

THE EVOLVING NAMES OF THE BURLINGTON HOSPITAL

Burlington's Mary Fletcher Hospital opened in 1879 and, after merging with another small hospital, was renamed the Medical Center Hospital of Vermont (MCHV) in 1967. In 1995, it merged with Fanny Allen Hospital (a smaller facility in next-door Winooski) and the University Health Center to become Fletcher Allen Health Care (FAHC). The facility retained that name until 2014, when the overall medical complex was renamed the University of Vermont (UVM) Medical Center.

This book generally refers to the facility simply as the Burlington medical center; but the proper names Medical Center Hospital of Vermont (MCHV), Fletcher Allen Health Care, Fletcher Allen, and FAHC do appear in quoted material, and in a few other instances referring to events in the medical center's history.

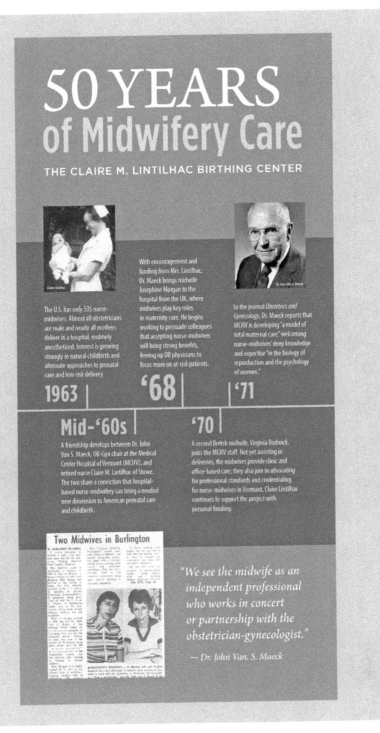

The first in a series of four display panels on half a century of midwifery care at the Burlington medical center, installed at the Lintilhac Birthing Center in 2018.

Crea and Phil Lintilhac at home in Shelburne, 2020.

2

"Not Being a Passive Funder"

A new generation expands on
Claire's approach to giving

Claire Lintilhac was the president and guiding light of the Lintilhac Foundation from its creation in 1975 until her death in 1984. A few weeks after her passing, the remaining trustees gathered at Claire's home on Mountain Road in Stowe, where they elected her son Philip as president and her daughter-in-law Crea as vice president, with attorney Thomas Amidon continuing as secretary. The three approved funding to underwrite a visiting lecturer series at the University of Vermont's Department of Botany, to expand the Stowe Recreation Path, and to support plans to develop a birthing center at Copley Hospital in nearby Morrisville.

With that, the foundation's work continued.

It has been shaped primarily since that meeting by Phil and Crea, with Crea taking on the day-to-day leadership. The two had this conversation with the author about the transition to their stewardship.

Phil, when your mother was still alive, you were on the board, but the foundation was really guided by what she was passionate about. It was her mission.

PHIL: Yes, and we weren't involved in as wide a diversity of things as we are now. It was the midwifery service. And Planned Parenthood.

CREA: And parent-child centers.

You were on the UVM faculty by then, Phil, as a plant biologist. And you were recently married.

PHIL: Yes. Just a year.

Crea, you're an environmentalist also. At that point, did you envision yourself on a whole different path?

CREA: Well, I had moved from an oceanographic institute in Rhode Island to work at IBM, in Essex Junction [Vt.]. I worked with tools in photolithography [a micro-fabrication process that creates patterns on thin film, similar to the printing of circuit boards]. Then I was pregnant with Louise, and IBM was chemicals from one end to the other — not a healthy environment for a pregnant woman. So I left there, and we started our family. We lived in Stowe at that time, because we were renovating the Waterbury Center property that we'd just purchased.

I stopped working, and I really participated in the foundation in a more peripheral way, because at that point Tom Amidon, Claire's lawyer, was acting as an executive director. His office manager was Nancy Brink. A couple of years later, Nancy said she'd be happy to work with us, and I said, "Well, let's bring the foundation home." So that's what we did.

Didn't Tom Amidon advise you not to do that?

CREA: He said it would be way too complicated for me. So that was the time for a transition.

PHIL: Crea's dad, Rae Sopher, and his lawyer worked out a rather forward-looking arrangement of using charitable annuity trusts to feed into the foundation. The charitable annuity trusts would be retained outside the foundation, and they would pay their income, annually, into the foundation for us to spend. These are an IRS-sanctioned charitable gift tool. After they run their course, and you've abided by the requirements of paying in a certain amount every year, then after that term the principal comes back, tax-free.

But you were confronting a complicated challenge. This is a sizable estate, and here you were a young couple with no background in financial management.

PHIL: That's right.

Were you sort of startled, like "Oh my gosh, what are we dealing with here?"

CREA: We became more astute after the embezzlement [see page 15]. Claire was still alive then, and it was very difficult. The lawyer and others — accountants — were not aware of it, and it changed how trust departments at banks did business in our state.

PHIL: It broke my mother's heart, because she loved this trust officer [George Sharrow]. She trusted him.

CREA: Even years later, accounts that he had taken offshore were still trickling back.

PHIL: It was heartbreaking for Mom. But I'm also thinking about the progression of how we started to get more involved. When my mom died, of course, there was the midwifery program, that was the original reason for starting the foundation, but she was also involved with UVM's Asian Studies Program. That was partly run by a professor in the History Department, Peter Siebolt, who was a Chinese scholar. So she supported that program. But I remember the particular thing that got Crea more involved — because Crea was a geologist —

CREA: And working in oceanography, on research vessels —

PHIL: We realized that UVM had finally got rid of their old lake research vessel, which was called the Melosira.

CREA: I had worked on it as a grad student.

PHIL: It was just a little tub. Crea realized that buying UVM a new Melosira would constitute a major advance in the programs the university could offer. We went to Maine, we went to the shipyard, we watched the design evolve, we watched the ship being built, and we watched the hiring of the captain. It all turned out so well. [See Chapter 5 for more.]

CREA: Part of the work I had done at UVM involved mapping the extent of the [prehistoric] Champlain Sea. We were doing coring, and part of my job was to look at the cores and identify the foraminifera, marine single-celled creatures. You could identify temperature regimes and everything by looking at these. When I came back to Vermont, I just couldn't believe that the whole lake studies program had ended, with the university sitting on the sixth-largest lake in the country.

PHIL: The new Melosira really changed my own and Crea's approach to the foundation. It made us realize that rather than acting as most foundations do — they sit back and wait for people to come forward with proposals — we could turn that on its head. We could say, "Give us a proposal on this topic. We think this is important for you." So we kind of took that as an operating principle for a number of years. We still do.

For instance, me being a botanist, one of the first things we did was to create an endowed fund for invited speakers, a seminar series, at the UVM Botany Department. We did that also in the business school, and in geology.

CREA: And Asian studies.

PHIL: So we maintained that attitude of not being a passive funder. Because we were both scientists and immersed in the university, we could see that it needed these things. And that's kind of driven the foundation in many ways.

UVM's research vessel Melosira, its second by that name, was launched in 1987.

CREA: It started with Claire, though, with the bike path in Stowe.

PHIL: Well, that's true!

CREA: She was just beside herself with the danger of people walking up and down Route 108. She probably wanted something like a sidewalk, but it morphed into something different — and what an asset for the community. She was the genesis of that. She funded the engineering plans, and hired somebody to work with the different landowners. She died shortly after the first bridge was put in. [See Chapter 7.]

Other foundations that are about our size in Vermont don't accept proposals unless they are solicited. We've thought about that, and we always say, "You know, things come in across the transom that you would never expect, from places you would never anticipate, and that adds some depth and interest for us." So we would not want to receive solicited proposals only.

Going back to those early days — Crea, when you were working on the new Melosira project, had you become the executive director of the foundation?

CREA: I never considered myself in that position until very recently, when we transitioned the foundation and brought the kids on board. [Crea and Phil's three grown children, Louise, Will and Paul, joined the foundation board in 2012.] We had a thoughtful year of conversation about our present areas of concentration, which are water quality, energy and conservation. At that point, a lawyer made it very clear that there is an executive director that gets voted on by the trustees.

You had never had that structure.

CREA: Not until then!

PHIL: I was president for most of those years, but Crea was doing the actual legwork.

CREA: With Nancy Brink, who's been by our side for over thirty years. She's the office manager. We are plugged in enough in our community, and certainly in academia and nonprofits; we're always checking with experts, getting opinions. We basically have a philosophy that the particular knowledge and talents of the individual trustees, those areas, that's what we pursue.

There was a decision [in 1989, as part of amending the bylaws] that the board would be family members only.

CREA: Yes.

And your father, Rae Sopher, joined the board.

CREA: Yes. Dad was a metallurgist, and one of the scientific advances that he had in his lifetime was the creation of the ultrasonic inspection that replaced X-ray inspection on submarines. He was working for Electric Boat in Connecticut, and I was about ten, when the USS Thresher went down. [The first U.S. nuclear submarine to be lost at sea, the Thresher sank while testing deep dives in April 1963. All 129 sailors and others aboard were lost.]

PHIL: The new system of testing that Rae was working on would have prevented that.

CREA: Yes, and I think Dad was heartbroken. He went immediately to work for IBM in Poughkeepsie [New York]. He was very analytical and mathematical, and very self-sufficient. He grew up on a dairy farm, went to Grove City College [in Pennsylvania] on the GI Bill, then to Ohio State for his master's.

He was on the board for many years.

CREA: Yes. And as a family, we're plugged in and have a network. We reach out to scholars and experts all the time. The Conservation Research Foundation was run out of this office for 20 years. That was an international science research foundation that administered projects around the world. It was a group of about eight of us, and I was the only one without a PhD. That allowed us to participate with other scientists, to really look at some international science projects.

But in the end, we want to keep it in the family. It's a philosophy that you go forward with this wonderful foundation, being able to support community endeavors where there is talent and knowledge, on the part of family members, to direct it. Where can we be most strategic in our community?

But at the same time that you broadened the focus areas of the foundation, you also maintained your commitment to Claire's mission. That was important to you.

PHIL: Oh yes.

In recent years, you've given a somewhat reduced level of support for the nurse-midwifery service at the Burlington medical center. You wanted to see that program become more self-sustaining.

PHIL: That's right. That's always been our goal.

CREA: We've also supported parent-child centers, maternal child health, the Visiting Nurse Association, and so on. Rather than create our own institutions, we like to work within existing institutions. I think that's important.

PHIL: We also helped start the midwifery programs at Copley Hospital in Morrisville, and at Porter Hospital in Middlebury. And a number of the midwives went on to the Central Vermont Medical Center in Barre.

CREA: It's better maternal/child health if you have somebody who is devoted to helping a woman through the birth, instead of intervention. A high-risk doctor is trained in intervention; they will intervene. A nurse-midwife's training is different. When I see a high-risk doc engaging in a low-risk birth, why is that? If you are low risk, your best choice is a midwife. They know how to usher you through.

PLANTING SEED GRANTS FOR A HEALTHIER WORLD

The Work of the Conservation and Research Foundation

For 20 years, the Lintilhac Foundation office administered the work of the Conservation and Research Foundation, founded in 1952 by botanist and conservationist Richard H. Goodwin. The trustees of the CRF were working scientists, mostly plant biologists and zoologists at various academic institutions across the country. The foundation's mission was to promote the conservation of energy and natural resources, and the limitation of population growth in countries around the world, by strategically directing moderate-sized "seed" grants to nonprofit organizations working in these areas.

"The trustees of the foundation met every year for 20 years at our home in Shelburne, for weekends of discussions about proposals," recalled Crea Lintilhac, who joined the CRF's board in the mid-1990s. "Every year the trustees were impressed by what could be accomplished with modest sums of money imaginatively expended in neglected areas of the world."

Among the media organizations the CRF supported was Population Communications International, which worked with broadcasters in developing countries to produce long-running soap operas with characters created as role models to promote the elevation of the status of women, the use of family planning, and the desirability of small families.

Grants also supported various efforts to protect and preserve biodiversity: the acquisition of natural areas, their protection and management, and the saving of specific endangered species around the world.

Some of the initial funding for the American Farmland Trust came from CRF, to preserve Vermont farmlands. The foundation helped finance negotiations by The Conservation Fund that led to its 1999 purchase of about 300,000 forested acres in the Adirondacks, northern Vermont and New Hampshire from Champlain International, Inc. About a quarter of that land was transferred to public ownership.

Other CRF grants were directed toward reducing the use of pesticides in Mexico and throughout Central America. Initial funding from CRF for Sandra Lanham, pilot and founder of the Environmental Flying Service — which transported organizations and individuals conducting environmental missions — led to Lanham receiving a $500,000 MacArthur Foundation fellowship.

The foundation also supported a number of projects related to the dangers of nuclear technology to humanity and the environment. Those included *Eight Minutes to Midnight*, an Academy Award-nominated film on Dr. Helen Caldicott's efforts "to stem the drift" toward nuclear war. Other CRF grants assisted efforts to reduce energy consumption and convert to energy generated from renewable fuels.

"The Conservation and Research Foundation has been a highly productive investment," wrote Goodwin, a longtime botany professor at Connecticut College, in his 2002 memoir, *A Botanist's Window on the 20th Century.* "An organization has been established that has gained an international reputation as a source of financial support for environmental projects. ... Over $1.2 million has been expended over the past 49 years in grants, contracts and awards."

The CRF was retired in 2015, with its assets delivered to the Goodwin Trust Fund at Connecticut College's Botany Department.

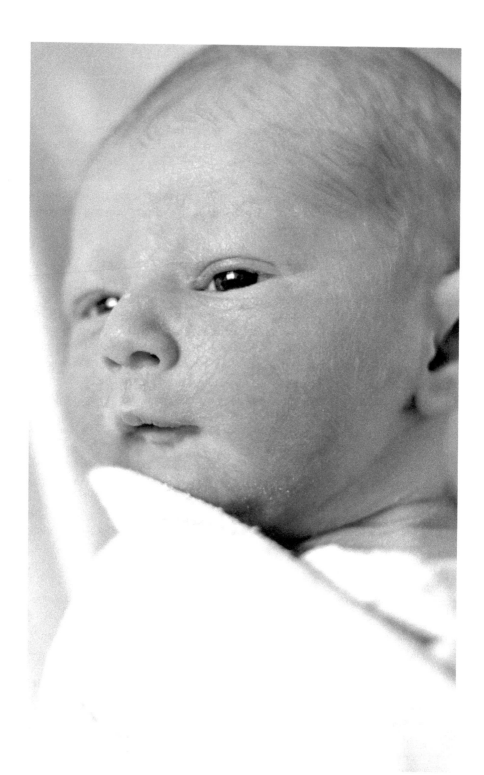

A newborn at the Claire M. Lintilhac Birthing Center, University of Vermont Medical Center.

3

For Mothers, Babies and Families

Standing by nurse-midwives as
they prove their value

nterest in natural childbirth had grown strong in Vermont, as it had in much of the nation, by the time Dr. Eleanor Capeless, a maternal-fetal medicine specialist, became medical director of the Nurse-Midwifery Service at the Burlington medical center in 1980. Elsewhere in the country, she said, OB-gyn departments often met that rising interest with "an incredible amount of resistance." But here, having nurse-midwives practicing alongside the physicians helped to smooth the adjustment.

"There was tension, but not to the degree that there was in other places," Dr. Capeless said. "The collaborative approach was there, which allowed the midwives to come and have a place. Then it just expanded on that.

"We docs had never been taught to sit with somebody in labor," she reflected. "I never rubbed anybody's back, you know? And that's what patients were then expecting — things we weren't trained to give, didn't know how to give, and didn't have time to give. So this worked well."

By the mid-1980s, though, the two visionaries behind the startup years of the nurse-midwifery service were gone. Dr. Maeck was in retirement, and Claire Lintilhac had passed away in 1984. Without them, the nurse-midwifery service "could have just gone by the wayside," Kathy Keleher, director of the service from 1985-1995, said in a 2017 conversation with Crea Lintilhac.

"But it was a devotion," Crea answered. "It was central."

\/

The Lintilhac Foundation renewed its support for the service in 1986, with a second five-year grant. The nurse-midwives continued the lunches they had begun with Claire, now meeting each year with Crea and Phil Lintilhac on the UVM campus to share a meal and present their annual report. "The reports showed what we accomplished for the community," Keleher said, "and what we did for the medical practice: how much time our work afforded to the physicians, so they could do more high-risk care."

Also with the foundation's support, "we became a training site for the clinical rotations of nurse-midwife students from Yale, and from several other programs," she recalled. "I was on the board of the American College of Nurse-Midwives for a number of years, and I encouraged programs to have students apply here for their clinical rotation. We'd take them from the Frontier Nursing Service down in Kentucky, and we had a student from Boston University. It was really fun. We loved that."

Nurse-midwives could also now apply for a three-month sabbatical, during which they were expected "to delve into something — to publish, to look at things from a different perspective, to get different training," Keleher said. "We wrote that into the grant, just to encourage everybody to have a break from the 24/7 work life."

From the late 1980s into the new century, the foundation also made a number of grants to other hospitals and health-care services in central and northern Vermont, always to support and improve care for women, babies and children. Beneficiaries included the hospitals in Berlin, Middlebury and Morrisville, Lamoille County's parent-child center, and the Visiting Nurse Association in Burlington.

In Morrisville, Copley Hospital serves both Stowe, where Claire lived, and nearby Waterbury, where Phil and Crea were now raising their family. A major foundation grant in 1986 helped Copley develop its birthing center, which it opened that spring — "one of the finest birthing centers in New England ... a tribute to the hospital and the communities it serves," said the hospital's news release on the new facility. Smaller grants each year from 1992 to 1996 supported the facility, where certified nurse-midwives joined the staff in 1996.

During that period, Copley conducted a community-wide survey, "asking women what they were looking for as it pertains to their healthcare," said a 2016 hospital article on the 20th anniversary of its nurse-midwifery service. "The response was overwhelming with women wanting a new care model."

"You don't need to be cared for by a midwife for just pregnancy; we treat the whole woman through every stage of life," said Jackie Bromley, CNM, Copley's first full-time nurse-midwife, who was still on staff for the 20th anniversary. She was joined by a second CNM in 1998, and a third in 2012.

"Part of the whole thing — establishing families"

n 1997, *Ladies' Home Journal* named Burlington one of the nation's ten best cities for women. Having evaluated the country's 200 largest cities "on the qualities women care about most," it ranked Burlington number one for health care, giving the city the only A-plus rating it awarded in that category.

By the time the medical center's Nurse-Midwifery Service joined the fast-emerging world of the internet with its own website in 1997, it had six full-time nurse-midwives, all part-time faculty at the UVM College of Medicine. The service had also become a site for the Community-Based Nurse-Midwifery Education Program of the American College of Nurse-Midwives.

The foundation's support for the Burlington nurse-midwifery service continued with a three-year grant, awarded in 1999, to help it develop a master's degree program, together with the University of Rhode Island, that in the end did not get off the ground. Then a four-year grant, awarded in 2004, devoted half a million dollars to the new Lintilhac Birthing Center, opened that May and dedicated to Claire's memory.

Movement toward a dedicated birthing center had begun in the late 1990s, when the nurse-midwives helped persuade the medical center to refit single-patient rooms as birthing rooms, where mothers on track for vaginal deliveries could go through labor, delivery and recovery in a single space, often with partners and other family members present.

"You'd walk in and the room didn't look like it had a surgical table, with stirrups. It had a bed, with a bed cover on it, that you could break apart if you needed to," Kathy Keleher said. "You could put stirrups on, but things were more hidden. There was a warmer for the baby in the room, so it was all self-contained."

"Those rooms were tiny," Dr. Capeless remembers. "It was a new hump to get over,

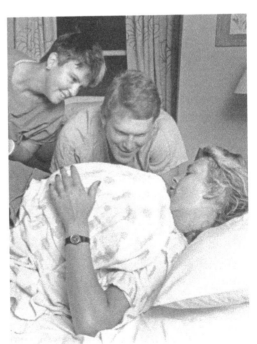

Linda Campbell, a nurse-midwife at the Burlington medical center, with a new mom and dad in the early 1990s.

because all of us were used to delivering in the delivery room, which was three times as big. Once we got birthing rooms that were a reasonable size, designed for that purpose, everybody felt more comfortable."

The nurse-midwives had also pushed to let fathers or other partners be in the delivery room. "That was part of the whole thing — establishing families," Keleher said. "When I first started, physicians wouldn't even let the husband in. It was their territory."

As the hospital developed more spacious birthing rooms, and then as it designed and created a new birthing center, it made sure that operating rooms were still nearby, in case of emergency or unplanned surgical deliveries.

"In obstetrics, you always have only about 30 seconds to say, 'Uh oh, something's going on and I need to do something,'" Dr. Capeless explained. "But the access was always there."

"When the proposal came up to build a birthing center," said Keleher, "there was a big discussion: Should it be outside the hospital or inside? We wanted it inside; we're nurse-midwives, we want to work in a hospital. Ninety-five percent of women deliver in the hospital, so let's go where the women are."

"The design came from the nurse-midwife model"

"Fletcher Allen Names New Birthing Center in Honor of Claire M. Lintilhac," read the headline of the medical center's announcement that it had dedicated the new facility. It was May 9, 2004, and it was Mother's Day.

The center was equipped with larger birthing rooms, a visitors' lounge, two operating rooms for C-sections or multiple births, deep soaking tubs in all birthing rooms, a room specially equipped for water births, a wireless fetal-monitoring system that would allow laboring moms to walk around or get in a tub, and "a labor lounge with fantastic views of Lake Champlain and the Adirondack Mountains," the announcement said.

"A person of great compassion and vision, Claire Lintilhac was instrumental in bringing a hospital-based midwifery service to our academic medical center in the late 1960s to serve the women of our community," said Dr. Melinda Estes, Fletcher Allen's president and CEO, in dedicating the center. "By naming this new Birthing Center in her honor, we are commemorating her dedication to perinatal care and paying tribute to her energy and spirit, reminding us all that one person really can make a difference."

"The whole design of it came from the nurse-midwife model — everything [for normal labor and delivery] in one room," Kathy Keleher noted. "The physicians were totally on board, but the nurse-midwives were very involved in planning that."

Even as the Birthing Center was being developed, the nurse-midwifery leadership understood that the foundation support, which had helped the service start up and grow strong, would not be continuing at such a high level.

"They were slowly needing to fund other things, and realizing that the department and the medical center needed to step up to the plate in terms of supporting the Nurse-Midwifery Service even more," Keleher said. "Getting that birthing center named after Claire was kind of, for me, the icing on the cake. She helped to grow the philosophy, and the practice, in terms of what goes on there."

\/

"Or will you fight?"

But then in September 2007, Fletcher Allen announced that it would close its nurse-midwifery service, laying off some nurse-midwives and folding the service into its low-risk obstetrics practice.

"As a result, the state's largest hospital, which handles about a third of all births in Vermont, will no longer provide 24-hour nurse-midwifery service," reported Ken Picard in the Burlington newsweekly *Seven Days*. This would mean, he wrote, that a mother's "chance of delivering with a nurse-midwife will be determined by fate — i.e., if a nurse-midwife is on call the day she delivers. And, since most physicians aren't trained in water births, that, too, may no longer be an option."

The service had been losing money; that was the reason given by hospital officials. "Between 2004 and this year, the program lost $482,278," *Seven Days* reported. Private OB-gyn practices had begun offering nurse-midwifery care in the area, and the number of women choosing Fletcher Allen's nurse-midwifery service had been falling, even as the total number of births at the hospital remained steady.

After the closure plan was reported in *Seven Days* and the *Burlington Free Press*, area mothers mobilized. Among them was Crea Lintilhac, who delivered her third child, Paul, with a nurse-midwife at the medical center, and had been alerted by the nurse-midwives to the hospital's plan.

"I would like this process to slow down," Crea told reporter Nancy Remsen of the *Free Press*. "We need to do whatever it takes to preserve this choice for women. It will not be the same if a couple of midwives are folded into an obstetrical practice."

Crea alerted the state's nurses' union, which objected that the hospital hadn't followed procedures that required every option to be considered before layoffs could be set in motion. A dozen mothers met in a Fletcher Allen cafeteria to speak up for the service. Mothers wrote opinion pieces and letters to the editor.

"With health-care costs out of control, women should be encouraged to use midwives rather than doctors," argued Emily Watkins of Burlington in a *Free Press* letter. Delivering her child with the Lintilhac service, she said, "was the highest-quality health-care experience I have had."

"The practice at the hospital allows women the security of laboring and delivering at the hospital while having the supportive and nurturing care of a nurse-midwife," said a letter to the daily paper by Regina Park of South Burlington. "To me, and to many other women, this strikes an ideal balance."

"Imagine having a woman that has been with you every step of the way through your pregnancy; who has taken the time to call you back immediately in the middle of the night with your fourth child because you were having false labor for the sixth time," wrote Lori Tarrant of Colchester. "Imagine having a qualified, caring midwife never leave your side for a 12-hour labor ... a midwife next to you who knows your desires and needs because she has taken the time for the past nine months to get to know what kind of birth is important to you. ... These women are truly amazing."

"Women came out of the woodwork that had had their babies with us 30 years before," recalled Martha "Marti" Churchill, CNM, who became director of the Nurse-Midwifery Service in the late 1990s. "I had women in my church come up to me and say, 'They can't close that practice!'"

Fletcher Allen reversed its decision, announcing on October 2 that it would keep the Nurse-Midwifery Service. "We have listened to the patients and worked with

Marti Churchill gets help checking in on a mom's condition in the Birthing Center.

the midwives to develop this agreement," said hospital spokesman Mike Noble.

"They gave us two years to make our numbers better — and we did," said Churchill. Fletcher Allen's CEO and its OB-gyn chair "underestimated what it meant to have a 24/7 midwifery service in this community — the legacy of it, and what it meant to lots of people still," she summed up. "With the help of the foundation, Crea, Phil and the union, we were able to save the practice."

"It was just an incident along the path," Crea reflected. "It kind of teaches you. Things go along, they flourish, then they might hit a spot. And you have to decide: Will you just go along with this, or will you fight?"

"That period, to me, set the stage for a really solid acknowledgment of the worth of the midwifery service — again," said Dr. Capeless, its medical director at the time. "That solidified it. And that then allowed people like Marti to say, 'We need to expand in this or that direction.' The administration listened, and you have to give them credit for that."

"Let's do more than we've been doing"

In 2012, a new chairman took over leadership of the OB-Gyn Department and brought stronger support for the nurse-midwives. The service's improving patient numbers got a big boost in 2014, when Champlain OB/Gyn, a popular practice in nearby Essex Junction, announced that its obstetrical care would now be provided primarily by nurse-midwives from the Lintilhac Service. Physicians would provide backup, ultrasounds and consults, but nurse-midwives would entirely staff the on-call service for deliveries.

"The FAHC midwives are the longest-standing midwifery group in Chittenden County with many years of experience," Champlain OB/Gyn wrote. "They are well-known for their individualized family-oriented prenatal care."

"We all rotate out there, the patients deliver there," Marti Churchill said. "The patients love it — and our patient numbers have more than doubled. The first year [after 2014], the numbers went to about 400, the next year it was 420, and in 2016 it was 450. We're now more than self-sustaining."

The foundation continued to support the Birthing Center with annual grants from 2010 through 2013. From 2014 to 2017 it made annual awards for two new programs the nurse-midwives wanted to add: a lactation clinic and a program of therapy, consultation and support for pregnant women and new mothers who were struggling with psychological or emotional challenges.

"It was the Lintilhacs' and the midwives' vision: Let's do more than we've been doing," Churchill said. "Let's do this breastfeeding clinic, let's do this mental health piece. The department supported it — because we had the funding."

"There was this hole in our community"

One day early in the 2000s, as the nurse-midwives were reviewing patient cases, recalled Sandra Wood, CNM, "we noticed that about a third of our patients were on psychotropic medications," for depression, anxiety and related disorders.

"At that time, SSRIs [selective serotonin reuptake inhibitors] were booming — Prozac, Zoloft," Marti Churchill explained. "We were getting lots and lots of women coming into the practice already on these. And everyone was having to stop cold turkey, because nobody wanted to touch a pregnant woman with them. We didn't know what would happen. There wasn't a lot of data."

Psychiatrists and primary-care doctors were often very reluctant to prescribe these meds to pregnant women. So were obstetricians, whose training generally gave them little background in psychotropic medications or their impacts.

"So there was this hole in our community," Churchill said. "Sandy took it on herself to get a degree, to meet this need — and she brought a huge resource to our practice."

With support from a state grant program, Wood returned to school at UVM and earned a second degree as a psychiatric-mental health nurse practitioner (PMHNP). By the time of the medical center's 2007 proposal to close the 24/7 service, she had submitted her resignation and was developing a private practice. When the closure plan was abandoned, she returned full-time to the medical center — and brought along her interest in helping pregnant and new moms cope with depression, anxiety and similar challenges.

"A lot of what I'm doing is what midwifery already does. It's relationship-based care," Wood said. "Having somebody doing this work who's just another part of the service normalizes it a bit, and it's just a normal part of pregnancy.

"Women often feel shame about what they feel," she added. "Symptoms of depression or anxiety are seen as selfish. 'I'm a bad mother, I should be able to do this, I should be happy.'"

"She's a midwife at heart, which is about treating the whole person and using medical intervention judiciously," Churchill said. "So in our practice she was doing more and more around perinatal mental health, not just medication management. I loved her expertise, and that's when the idea came to me: 'Let's see if the foundation will fund this, so Sandy can really dedicate herself to it.'"

Crea Lintilhac was already aware of how common depression and anxiety had become, both during and after pregnancy. "I was reading these articles in the *New York Times*," Crea said. "Then Sandy Wood and the midwives met with me, and I was just shocked by how little we know, and how hard it is to help people. It takes somebody being there to give a helping hand."

Since 2014, Lintilhac Foundation funding has enabled Sandy Wood and the Nurse-Midwifery Service to offer extra care and support to pregnant women, with screening for mood and anxiety spectrum disorders. The service provides clinic appointments for these issues, with Wood; postpartum phone calls after every birth, again to screen for mood and anxiety challenges; a third screening at the six-week postpartum visit; and a mothers' postpartum support group. As a research project, Wood and a medical center psychiatrist have conducted an eight-week teaching series, "Mindful Motherhood," for pregnant women.

Many or most of these services did not qualify for reimbursement through conventional health-care plans. Many still don't. So the foundation's support has been critical to developing the services and demonstrating their value.

Sandy Wood also shares her expertise and experience with other health practitioners around Vermont, "trying to educate everyone I can." She does that through a state-funded "warm line" and by traveling around the state, talking with providers about perinatal mood and anxiety. At the medical center, she said, "I do normal midwife stuff — I just have more time to do it. I can spend a whole hour talking with someone about their mental health, their fears, their childhood.

"The Lintilhac grant has allowed me to be here, doing this work," Wood summed up. "I wouldn't have been able to build that, without this support. My goal now is to spread this knowledge."

Across the community served by the Burlington medical center, many pregnant and new mothers are still going without treatment for mood and anxiety issues, said Dr. Nathalie Feldman, an assistant OB-gyn professor who is also director of the Learning Environment at the Larner College of Medicine, as UVM's medical school is now called.

"Today there are so many issues — social issues, opiate addiction issues — that make for a very high-risk population," Dr. Feldman added. "So those really need to be addressed. It's gotten a lot better, but I think we're just scratching the surface of really meeting the needs of patients when it comes to postpartum depression."

A psychiatrist is now embedded in the medical center's

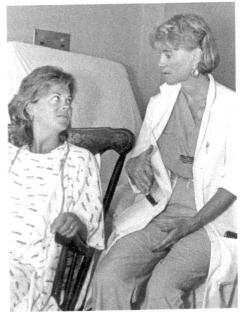

Kathy Keleher with a mom in the late 1980s.

perinatal clinics, she said, "and Sandy is available for consultation. She also does some teaching to our residents, on postpartum depression: how you recognize it, how you might prevent it, how you treat it."

"This is what is so incredibly necessary in health care, in integrated medicine," said Crea Lintilhac — "having a support system that makes people feel, at least, that their fellow citizens care about them. It's that basic. And that can improve the health care system overnight, by leaps and bounds."

$$\sqrt{}$$

"We've learned from midwifery. This is part of who we are"

Since 2014, nurse-midwives have also played an integral role in helping to educate residents — and, more recently, medical students as well — at UVM's Larner College of Medicine.

"We really saw a need for our residents to learn a bit about the stylistic differences with how nurse-midwives approach laboring moms, and the support they provide, the time they spend with patients in labor," said Dr. Nathalie Feldman of the medical school. "If a patient comes in who's in labor, a first-year, sometimes a second-year resident might be working with that midwife in the care of that patient. It's very active. They participate in the delivery, and they build a relationship with the patient so that trust is established over time.

"In an academic tertiary care center, we get a lot of referrals of very high-risk patients. The risk is that the residents graduate feeling as if every pregnancy, and every laboring mom, is sort of a complication waiting to happen, as opposed to looking at pregnancy and childbirth as a very natural, kind of holistic experience where so much of the time, most of the time, things go very well — and we really just need to stand back and not be interventionist, allow families to go through labor in a way that feels right for them. I think that midwives offer that perspective.

"Midwives also help teach our medical students how to provide labor support, as well as the basics and fundamentals of labor and delivery, and how to support a family. It's so important in establishing trust, and in developing a relationship with patients. For our trainees to understand the benefits of that, and experience that and learn from experts in that, is such a wonderful relationship to foster."

"Our residents get to learn how to communicate more effectively, how to support women in labor, in ways they don't necessarily get from the docs — because we're busy running around, doing C-sections, giving talks," added Kelley McLean, M.D., an obstetrician and maternal fetal medicine specialist at the UVM Medical Center, assistant professor at the College of Medicine, and medical director of the Nurse-Midwifery Service. "They really get to focus in on caring for women, especially women who choose natural birth."

How do residents feel about working with midwives? To find out, Dr. Feldman approached a number of them and asked.

"They really appreciated the opportunity to learn the art of midwifery — that approach to labor and the support during labor," she said. "Midwives spend more time. The residents see that as a role model, as opposed to being in clinic all day and then coming for the last few minutes of a delivery, which is a common scenario for busy obstetrician-gynecologists."

Dr. Feldman shuffled through the notes she had made from her conversations.

"The historical perspective, the ancient art of midwifery: They appreciate getting a little knowledge about that," she said. "They also mentioned a certain art of positioning. When to get on all fours, or different positions. Midwives have much more tolerance for allowing a patient to get in a comfortable position, whatever that might be.

"The nurse-midwives are part of the faculty here — and that sends a very important message, I think, for medical students, trainees, hospital staff, the entire community," Dr. Feldman concluded. "We've learned from midwifery. This is part of who we are."

The certified nurse-midwives at the University of Vermont Medical Center, in 2020. First row, from left: Cory Simon-Nobes, Marti Churchill, Bonny Steuer, Lucy Chapin. Second row: Meredith Merritt, Whitney Smith, Krista Nickerson, Mary Jo Gehrett.

"I think they'll be a force in the future"

n 2016, Dr. McLean put together a presentation titled "Obstetric Care in the U.S.: *Less* Appears to Be *More*."

Presenting at the annual conference of the Maine Medical Society, Dr. McLean said she would "discuss the growing recognition that increased intervention has not reduced maternal and/or neonatal morbidity." As a September 2016 article in the journal *Obstetrics & Gynecology* had reported, "the reported (unadjusted) maternal mortality rate in the United States more than doubled from 2000 to 2014"— a 26.6 percent increase — "at a time when the World Health Organization reports that 157 of 183 countries studied had decreases in maternal mortality."

"Maternal mortality is the death of a mother from pregnancy-related complications while she's carrying or within 42 days of birth," the news website *Vox* explained in 2017. The 2000-2014 maternal-mortality rate in the U.S., it said, was "more than three times the rate of the United Kingdom, and about eight times the rates of Netherlands, Norway and Sweden."

What was going on? There appears to have been multiple factors, Dr. McLean said in her talk. In the U.S., these included women delivering later in life, the obesity epidemic, "lack of nationally coordinated health-care systems, with resultant decreased access," "racial and socioeconomic inequality of care," and other contributors — including the prevailing American model of obstetrical care.

In the U.S. from 1993 to 2003, the rate of cesarean deliveries (CDs) per 1,000 live births rose by 35.5 percent, then leveled off somewhat from 2003 to 2013, increasing by just 11.3 percent. Twenty other industrialized countries reported similar rates of increase, according to the *American Journal of Obstetrics & Gynecology*.

"Ninety percent of women who have a first CD will go on to have a CD for their next delivery," Dr. McLean said. And "while cesarean delivery can be lifesaving (for mom and baby), cesarean deliveries are also associated with increased risk for maternal and neonatal morbidity."

Others have put the issue even more strongly. "Put simply, women who give birth in the U.S. have a greater risk of dying relative to other rich countries — and the problem has been growing worse at a time when America's peers have continued to make pregnancy safer," declared *Vox*.

"Severe maternal complications have more than doubled in the past 20 years" in the U.S., the investigative-journalism site *ProPublica* reported in February 2018. What's more, "shortages of maternity care have reached critical levels: Nearly half of U.S. counties don't have a single practicing obstetrician-gynecologist, and in rural areas, the number of hospitals offering obstetric services has fallen more than 16 percent since 2004."

One approach to addressing this, Dr. McLean suggested, may be a team that integrates care by certified nurse-midwives with that of physician specialists and other professionals. She noted a February 2017 "Committee Opinion" from the American College of Obstetricians and Gynecologists, titled "Approaches to Limit Intervention During Labor and Birth." Its abstract, or summary, begins: "Obstetrician-gynecologists, in collaboration with midwives, nurses, patients, and those who support them in labor, can help women meet their goals for labor and birth by using techniques that are associated with minimal interventions and high rates of patient satisfaction."

ProPublica's 2018 report focused on a new paper, published that February, from a multi-disciplinary team that studied regulatory data across all 50 states. "Poor coordination of care across providers and birth settings has been associated with adverse maternal-newborn outcomes," the team concluded. "Research suggests that integration of midwives into regional health systems is a key determinant of optimal maternal-newborn outcomes."

In other words, the model that Dr. John Maeck and Claire Lintilhac conceived in the late 1960s, the one they promoted and developed at the Burlington medical center — where certified nurse-midwives work with obstetricians and others to serve women in low-risk pregnancies, across the full range of pregnancy and labor — could be a model for other medical centers across the nation.

"Vermont has very good birth outcomes, one of the lowest primary C-section rates in the country," Dr. McLean said in an interview. There are lots of probable reasons, she said, including a more homogeneous population than in many U.S. urban centers. But, she noted, "there's a growing body of data pointing to the importance of integrated CNM care.

"I don't know how many places have integrated nurse-midwifery into obstetric care in the way that we have," Dr. McLean said. "We now have a good-sized midwifery service that is delivering 400 babies a year in this institution. A fifth to a sixth of all the kids delivered in this hospital are delivered by our midwives. And they're now teaching our residents."

A summary of research on midwifery practices in the U.S., published in 2012 by the American College of Nurse-Midwives, found that the number of midwife-attended births more than doubled nationally from 1991 to 2012, to about 11.3 percent of vaginal births and 7.6 percent of all births. And, said the summary, "a recent systematic review of studies comparing midwifery care to physician care" found "that women cared for by CNMs, compared to women of the same risk status cared for by physicians, had lower rates of cesarean birth, lower rates of labor induction and augmentation, ... lower use of regional anesthesia," and "a significantly higher chance for a normal vaginal birth, fewer interventions, and successful initiation of breastfeeding.

"Today, approximately one in three women gives birth by cesarean" in the U.S., the research summary declared. "To date, no published research demonstrates that significant maternal or child health indicators have improved in the wake of the increased cesarean rate." It noted that "New Mexico, where CNMs attend one third of all births, has the lowest cesarean rate of all 50 states." (Vermont's rate was seventh-lowest in the country in 2015, at 25.8 percent, compared to New Mexico's 23.8 percent. The national average was 32.2 percent.)

"We're incredibly lucky," said Marti Churchill, lead midwife today at the Lintilhac Birthing Center. "I think midwifery wouldn't be here, where it is today, without the Lintilhac Foundation and Claire's vision. It was really Claire that inspired midwifery to be here. She approached John Maeck in 1968, and the two of them came up with an idea that shaped everything."

"I love the relationship with the nurse-midwives — and I do think it's under-recognized," Dr. McLean reflected. "We have really great outcomes, in terms of patient care; and the midwives change the conversation a bit, around obstetric care, in a way that's hard to measure. I think they'll be a force in the future. And if the foundation hadn't kept them going when they were in danger, I don't know if we would have a midwifery service here today."

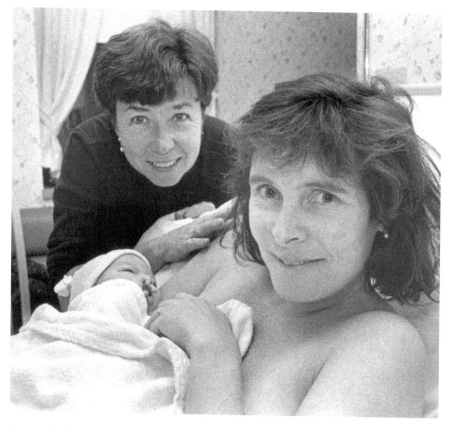

Nurse-midwife Nancy McLellan, CNM, with mom Kathleen Hegarty and newborn Rachel Swanson, at the Burlington medical center in 1993.

FOR NEW MOTHERS COPING WITH DEPRESSION, EXPANDING THE REACH OF TREATMENT EXPERTISE

Funded initially by the foundation, the work by Sandra Wood, CNM, PMHNP, that offers consultation and advice to other Vermont health-care providers on treating pregnant and new mothers with depression, anxiety or other mental-health issues is now half-funded by a federal initiative and half by Medicaid, allowing Wood to reach a bigger network of providers around the state.

Sandra Wood

"During pregnancy and the first year post-partum, a wide spectrum of emotional compli-cations [is] possible," notes the UVM Medical Center's description of Wood's Perinatal Mood and Anxiety Consultation Service. "Postpartum depression, a well-known term, is just one of the Perinatal Mood and Anxiety Disorders. ... As many as one in five women suffer from the symptoms of these disorders, making this one of the most common complications of pregnancy."

After Wood began offering perinatal mental-health treatment to women at the Lintilhac Birthing Center [see page 34], the foundation in 2013 made a contribution that enabled her to spend nearly half her time providing this important form of care. Then in 2018, a federal initiative through the U.S. Health Resources & Services Administration chose Vermont as one of seven states to receive multi-year funding through its Screening and Treatment for Maternal Depression and Related Behavioral Disorders Program.

"This is an initiative to improve screening and access to care for pregnant and parenting moms," Sandy Wood said. In Vermont, she explained, "They've been educating therapists and clinicians that work with pregnant moms. A lot of therapists in the state are being brought up to speed on perinatal mood and anxiety disorders; and through the initiative, some of the funding was funneled to UVM Medical Center to support my position.

"This has grown my ability to help other providers," she said. "I am getting way more consults from other providers around the state, so my reach has really expanded. More people know I'm available now."

"Sandy's service has been very well-received," said Laura Pentenrieder, MPH, the manager of Vermont's initiative under the federal program. "The training she provides to the medical community through grand rounds (pediatrics, family medicine and psychiatry in 2020) and meetings with community-based providers (mental health, home visiting, hospital groups, maternal mental health coalitions, parent child centers, etc.) has contributed to elevating the importance of perinatal mood and anxiety disorders, and growing the knowledge of many of the providers in the state who work with pregnant women and young families. And she graciously answers questions regarding maternal mental health care from anyone."

For Mothers, Babies, and Families

STORIES OF MOTHERS AND MIDWIVES

SUSAN SHECKLER LEFF

Susan Leff delivered four babies with the nurse-midwives at the Burlington medical center: Rachel in 1979, Alex in '83, Jay in '87 and Asher in '89. The first time she was pregnant, "I was happy to hear about this as an option," she recalled. "It was a time when people were first interested in natural childbirth, and I definitely was. All four of my children were born without medication."

A community organizer by profession, Susan was director for ten years at UVM's Hillel Center, the hub of Jewish student and community life on campus; she's currently executive director of the Jewish Communities of Vermont. "My work is all in interpersonal relationships," she said, "and I liked the idea of having someone with me while I was giving birth, not just coming in at the very end — and having a relationship with that person.

"A lot of my friends at the time were having home births, but we lived close to an hour from Burlington. I was uncomfortable having a home birth that far away from a hospital.

"When Rachel was born, it was ten days early when my water broke. We did have to induce, and I was hooked up to a fetal monitor, which meant I couldn't walk around or take a shower. It would have been terrible if I had been in the hospital by myself. But there was a midwife there with me, and my husband was there. It was more relaxing, and less scary. When the monitor started beeping, she was right there."

After her second child was born, Susan and her family moved to Burlington. Delivering her fourth baby, she said, "was a very different experience.

"There were three babies born within five minutes, at the hospital. I came in around 12:30 a.m., and he was born at I think ten after one. I said, 'This baby is coming, this baby is coming!'

"The midwife came in from the room next door, where she had just delivered a baby, and said, 'Let me check you.' Then she said, 'Oh, here he is!' So she caught him."

The Leff family, at the 1992 bat mitzvah for Rachel. First row, from left: Alexander, Asher and Jay Leff. Second row: Rachel (now Rachel VanOrnum), Susan and the late Richard Leff.

In the years that followed, Susan sometimes saw the nurse-midwives she had worked with, just in and around town. "We were part of the community," she said.

✌

JULIA MELLONI

All three of Julia and Thomas Melloni's daughters were delivered by nurse-midwives at the Burlington medical center — and the family became, for a time, the face of the nurse-midwifery program.

That's because their third child, Bianca, was the first baby born in the medical center's first dedicated birthing room, which it created in 1996 by expanding a patient room and equipping it with homestyle furniture and a non-institutional bed. A photo taken after Bianca's birth, showing Julia and her three girls together in the new birthing room, went onto the cover of the brochure the medical center produced to tell the community about the new delivery option.

"About a half hour after Bianca was born, the two older girls were up on the bed with me and the new baby — and they were able to spend the night," Julia recalled. "They sat at the table and drew with crayons. It was a really nice family setting.

"Having a baby is still one of the most risky endeavors that a woman can undertake," she noted. "The beauty of what this organization did is that it married the natural, no intervention whatsoever, with the best medical personnel and knowledge, there at a moment's notice."

A middle-school teacher at the Mater Christi School in Burlington, Julia did a lot of research when she was pregnant with Marcella, her first daughter. When her family physician said she might consider the midwifery option, she said, "I didn't even know that existed."

The Melloni family: Marcella, Julia, Thomas and Elena, with their newborn Bianca.

But she learned. "They were excited about educating me about the whole process, everything from nutrition to physical activity. They framed it in such a way that my whole life, my body has been getting ready for this. I had the confidence of these women empowering me, that I could give birth naturally. And it all worked."

SUSAN WARGO

Susan Wargo's first pregnancy and delivery, in 1978, went fine. When she became pregnant a second time, in 1983, she was in her mid-thirties, and her nurse-midwife friend Kathy Keleher agreed to follow the pregnancy and to be with Susan for the birth.

"They had just added birthing rooms, so I was really looking forward to that," Susan said.

The Wargo family: Emily, Susan, Buddy the dog, Ben and Bill.

The baby was two weeks late. Routine testing, done the day before she went into labor, showed that the baby was in good health.

"I went into labor, I went to the hospital," Susan said. "Kathy was there."

During the delivery, the baby was in some distress. But there was no immediately apparent reason why, suddenly, he was a stillborn.

"It was all a blur," Susan said. "It happened really quickly."

An autopsy later showed that a blood vessel that connects two major heart arteries in an unborn baby, and usually closes up a few hours or days after birth, had closed too soon, causing the fatality.

Susan and Bill, her husband, were devastated. "Even though the hospital staff encouraged us to view him, it was too hard for us to do this," she recalled. "Kathy understood that we might have second thoughts and took a picture of him, which I have, and that has been a really special thing.

"That morning, she helped me get out of the hospital as soon as possible. She was always available, in the following difficult months and years, to talk about his death — which, in retrospect, I know was very hard for her as well."

In 1988, Susan, who lives in South Burlington, became pregnant again. She was 40 now. She asked Kathy to be there, again.

"Because of my age and previous stillbirth, all the doctors considered me very high-risk. I had every possible test. But I wanted Kathy there — and I think it was really hard for her. But I trusted her."

Again the baby was two weeks late. Kathy asked Susan to come in for testing, to make sure the baby was healthy.

"At one point the heart rate fell, and Kathy made the decision that we had to get the baby out," Susan recalled. The attending physician agreed. "I was whisked into the

OR, I had an emergency C-section. He was also born in distress; he wasn't breathing, and he got whisked away — but Kathy was right there, saying 'It'll be okay.'"

Susan and Bill's son, Ben, was in neonatal intensive care for a week. But he came through.

"I feel like she saved his life, making that call to go to the OR," Susan reflected. "It was really hard for her to see that this second baby was struggling — but she was sure that he would be okay. And she conveyed that to us."

⅍

LISA SIMON

"**I** was sick as a dog," recalled Lisa Simon of her 1983 pregnancy with Cory, her first child. "I was aware of problems with the medication that was used at the time for morning sickness, so I was trying to not use it. I was losing weight and I was just miserable."

"There are problems of pregnancy where there's often not an instant cure," noted Kathy Keleher, who became director of the Nurse-Midwifery Service two years later. "That's an advantage of being in a group practice: When you run out of ideas, someone else might say, 'Have you tried this?' The physicians might say, 'She might need to be admitted for fluids.' So you'd get the whole range of options."

The baby was three and a half weeks late. Medication to induce labor didn't work. Lisa, a Charlotte resident who worked for many years with the Visiting Nurse Association in Burlington and helped establish the VNA Family Room, went home to relax. Then she rushed back, ready to deliver.

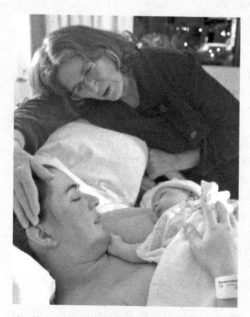

Lisa Simon with her daughter, Cory Simon-Noles, and Cory's newborn son Simon Newcomb.

"I had to stay in the labor room, couldn't walk around or anything," Lisa said. "The birth went very quickly. The baby part was fine."

But soon after, Lisa suffered a postpartum hemorrhage. There was a whole lot of blood.

"You can feel the panic, but you're there to do a job, and you know what's happening," Kathy Keleher said. "A fist in the vagina and one on top of the uterus, and plain old compression. It's a serious thing; you can bleed to death in ten minutes. If you can get it right on the spot — get an IV going, get the compression going, get the right medications to help contract

46

the uterus — you can stabilize.

"In that setting, the doctor's always there. You and the nurse know what to do; the important thing is that you do it just like this," she said, snapping her fingers. "A lot of things are happening, and you're at the end of a 24-hour shift — and you don't want the mother to freak out. But it just kicks in: this is what you do. The doctor knew that I knew what to do, and that I knew to ask for help if I needed it."

Lisa stabilized, and came through unharmed. Cory, her daughter, was fine.

Today, Cory Simon-Nobes, who lives in Shelburne, is a CNM with the Lintilhac Nurse-Midwifery Service. She delivered Simon, her first child, with the service.

"Unlike my mom, I had a very easy pregnancy," Cory said.

In the service today, she added, "we consult with the physicians, and they in turn support us and are respectful in standing by if we need them, but not jumping in. In the vast majority of cases, pregnancy and birth are just a normal part of the woman's life cycle. We want to keep her safe through it."

⬇

DOMA SHERPA

Doma Sherpa and her husband, Lapka Lama, are both from Nepal; he came to the U.S. in 2002, and she followed the next year.

"We met back home, and got engaged back home," Doma says. "He moved here when I was in high school, then I came here to go to Champlain College."

Married here, living in Burlington and running a Nepalese restaurant downtown, the couple had a first pregnancy that ended in a miscarriage. "After that," Doma says, "it took me two years to conceive my older son."

Doma and Lapka visited a Tibetan Buddhist lama, "to bless me," she says. "He told me to stay as clean as I could, spiritually, and I did. He told me that I could conceive in August, and I did. Right in August, I conceived Norbu." Having experienced the miscarriage, she added, "Lapka was so scared that didn't want to tell anyone until the first trimester was over."

This time, the couple chose to work with the nurse-midwives.

"They were very supportive," Doma says. "I didn't feel too much pressure — they were

Lapka Lama and Doma Sherpa with their sons Jordan, at left, and Norbu.

very helpful for the delivery. Oh my goodness, they were the best.

"The midwife said, 'If there's any complication, a doctor will be there,' but I really just wanted the midwife. She was so nice, so supportive." Doma was diagnosed with gestational diabetes, so the birth was induced — but "there was no complication," she says. "Everything went so fine. A healthy baby."

Norbu was born in 2014. Three years later, the couple was able to conceive again; Jordan came along in 2017. Again, the pregnancy and delivery were uneventful.

Doma still goes in to see the nurse- midwives, for an annual checkup.

"I just like them so much," she says. "They're very relaxed, very reassuring. They were there the whole time. Just like a family member."

VANESSA MELAMEDE BERMAN

"When you're pregnant and when you're giving birth, you are so exposed. You see the core of who you are," reflected Vanessa Melamede Berman, who delivered her first child in 2007, and then a set of twins in 2010, with the Nurse-Midwifery Service.

"I really just wanted people who viewed pregnancy as a healthy normal process, and who were going to be supportive of the things I wanted for my pregnancy, and for the birth experience and the postpartum," she said. Pregnant in 2007 with her daughter Samara, she decided after a careful search to work with the nurse-midwives. She soon developed a special bond with Martha Churchill, who would soon become the service's director.

Vanessa, Samara and Dave Berman.

It was a bond that would be tested. After what Vanessa called a "standard, normal pregnancy," her daughter was overdue. Well overdue.

"She just wasn't coming out. Most doctors would have induced me much sooner than the midwives did — but when it was 17 days after my due date, Marti Churchill said, 'We have to get this baby out.'

"I remember it was six in the morning," Vanessa said — "I was on the phone with Marti, hysterically crying. 'I don't want to do this! Why aren't I going into labor?' We had tried all the crazy natural things, to kickstart labor.

Even the induction we did in a very slow-acting way.

"At that point, because my labor had been so long, Marti was no longer with me. She had stayed hours beyond her shift, but then it was Krista Nickerson, another midwife. She let me push for five hours, so I could have the vaginal delivery that I wanted, without an epidural."

The next pregnancy came three years later. When Vanessa and her husband David went for an ultrasound exam, they learned they were having twins.

"I was freaked out; my husband and I were in shock," she said. "That automatically meant my pregnancy was high-risk. Could I still use the midwives? What did this mean?

"Late that night the phone rings, and it's Marti. I hadn't called her, she just cared, and she knew my head was probably spinning. She was able to provide information, and for me information is comfort. That's why having somebody who is not only skilled but is patient and therapeutic is the full package that I really needed, and that I think a lot of women need."

When it came time for delivery, a medical team was on hand, but "Marti delivered them," Vanessa said. "It was the first set of twins she'd ever delivered.

"I was in a room with probably 20 people in scrubs and masks. The babies each had a team of specialists, I had a team of specialists, and I think there were all these residents there who wanted to see this rare, unmedicated vaginal twin delivery. But it still felt like it was me, my husband, Marti and our doula," a birth coach.

"I felt like we were in a bubble. And Marti created that bubble. She made it exactly the way we wanted it to be.

"Alana came out first, and seven minutes later was Hazel. That's the story."

⅋

CARINA MCCAULEY

After the first of Carina McCauley's two boys was born in 2009, "I joked that I had postpartum elation," she said. "I had waited my whole life to be a mom. Even though the birth had complications, I still felt very supported by the staff."

The second experience was not the same.

"I became extremely emotional," said Carina, a registered nurse who lives in Richmond, Vt. "Everything felt excessively hard. I did not find joy in much."

She had just changed jobs to work the night shift on the medical center's maternity floor. Leaving home each night at 10 p.m. was tough. She was crying a lot.

"I remember thinking, maybe I'm depressed — but I thought everything would be better when I had the baby. I just kept blaming it on my shift."

Having had her first child by cesarian section, Carina very much wanted to deliver her second by vaginal birth. She again saw the nurse-midwives. But this birth, in April 2012, did not go as she'd hoped.

She developed a slow water leak. After 24 hours she hadn't gone into labor, so the midwife on duty induced her with Pitosin, a hormone-like compound. With her labor now in full swing, she received an epidural anesthetic for pain relief. But she

The McCauleys, from left: Brayden, Carina, Ethan and Ed.

developed a fever and her cervix would not open further, in spite of her contractions. She was wheeled into the OR for a cesarean, her nurse-midwife at her side.

The epidural usually provides pain relief during the cesarian, but this time it did not. At the last moment, Carina was given a general anesthetic.

"It's rare to be given a general, and we try hard to avoid it," explained Marti Churchill. "It's hard to wake up groggy and sore and make sense of meeting your baby for the first time."

"As I was waking up, they put Ethan on me to nurse," Carina said, "and Krista, the midwife, held him on me, which is beautiful and amazing — but all I could think was, 'Get this child off me.' After, I cried for days. I felt guilt that I couldn't birth him, guilt that I couldn't be present for his birth, guilt that I wanted him off me. I was showing up, my kids were well taken care of. But I wasn't."

Months went by as Carina, working evenings now in the maternity unit, saw moms who'd had the vaginal birth she had so wanted. Driving home, the events of Ethan's delivery played through her mind, night after night. She saw a therapist, but that provider wasn't trained in postpartum depression. Finally, she shared her struggle with a nurse-midwife.

"She was amazing. She said, 'I'm so sorry that happened.' She put me on meds, and set me up with an appointment with Sandy."

Sandra Wood, CNM, had become a psychiatric nurse practitioner to help new mothers who were having mental-health struggles. But the medical center had no program or budget support for that sort of work; Wood could only get reimbursed for seeing Carina on two medication consultations. Yet she continued to work with Carina, on her own time, every week. For months.

"She helped me deal with the postpartum depression, with the post-traumatic stress syndrome," Carina said. "I wanted to understand: What is going on with my brain? She brought me books, drew me pictures. She went way above and beyond.

"I came around. I got to where I could bond with my son, and I could enjoy being with him. Sandy saved me."

The year after Wood's work with Carina, the Lintilhac Foundation approved the first in a series of significant grants devoted, in large part, to funding her efforts to provide and develop mental-health services to pregnant and new mothers, at the medical center and throughout Vermont.

"I remember telling Sandy, I will do anything to help you get a program going," said Carina, who now works in a pediatrician's office. "I will be on any panel. I will talk from a nurse perspective, I will talk from a patient perspective. But this needs to be here."

✇

ASHLEY OLINGER AND MAUREEN MCGRATH

Ashley Olinger and Maureen McGrath of Waterbury Center went to UVM for their first insemination, "and they were great," Ashley says of the staff. "So we got into the midwife program. We cycled through all of the midwives; we wanted to meet them all."

Ashley bore Martin, their first child, in 2015. She got through 24 hours of painful false labor, then almost 24 hours of real labor. "We tried everything, the tub, the stool," she says. "I was getting exhausted and dehydrated."

Doctors began discussing a cesarean. But with help from the nurse-midwife and the on-duty nurse, Ashley brought the baby down into the birth canal.

"By this time they were worried about her health, and now the baby had to come out," Maureen recalls. "At this point, the only options were the vacuum or the forceps."

Ashley began to panic. But the nurse-midwife assured her, "We're going to get him out. It's going to be fine." A perinatal specialist began the vacuum procedure.

"'We can see his head! Two pushes and we'll grab him,'" Maureen says. "She did it — and we got him in one."

The nurse-midwife, Ashley adds, "was the constant, and the calm."

Maureen bore Oisin in 2017. The birth took hours of hard pushing, and soon after she began bleeding from torn muscles inside. A surgeon quickly repaired the damage.

"That's why it was really good we were in the hospital," Ashley notes.

"It's very personal care," she adds. "You literally feel like they're family — and they're very respectful of your wishes. That's one of the biggest things."

Oisin Olinger, Maureen McGrath, Martin Olinger and Ashley Olinger.

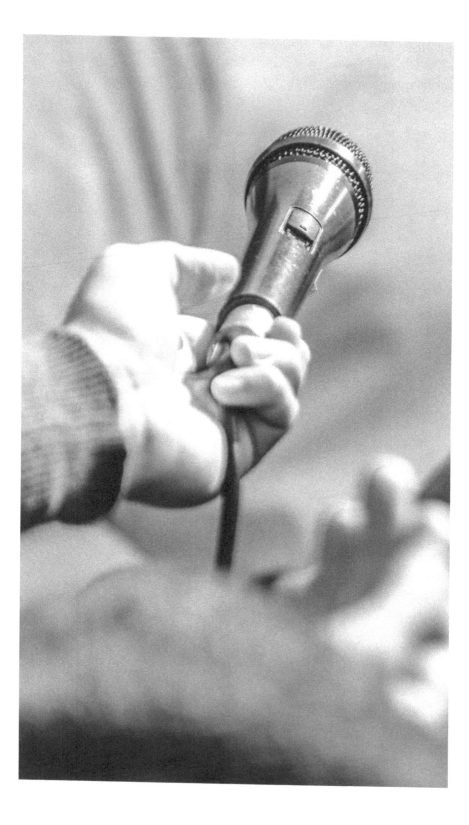

4

In Pursuit of Truth

Supporting informed public discourse in a tough time for journalism

———— ☙ ————

Under the leadership of Crea and Phil Lintilhac, the foundation has continued to support nurse-midwifery and maternal/child health. It has also expanded its focus, especially into four priority areas: informed public discourse, lake science and water quality, land conservation, and clean energy. This chapter and those that follow examine these priorities, and the impacts that Vermont nonprofit organizations have helped to generate with the foundation's support.

Inside a Miami hotel ballroom in February 2018, Vermont editor Anne Galloway stepped, for the first time, onto a national stage.

Galloway is the founder and editor of *VTDigger*, a news website based in Montpelier that covers the state. The occasion was the Knight Media Forum, a gathering of leading journalism funders and practitioners organized by the Knight Foundation. The program's second day featured a panel on how foundations are supporting efforts around the country to meet the need for local news, often in innovative ways. Galloway's opening remarks were set to lead off the panel.

Her news site fit the bill. Founded in 2009 with virtually no budget through the Vermont Journalism Trust, a nonprofit publisher also started and led by Galloway, *VTDigger* now had an annual budget of $1.85 million and the state's largest news team, with 16 reporters and editors plus five business staffers.

Anne Galloway, right, with *VTDigger* reporter Kit Norton in the Vermont State House, 2019.

Soft-spoken but determined, Galloway had worked enormously hard to build *VTDigger*, and this conference was the first time she had been asked to describe that work to an audience from across the country. She was joined on the panel by funders and editors of the online *Texas Tribune* and the radio station WHYY in Philadelphia.

"In 2009 I was an editor at the *Rutland Herald/Times Argus* and I was laid off, just like a lot of other journalists around the country," Galloway began. "I wanted to stay in journalism — and I decided that day, when I got my pink slip, that I wanted to start a news website. I didn't have any money, I didn't have a big reputation, but I had an idea."

She wanted her new site to focus on investigative reporting and watchdog coverage, both in the capital and, if possible, elsewhere around the state.

The Vermont Community Foundation gave the startup $6,000. A few years later, Galloway hired *VTDigger's* first reporter with funds from the Knight Community Information Challenge Program. One of the Lintilhac Foundation's funding priorities is supporting informed public discourse; it began to support *Digger* with a $10,000 grant in 2014, and has continued making larger grants in the years that followed.

During those same years, *Digger's* growing reputation for hard-nosed and relevant reporting helped the operation broaden its base of support. By 2018, 40 percent of its budget was coming from membership, 40 percent from underwriting, 15 percent from grants, and the rest from news-related revenues. (*Digger* contracts to provide its coverage to local and regional news outlets around the state.)

"I think our success is about the trust we've developed with the community," Galloway told the panel, "and the reason people trust us is we're hard on everybody. We're really aggressive in our reporting; we break investigative stories quite frequently. We broke a huge story about a $200 million fraud at a resort in northern Vermont," she said, referring to the EB-5 Immigrant Investor Program fraud at Jay Peak Ski Resort. "We started on that story two years before the SEC brought 52 counts of securities fraud.

"People give us tips every day, and we follow those tips — because at the end of the day, when we expose what's going on, things change."

When *VTDigger* started, "I thought 'Wow, if we had ten reporters, we could cover everything in the state,'" Galloway told the forum. "But even with a newsroom larger than that today, she said, "we're still not cutting it. We're still not covering everything. We're missing 20,000 reporters in this country now. In my state, we're missing 50 reporters. We're not making up the difference — it's not enough."

"At *Digger*, half of our readers are conservatives, half are liberals, and the same is true of our donor pool," she added. "We give everybody a hard time. We're doing that in pursuit of truth, and that's a moving target. When we get it wrong we fess up to it, and we correct it. It's important to engage in customer service, because this really is about service to the reader.

"Sure, I love to break big stories, I love to win awards," Galloway concluded, "but that's not what this is about, is it? It's about making sure that we're serving our communities."

"Our common connections"

The Lintilhac Foundation began supporting fresh efforts to bring news and issue analysis to Vermonters in 1986, when it granted $25,000 to help Vermont Public Radio research "a possible ... regional news and public affairs service." That led to the launching of "Switchboard," VPR's 90-minute

Vermont Public Radio and Vermont PBS became Vermont's largest news organization when they merged in late 2021. Veteran broadcast journalist Stewart Ledbetter continues to host the "Vermont This Week" TV news program, now from its new studio in downtown Winooski. *Photo courtesy of VPR and Vermont PBS*

call-in program, to which the foundation gave yearly grants from 1988 through 2008. The foundation has since been an annual supporter of "Vermont Edition," the daily hourlong interview and call-in program that replaced Switchboard.

Since the mid-80s, the foundation has also helped fund a variety of other news and public-issue initiatives — from Vermont PBS's news discussion show "Vermont This Week" to a variety of documentary films, publications on state government and citizenship, an environmental news program, the radio broadcast "Democracy Now," VPR's endowment fund, the Vermont Democracy Fund's "Equal Time Radio," and *VTDigger*.

Vermont PBS's relationship with the foundation goes back to 1985, when it began supporting children's educational programming on what was then called Vermont ETV, the state's public television station. "But for quite a while it's been 'Vermont This Week,'" said M. J. Reale, a PBS development officer. "They're one of four underwriters on the program; and of all their investments, this one is reaching hundreds of thousands of people on an annual basis."

Journalists discuss the state's news and issues on the weekly program, which "is consistently nonpartisan," Reale said. "And isn't that important, especially in times like this when we feel more entitled to go back to our respective corners and reinforce our preconceptions. More than ever, we need to re-emphasize our common connections and shared goals."

For Vermont Public Radio, Bob Kinzel has been a host of the midday public-affairs show since 1993. "I met with the Lintilhacs very early on, after I'd joined 'Switchboard,'" he said, "and their main message was encouraging me to have as much dialogue about important public policy issues as possible. They didn't say 'Do this, do that,' but it was very important to them that 'Switchboard' as much as possible present different points of view on issues that are important to Vermonters.

"I always appreciated that," Kinzel added. "They have a hands-off approach to different topics, but not to the idea of having an informed public debate."

VPR "Switchboard" host Steve Zind, right, interviewed Vermont actor, writer and humorist Rusty DeWees for the radio program in 2000.

Crea Lintilhac responded, "I write op-eds in opposition to a point of view, but I will remain supportive of organizations and people I disagree with. I think it's important, in terms of just the integrity of the foundation and the integrity of the institutions we support.

"Local news, small-town journalism, is disappearing," she reflected. "That's why we need *VTDigger*, Vermont Public Radio. Investigative journalism that digs deep is extraordinarily important for our democracy, for our lives and for getting information — and it often takes a lot of courage and tenacity."

Behind the mics at "Vermont Edition"

I n a 2016 report, "The Modern News Consumer," The Pew Research Center said: "As of early 2016, just two in ten U.S. adults often get news from print newspapers. This has fallen from 27 percent in 2013. This decrease occurred across all age groups, though the age differences are still stark: Only 5% of 18- to 29-year-olds often get news from a print newspaper, whereas about half (48%) of those 65 and older do. Compared with print, nearly twice as many adults (38%) often get news online, either from news websites/apps (28%), on social media (18%) or both."

The changes in Vermont's journalism landscape seem just as stark.

"Going back ten years, the three dominant news sources in Vermont would have been the *Burlington Free Press*, Channel 3 and the AP," said Bob Kinzel, reflecting on VPR's history. "Without giving ourselves too much credit, I would say that if you picked three today, you would pick *Digger*, *Seven Days* and VPR. The landscape has totally changed. The AP has gone from five or six people down to two. They don't really have a reporter in the State House full-time any more. They have us; we have a collaboration with them."

Does that mean the role, and value, of a program like "Vermont Edition" has changed?

"I think it's more valuable," Kinzel said. "The goal of the program is the same — if it's an issue that has two sides, you know you're going to hear both sides. So I think it's become more important to have a show like 'Vermont Edition.'"

A veteran State House reporter, Kinzel hosts "Vermont Edition" from Montpelier for its noon-to-1 p.m. broadcast on Friday. From 2007 to early 2021, Jane Lindholm hosted the Monday through Thursday program from VPR's headquarters in Colchester (each show is rebroadcast at 7 p.m.). Together, the two broadcasts average 63,000 listeners each week; distributed also as a podcast, the program also draws 35,000 downloads per month.

VPR's large newsroom in Colchester is full of reporters' and producers' workstations, plus a round table stacked high with newly published books. The newsroom has high ceilings and tall windows, and the First Amendment is displayed in big type on a high wall.

On a Monday in early March 2018, it was a gray, snow-mottled day outside —
and in here, Jane Lindholm and her colleagues were getting set to do the program's
annual Town Meeting Day show.

Jackson Evans, a young farmer and town moderator in tiny Braintree in Orange
County, had come in to be a guest. Set to join the program by phone were Susan
Smallheer, a longtime *Rutland Herald* reporter who had covered Town Meetings
in 46 Vermont communities over 40-plus years, plus David Plazak, a professor at
Northern Vermont University in Johnson who, with his students, had been collect-
ing data on present-day Town Meetings in the Northeast Kingdom.

Lindholm had been in the studio since 9 a.m., studying, reading links she'd
been given and generally preparing. "For me it's like cramming for a test," she
said. "The producers do all the legwork, with figuring out who should come on the
show. My role is to cram for the test and figure out what angle we're going to take."

Inside the control room, a big window looked into the "talk studio" next door,
where Lindholm sat down at the long table and put on her headphones. The table
had four microphones on swing stands, two monitors and a keyboard. In the control room, a UVM intern, Lydia Massey, had begun screening calls. Producer Matt
Smith called her "the unsung hero of the show. The interns are going to get the
brunt of the abuse from a caller who's cranky."

Lydia collected information on each caller, then posted it — name, town,

On Vermont Public Radio, Bob Kinzel (right) has been a host of the midday public-affairs program —
first "Switchboard," then "Vermont Edition" — since 1993. Jane Lindholm was a "Vermont Edition"
host from 2007 to 2021.

"THERE'S STILL A NEED FOR GOOD REPORTERS"

UVM's Community News Service helps fill the local news gap

In summer 2019 the University of Vermont launched a new minor, Reporting & Documentary Storytelling, with a program called the Community News Service that lets students earn publication credits and experience by developing and filing stories, with an editor's guidance, for Vermont weekly newspapers and *VTDigger*.

"Instead of inventing a program from scratch, we thought, 'Let's just partner with all these great media enterprises that exist in Vermont,'" said Richard Watts, who co-directs Reporting & Documentary Storytelling with two UVM colleagues, and is director of the university's Center for Research on Vermont. "So along came the idea of this Community News Service, in which students write for these small, struggling community papers."

"It's really important for the university to develop a pipeline of students who've gotten the journalism bug, who want to devote their lives to this important public service," said Anne Galloway, *VTDigger's* founding editor. "It has already helped us, in identifying students who want to serve as interns — and we turn to those folks over time as potential sources for jobs we're hiring for. So it's absolutely critical what Richard is doing."

The foundation has helped to fund the Community News Service, which is working with about ten news outlets, all of which except *Digger* are local weeklies. "Their freelance budgets were super-tight, so it was really hard for them to pay a lot of others to contribute," said Lisa Scagliotti, a veteran Vermont journalist who served as the service's first editor. "So I told them, I'm going to send you stories every week.

"We'd hammer out what the assignments are, and I worked with the students to mark up their copy, ask them questions and have them turn out a story that was ready to go into print — and deal with photos and captions, all the details, so I could hit Send and ship it to the editor."

In spring 2020, Scagliotti moved on to create a new, online news outlet for Waterbury, her home community, after the *Waterbury Record* had printed its last weekly issue and folded in March. As the so-far-unpaid editor of the *Waterbury Roundabout*, Scagliotti has enlisted UVM students to design the website as well as contribute articles.

"Whether they are inspired to take on journalism as a career varies," she said. "But what we're doing isn't 'fake news.' There is a lot of care and time that goes into getting the details right. If these were classroom assignments, I could give them a grade and tell them to do better next time. Instead, they are turning in stories on deadline, and they need to be ready to be published and for real people to read them."

UVM 2020 graduate Sunny Nagpaul worked with Scagliotti on the Community News Service. "I landed some stories all over the place," she said. "It was mostly community stories, like local businesses. I did a feature on hair salons in Hinesburg, I went to the Champlain Valley Fair and wrote on local musicians who were performing, a cooking demo by Shelburne Farms, and Al's French Frys. That was pretty cool, because the family had been doing that at the fair for like 70 years."

After graduating, Nagpaul got an internship at *VTDigger*, where she was able to do some reporting on political subjects. "I definitely have more of a passion for politics and social reform," she said. She has hoped to build a career in journalism; but "I'm kind of worried," she said. "I applied for a lot of jobs when I was still in school, and a lot of them were like, 'Oh we're firing, not hiring.' Even the newer programs were saying, 'You need more experience.'"

In talking with aspiring journalists about building a career in the business, "I tell them it's hard," said Lisa Scagliotti, who hopes her *Waterbury Roundabout's* appeal for local funding support will help the startup become a sustaining, salaried operation. "A lot of our conversations have been around how many papers are scaling back, and laying people off. They're seeing that in real time. They know how hard it is.

"But what I also tell them is that if they're good at it, there's still a need for good reporters out there. I'm trying to fill a void in a little town that just lost its paper. There's still news that needs to be covered, so we've got to figure this out. I think if we do it well, people will respond and we can survive."

At the University of Vermont's Patrick Gymnasium, Katie Jickling, health care reporter for *VTDigger*, gathers information on the coronavirus outbreak, in 2020.

"comments"— to an on-screen form that both the producer in the control room and Lindholm in the talk studio could see. Smith, meanwhile, monitored the program's two Facebook pages, its Twitter feed, the VPR websites, and the comments coming in by email. He put comments into an order he thought would work; Lindholm then decided which ones she'd read on air.

"I'm going to put you on our screened call list," Lydia told a caller named Sylvia, who like today's guest was from Braintree. "If you hear Jane say your name, that means she's about to take you on the air."

After the noon news, at precisely 12:07 p.m., Lindholm read her lead-in.

"One tradition that seems to be almost as old as Town Meeting itself is questioning Town Meeting Day's relevance as times change and towns evolve," Lindholm said. "But it's more than just hand-wringing. Times *do* change — and it's okay to question where and whether and how to conduct some of the most relevant civic and political business people face, the things that happen to them on a very local scale."

This year's broadcast was airing on Monday, she noted, so that it wouldn't conflict with the meetings that towns across Vermont still convene during the day on the traditional first Tuesday in March.

"There's a lot of emphasis on national politics, state politics," Jackson Evans observed, "but there's really not a lot of opportunity for people in small towns to get together and talk about things that will affect them on a day-to-day basis. So I think it's vital."

But, Lindholm asked, isn't the relatively small group of people who show up at Town Meeting making decisions for the rest of the town?

That's so, Evans says; not everyone can get to a Tuesday daytime meeting. "You really have to make a commitment ... if it's important to you."

A number of Windsor County towns have switched to Saturday meetings, noted Smallheer of the *Herald*. "They have the time, and they really air out the issues." Evans said that whether to make that shift was on the Braintree meeting's agenda. He expected a lively discussion.

"I can tell you've really thought about this"

Not everyone who called in to discuss Town Meeting argued for continuing the traditional in-person format. "Our town increased voter participation by almost 25 percent when we went to Australian ballot," one caller said. "Every citizen should have that opportunity, even if they can't take the day off."

"Democracy is about participation and governance — not the form it takes," said another.

A Salisbury caller said that in her town, as in many others, school region-alization has taken the school portion off the Town Meeting agenda. The town elections and major funding questions are decided by Australian ballot; so Town Meeting in Salisbury has become mostly informational, with presentations by the fire and ambulance squads and Girl Scouts selling cookies. Those still devoted to the tradition, the caller said, were struggling to keep others interested.

"Sometimes it's not what people would call easy," she declared, "but it's critical to building community and sustaining the social fabric of a community, I feel. Making meaningful decisions together, and having meaningful conversation. Otherwise it's just a bunch of people living together."

"Wow, I can tell you've really thought about this," Lindholm responded. "And what an articulate way of putting it."

Sylvia from Braintree was the last caller to go on the air. "Hello, Jackson," she said.

"Hello, Sylvia," responded Evans, the Braintree moderator, as Lindholm chuckled.

Sylvia wondered if Town Meetings could be coordinated with local high schools. Then students could attend, "to know how important this is — to our town government, but also to a better understanding of our state and national democracy, and perhaps an interest in taking part in those."

After the program wrapped, Lindholm, producer Smith and other staffers stood around her newsroom desk to debrief. Flyers and printouts were taped to the newsroom wall, along with a quote: "Your character is defined by your capacity to meet a deadline."

Lindholm observed, "If you live in a small town, it's, 'This is going to cost me money in taxes — why do we need a new fire truck?' You really get to know things about your town. It all comes down to connection."

And the conversation moved on, to tomorrow's topic: the invasive emerald ash borer. The tree-killing insect has devastated forests elsewhere in the U.S., and now has come into Vermont. Experts would be joining the next day's show to talk about what to do.

"We have a forum on our 'Vermont Edition' web page saying, 'What's a conversation you wish you were having in your community, that we could facilitate?'" Jane Lindholm said later. "We're getting better, but we don't have a particularly diverse staff when it comes to socioeconomic diversity, cultural diversity, geographical or racial diversity — so I struggle with that a lot. I try to cultivate different sources in different communities.

"I read papers, read Facebook groups, try to eavesdrop on conversations digitally, and we rely on our callers," she said. "That's the value and joy of our show, that we have people who call in and tell us things. You open up the conversation, and people will always call."

Putting marriage equality on screen, and into law

The foundation has also supported a number of documentary film and video projects. Its first grant of that type was $5,000, awarded in 2006 to the Vermont Freedom to Marry Taskforce for a video the group produced and used in its long, successful campaign to achieve marriage equality in this state for same-sex couples.

Produced and directed by Vermont filmmakers Deb Ellis and Nora Jacobson with funding from both the Lintilhac and Vermont Community foundations, the film, *Freedom to Marry: Voices of Vermonters*, was shown all over the state.

"We have distributed this DVD to every public library in the state, public access televisions, and schools; have run the video at our county fair displays, and will be distributing the video to elected officials, opinion leaders, coalition partners, churches and clergy persons, business organizations, and a variety of other recipients," Freedom to Marry reported to the foundation, which provided a second grant in 2007 in support of the marriage equality campaign.

By then, much had been achieved, but full marriage equality had so far eluded same-sex couples and their champions, in Vermont and elsewhere around the U.S.

In December 1999, the Vermont Supreme Court had declared, in its landmark *Baker v. Vermont* decision, that "in recognition of our common humanity," same-sex couples were entitled to receive "the same benefits and protections as married opposite-sex couples." In response and after intense debate and controversy, in 2000 the Vermont Legislature passed legislation granting same-sex couples the

An image from Jeff Kauffman's 2015 documentary film *The State of Marriage*, about the struggle for marriage equality in Vermont.

right to enter into "civil unions" that gave them legal recognition. Over the next several years, civil union ceremonies all over Vermont would legally join some 8,600 couples from Vermont, 48 other states, and a number of other nations.

But the long campaign had only partly succeeded. The Lintilhac grants of '06 and '07 came at a time when Vermont Freedom to Marry had very little money, and even many of its strongest supporters were skeptical that full, complete marriage equality could be achieved in anything like the near future.

Yet it was.

Almost a decade after the *Baker v. Vermont* decision, in April 2009 the Vermont House of Representatives overrode by a single vote Governor Jim Douglas's veto of a bill that allowed same-sex couples to marry. It was the first time in American history that marriage equality was enacted by a state legislature rather than through judicial action, as Vermont became the fourth state overall to grant full marriage rights to same-sex couples.

"Our victory here in Vermont was by no means inevitable — as evidenced by the razor-thin override margin and up-to-the-finish-line drama," wrote attorney Beth Robinson, then chair of Vermont Freedom to Marry, to Crea Lintilhac in April 2009. "Your early support for our video project back in 2005 helped us lay the groundwork for the past two months' events. Your ongoing generosity through the ensuring years likewise contributed to a solid foundation for our final push."

Instrumental in the Vermont Legislature's pioneering approval in 2000 of "civil unions" between same-sex couples in 2000, then of full marriage equality in 2009, were, from left: Beth Robinson, then chair of Vermont Freedom to Marry, now an associate justice of the Vermont Supreme Court; State Rep. Bill Lippert of Hinesburg, who chaired the 2009 hearings on marriage equality in the Vermont House, and led the House's passage of the marriage equality bill; and attorney Susan Murray, co-founder with Robinson of the Vermont Freedom to Marry Task Force. In 1999, Murray and Robinson won the *Baker v. Vermont* case before the state Supreme Court, whose ruling led to the passage of civil union legislation, the first of its kind in the nation. *Photo by Kym Boyman.*

Documentary filmmaker Jeff Kaufman was living in Middlebury and working as a radio host during the time when the debate over marriage equality was consuming Vermont. After the law's final passage, he set about filming *The State of Marriage*, a full-length documentary about Vermont's breakthrough on the issue. During editing and post-production, sorely in need of new funding for his project, Kaufman got a form of support the Lintilhacs have often provided, but rarely described publicly: a fundraiser at their Shelburne home.

"We had just done a fundraiser in a different state that we thought was going to be gigantic, and it did almost nothing," recalls Kaufman, who now lives in Los Angeles. "Then we came to Vermont for the one that Crea and Phil hosted along with Lola Van Wagenen," a resident of Charlotte, Vt. who was co-executive producer of the film.

"We didn't know what expectations to have," Kaufman said, "but it was fabulous. It brought so many people who were in the film together, and it ended up bringing in a substantial amount of money that really helped us finish the film. Trying to get across that finish line was complicated, and we would not have gotten there if it wasn't for the help of Crea and Lola."

The State of Marriage was released in 2015. In a landmark ruling that same year, the U.S. Supreme Court guaranteed marriage rights to same-sex couples throughout the nation. Also that year, *Entertainment Weekly* mentioned the film — along with the TV shows "Will and Grace" and "Modern Family," and the feature film *The Kids Are All Right* — in an article about "key moments that helped shape America's opinion" on marriage equality.

"It starts a conversation"

On a frigid winter night in early 2018, about 50 University of Vermont students gathered in a campus auditorium to see a new documentary, *Waking the Sleeping Giant: The Making of a Political Revolution*. Their host was film co-producer Jon Erickson, a UVM professor whose first documentary project, *Bloom: The Plight of Lake Champlain*, was created with major support from the foundation and won a regional Emmy Award [see page 116].

Waking the Sleeping Giant tracks the progressive activism that surged in places around the country during 2016's national election campaign. The film centers on that year's presidential campaign of U.S. Senator Bernard Sanders of Vermont.

"The initial idea was to kind of tell the story of a rebirth, a revitalization of the progressive movement, but through the Sanders story," Erickson said. "We had pitched to Bernie's staff about doing more of a traditional campaign documentary — something like *War Room*, where you talk to people behind the scenes, and a lot of the camera work was fly on the wall, and you get some access to the candidate.

"He had absolutely zero interest in letting people follow him around. He's a very, very private person. So then we sort of pivoted to the idea of, 'Well, let's use the backbone of his campaign to tell all the side stories around what a progressive movement would look like.' They more or less treated us as a group of reporters, and gave us press access when they could.

"From there, it turned into a more compelling story. We developed a storyline

Jon D. Erickson, right, and his son Jon E. Erickson, with two of the regional Emmy awards won by their "Bloom" series on cyanobacteria in Lake Champlain. Jon D. was executive producer on the series; his son contributed photography.

around a woman in West Virginia, around economic justice issues. We developed a storyline around Black Lives Matter when that became a major story in the race, and we developed a storyline around money in politics, and the millennial generation getting involved in protesting. It was very organic. It didn't turn out how we had originally planned it, that's for sure."

Along with providing a modest grant, Crea Lintilhac and the foundation assisted the project as "sounding board, facilitator, connector," Erickson said. "For the whole film, we didn't raise much more than $120,000. All the producers' time, the directors', the writers', none of that was covered. It was my own nights and weekends." For a time in summer 2017, the Lintilhacs' Shelburne home became the project's temporary home, as Erickson and co-director Jacob Smith did the initial editing.

"Real change never happens without struggle," Sen. Sanders says in the film. "When we come together as a people, there is very little that we cannot do." After losing the 2016 Democratic nomination to Hillary Clinton, Sanders says in the film, "Our attitude has got to be not to look back — we have got to look forward. ... The struggle continues, and we have got to roll up our sleeves and maintain the pressure."

After the screening, Erickson said to the student audience: "As you probably know, campuses like ours are places of passion and organization, of leadership."

"How can various identity groups come together?" a student asked.

"I think we are at a moment of intersectional coalition-building," the professor/filmmaker responded. "If this film and these kinds of movements inspire you, it's hard work — it's not going to happen overnight. Part of it is to step outside your own comfort zone."

"People don't get involved because they don't think they have a voice," a student reflected. "It was cool to see similar people get a voice."

"People can like it, people can hate parts of it," Erickson said of his film. "They can throw darts at each other. But it starts a conversation."

Committed to public-service journalism

Jay Rosen is a journalism professor at New York University who monitors and reports on innovation in the field, especially those that involve technology. He "has been one of the earliest advocates and supporters of citizen journalism, encouraging the press to take a more active interest in citizenship, improving public debate, and enhancing life," says his Wikipedia page.

"Two years ago," Rosen said in early 2018, "I was in Vermont to speak at Saint Michael's College, and while I was there I also visited the *Burlington Free Press*, which used to be the biggest news organization in the state. I met with the entire staff, which is not very many people, and most of the discussion was about how diminished they were, compared to years before.

"I said, 'Well, you're a lot smaller than you used to be, but you're still the biggest newsroom in the state.' And they all said in unison, 'No we're not.' And I said, 'What do you mean you're not? Who is?' And they said, '*Vermont Digger*. They've got three people in the capitol!'"

Having heard that, Rosen arranged to come back to Vermont. He spent a late-winter afternoon in 2018 at *VTDigger's* Montpelier headquarters, learning about and discussing the operation. Gathered around a long table with editor Anne Galloway and the newsroom staff, Rosen asked why so many Vermonters were supporting the online news provider.

VTDigger reporter Xander Landen, third from left, interviews Vermont Attorney General T.J. Donovan, at right, in the State House in 2019.

"It filled a void," Galloway responded. "Nobody was doing investigative reporting, and people wanted that void filled. People just responded to that."

Rosen asked if there was any connection between support for *Digger* and Vermont's democratic tradition. Everyone around the table nodded.

"We do have Town Meeting here," Galloway said, "and I think there's a perception that we have a stronger democracy."

"People have a sense of belonging here, and of caring," added staff writer Ellen Bartlett. "They're invested. People are involved."

"It's pretty widely known that economic forces have hollowed out the daily newspaper," Rosen reflected after returning to New York. "Among the solutions has been the growth of these statewide, nonprofit newsrooms that try to replace just one aspect of the local papers, the accountability journalism and public policy reporting. You have the *Texas Tribune* in Texas and the *MinnPost* in Minnesota, and I would put *VTDigger* into that category.

"There's just a small class of these sites — those are three of the most prominent, and most successful," he added. "*VTDigger* is particularly distinctive because of its single-mindedness about investigative reporting."

The news site has also stood out for moving away from dependence on foundation funding, such as the annual Lintilhac grants, to a broader base that also includes substantial public and membership support.

"They really hunger for local news"

There are some 172 nonprofit news outlets of various types around the country, the Pew Research Center reported in 2013. Most sprang up during or soon after the recession of 2008-2009, when traditional news outlets across the U.S. cut back severely on reporting staff.

"All but nine states in the U.S. have at least one nonprofit news outlet," the Pew report said. "Nearly two-thirds ... began with a start-up grant that accounted for at least a third of their original funding. ... About half of those organizations are still generating at least 75% of their income from a single revenue stream, almost always foundation grants."

More and more Americans are getting at least some of their news from online sites like *VTDigger*, whose motto is "News in pursuit of truth." Around the nation, nonprofit news sites "grew Web traffic by an average of 75% from 2011 to 2013," the Knight Foundation reported in 2015. Within that same period, it said, "75% of sites increased total revenue. Three sites experienced revenue growth of greater than 100%: *Oakland Local* (601%), *The Lens* (333%), and *VTDigger* (198%)."

"People get disenchanted with the D.C. nonsense, but I think they really hunger for local news," Anne Galloway reflected. "I do think that creates an opportunity for journalists, like those at *Digger*, who have a commitment to a cause, to public service journalism, and who understand that the business side is really important — that you have to spend time making the money to do the journalism. And people are willing to make donations. They're willing to subscribe."

Can an operation like *VTDigger* be replicated elsewhere around the country?

"I think it could be, but it's hard to know," Galloway said. "The difficulty is that there isn't, at this point, a lot of funding available for startups.

"When I started *Digger*, I started with almost nothing. I got through it — and it's really because of people like Phil and Crea, and Tom and Ina Johnson [fundholders at the Vermont Community Foundation], the Block Foundation [the Harris and Frances Block Foundation of Marshfield, Vt.], the Vermont Community Foundation, and the Knight Foundation that we were able to get started. Because people believed in the concept.

"Once we were able to get off the ground," she concluded, "then we were able to raise money from readers, and underwriting, and really stand on our own two feet."

VTDigger's staff in September 2021. Seated, from left: Emma Cotton, Maggie Cassidy, Lana Cohen, Anne Galloway, Grace Benninghoff, Jim Lehnhoff. Standing, first row: Lola Duffort, Taylor Haynes, Libbie Sparadeo, Erin Petenko, Marnie DeFreest, Fred Thys, Alan Keays, Jake Perkinson, Grace Elletson, Natalie Williams, Shaun Robinson. Standing, second row and in back: Jacquelyn O'Brien, Sadie Goldfarb, Libby Johnson, Jim Welch, Florencio Terra, Mike Dougherty, Paul Heintz, Glenn Russell. Not pictured: Tiffany Tan, Auditi Guha, Liora Engel-Smith, Kevin O'Connor, Stacey Peters. *Photo by Caleb Kenna.*

NEWS, COMMUNITIES AND *VTDIGGER*

A conversation with Anne Galloway

The American Journalism Project, a new philanthropy created in 2019 to help community news providers find a way to survive and even thrive, announced in spring 2020 that it had raised $46 million, and it named *VTDigger* as one of 11 news organizations to which it would make its first grants.

The initiative "aims to build financially stable, nonpartisan news outlets across the nation by supporting their business and revenue operations," the American Journalism Project (AJP) said. "The idea is that resources for the newsroom will follow once news organizations have stable, diverse sources of funding."

As ad revenues for traditional print newspapers have plummeted across the nation, "60 percent of jobs in journalism have disappeared and over 2,100 communities have lost newspapers, journalists, and access to local news," wrote John Thornton, founder of the online *Texas Tribune* and co-founder of the AJP, in a letter to readers and supporters of *VTDigger*.

As Vermont's only statewide online news outlet, "*VTDigger* is inspiring to AJP," Thornton wrote. "It works to fill critical information needs of your community and create greater civic engagement. ... We've seen this be even more front and center during our national and global pandemic."

Here is a conversation with Anne Galloway, founding editor of *VTDigger*, about her organization and the future of community journalism.

How are you using this grant?

It's tied to really building capacity in our business office, and in other areas of the company. The idea is that if we have additional help with our sustainable sources of revenue, we'll be able to become more sustainable going forward, and we'll be able to deepen our coverage in Vermont. It's $900,000 over three years, and it also comes with a lot of technical support and other resources they bring to bear to help everyone in the cohort build on what we have created so far.

AJP sees *VTDigger* as a national model they want to invest in, and possibly replicate in other places. They're experimenting with three or four different models around the country, and they're going to be investing in more newsrooms. They're taking the best bits and trying to synthesize what they learn, so they can help to build news organizations all over the country over time to replace the failing newspapers.

I share their vision. It's all about reporting the news that people really, really need, and developing a community, a reciprocal relationship between the newsroom and the people we're reporting for. As part of that effort, we grow. We have more people on our site; that enables us to raise more money through membership and underwriting, which are two major sources of sustainable funding; and that enables us to do other things, like start an obituary section, that really enhances our connection to the community. So it's really a powerful model, and it's quite different from the newspaper model in that it's less top-down. It's more of a grassroots approach to news gathering.

Did the Covid-19 pandemic and your response to it change your operation?

It completely revolutionized the way we operated, because the need was so great. We were bombarded with questions from readers; they were calling, they were emailing. We took their questions, and we got answers. We went to experts, we published an FAQ section that was updated repeatedly, and we increased our story production by 50 percent over two months. We started a live blog, and updated the [Vermont Covid] numbers sometimes more than once a day.

We also, behind the scenes, really pressed the [Gov. Phil] Scott administration to provide us with their plan for the surge. We pushed them, they gave us the plan, and then they released it to the public. We pressed them to hold press conferences every day. They decided to hold them three times a week, and I think it was one of the most successful things they did. We really questioned them on the state ethics policy regarding advance directives — who gets a ventilator, how they would make crucial decisions at hospitals as the surge hit. We also pressed them for PPE [personal protective equipment] numbers.

We formed a group of reporters who were dedicated to ensuring that we covered every aspect of the pandemic, every day. That team met for half an hour every day, to make sure that we were on top of everything. We also started a Covid newsletter, a daily rundown of what was happening.

Our readership went from 350,000 readers per month to 1.2 million in March. That held steady in April; in May it went to 1 million, and now we're at about 700,000.

If community journalism is to find a new future in this country, what are the keys to making that happen?

Number one, it has to move forward as a nonprofit industry, because there are no profits in journalism now. It's more about public service. Number two, it's about keeping the public trust — and I think at a time when fake news continues to dominate, it's even more important for news organizations to produce highly nonpartisan content.

And by "fake news," you mean ...

I mean social media, mostly. More than 160,000 people are on Facebook in Vermont. That leads me to my third point, which is that at this juncture, the kind of hyper-local journalism that we saw with local newspapers is going to be even less feasible than it was before. Because of the way the web works, if you're a small-town paper and you have 3,000 readers and a small number of advertisers, you don't get enough traffic on your site to generate the income you need.

You know, I just guessed at this when I started *Digger*, but it turns out that for us the statewide model is really important. We're big enough that we can attract enough readers to support membership, underwriting and other programs, and philanthropy. If we were in one small town, that would be really, really difficult. And Vermont's small. In other places, an online presence in a midsize city might work, but for rural areas it's particularly hard. You just can't generate the eyeballs to raise the revenue if you're too small. So I think the economy of scale of having a centralized operation, and of setting objectives based on a larger audience, is absolutely vital.

For us it's going to become a more distributed model, because we need to be in more communities. We have a Report for America reporter in Rutland and Bennington counties now; we've got reporters in Windham County, the Northeast Kingdom and Burlington. I can foresee a time when we will need to step up our game, to cover more areas.

Ellen Marsden, fisheries biologist at the University of Vermont, at work on the R/V Melosira.

5

Understanding the Lake

Three decades of Champlain science and archeology

———— \/ ————

t's an August weekday morning on Lake Champlain, a cloud-drifting summer day. The University of Vermont's research vessel R/V Melosira is on the water west of Burlington Bay. A reporter and videographer from local Channel 5 are on board, working on a feature for the TV nightly news.

On the open work deck of the research vessel, two powered winches have just hauled up a net that was trawling the lake bottom about 50 meters deep. Now Prof. Ellen Marsden, a UVM fisheries biologist, is measuring fish — and hoping to solve a mystery.

On a large worktable is the net's catch, a wriggling pile of lake trout mingled with smaller whitefish, alewife, smelt and lamprey. As Marsden calls out measures of length to a graduate student taking notes on a clipboard, she notes whether each trout has a clipped left pectoral fin. That would show it was a farmed fish, introduced into the lake from a state hatchery.

"That's a no-clip — the fins are intact," she calls out, grinning as she lifts and admires a mature wild trout. "That's a beautiful fish!"

Since the early 1970s, the state has been stocking Lake Champlain with both lake trout and landlocked salmon; and until recent years, the vast majority of mature trout pulled from lake waters were hatchery fish. But there's no clear reason, Marsden says, why this population hasn't become self-sustaining, why stocking is still necessary.

"We shouldn't have to spend so much time and money," she says. "The lake is a perfectly good place to live."

So in 2015, she and her grad students began looking for answers.

"Have we destroyed spawning sites? No, lots of spawning sites," she explains. "Are they using them? Yes. Are they producing little fry the next spring? Yes — and then we never saw them again. So that was the big worry."

Going out regularly in the warm months on the Melosira, the team has been amassing data: where the trout are, how many there are, how mature they are, and at what depths they're living. Unexpectedly in this process, they began to notice something. The numbers of lake trout with intact dorsal fins, showing they had grown to maturity after spawning in the wild, were increasing steadily.

Even dramatically.

"The first year, 2015, 23 percent of the fish we caught were wild," Marsden says. "Next year it was about 33 percent. Today, we caught about a hundred lake trout — and 89 of them were wild. And oh my gosh, the growth is spectacular; they're feeding, and they're maintaining their condition." (Other researchers have started to record growth, though more limited, in the wild spawning of salmon in the lake.)

For a young trout, the first winter is make-or-break, and now the fish are making it. All along, their food supply has been healthy, so what has changed? That's what the research team is working to understand.

"We just need to keep asking questions, keep trying to figure out why now," Marsden says. "We can't stock a carrying capacity's worth of lake trout and Atlantic salmon and then add this huge number of wild fish, and not collapse the forage base."

The findings from this research may also have wider usefulness. "What we're finding with lake trout is applicable to the Great Lakes, and to lakes in the West," the biologist notes. "We're all tied into colleagues globally."

The Lintilhac Foundation has helped fund UVM research into the invertebrates on which the lake trout feed. It has not directly supported Marsden's work, but the Melosira came to the university through Lintilhac support in the late 1980s. Since then the research vessel has been an indispensable platform, both for learning and for teaching about the nation's sixth-largest lake.

"UVM would never have been able to make its name the way it did, in the '90s and 2000s around lake health, if we hadn't had the Melosira to be that visible focus of all the work that was going on," observed Mary Watzin, an aquatic ecologist and watershed management specialist who joined the UVM faculty in 1990. Watzin directed the university's waterside Rubenstein Ecosystem Science Laboratory from 2005 to 2012, and from 2009-2012 she was dean of its Rubenstein School of Environment and Natural Resources.

"Increasing the understanding of what's going on is what drives forward public policy to promote lake health, and environmental health in general," noted Watzin, now dean of the College of Natural Resources at North Carolina State University. "And the Melosira is just iconic in that way: It represents attention to the lake's health and to science. When people see the Melosira on the water, they know there are people with credibility out there working on the lake."

Philip and Crea Lintilhac began to guide the foundation following Claire's death in 1984, and its focus has since expanded to supporting work on the Vermont environment — in scientific research, education and public-policy activism. Those same years in Vermont have seen a striking growth in public investment and attention devoted to better understanding Lake Champlain: its physical realities, its ecology, its historical treasures, and the challenges it faces.

Sometimes with fairly sizable grants, but often by making modest investments that helped programs and initiatives get going and find other support, the foundation has played a key role in the ongoing effort to better understand and safeguard the lake.

Along with supporting the Melosira, the foundation has:

- Helped make possible the development of the Lake Champlain Maritime Museum, and its Nautical Archeology Center.

- Provided early-stage funding for the Whole Lake Survey, a ten-year collaboration between the museum and Middlebury College that developed a sophisticated digital map of the lake bottom and depth readings, and discovered 85 under-water shipwrecks in addition to the 225 already known in the lake.

- Helped fund publication of two book-length collections of papers on new scientific research relating to the lake.

- Contributed the seed money that enabled Middlebury College to develop and fund its own sophisticated research vessel, the R/V Folger.

- Supported research into two urgent ecological challenges. The first is the destructive spread of one invasive mussel species, with invasion by a second species seeming imminent.

- The second challenge is the growing presence in warm weather of cyanobacteria. Often called bluegreen algae, this is a hardy phytoplankton that can produce dangerous toxins, is well-adapted to a warming climate, and poses a concerning hazard in this and other lakes around the world.

"I see the Lintilhac Foundation being really key here in Vermont, because we're a small state. We don't have a lot of resources when it comes to funding," said Angela

Shambaugh, a senior environmental scientist with the Vermont Department of Environmental Conservation who worked on a foundation-supported survey of lake plankton in the 1990s.

"We also, because we're small, don't necessarily rise to the standards of some of the bigger federal grants," she said. "So the Lintilhacs have been really good at helping some smaller projects, building an understanding of Lake Champlain and the basin that might have not happened otherwise.

"They've been a strong supporter of the Lake Champlain Research Consortium, and Crea has been active and involved in this for a long time," Shambaugh continued. "Very passionate, asks lots of good questions, and stimulates a lot of discussion. At a time when there was very little foundation support for work on the lake, the Lintilhacs helped it get started.

"They've been the seed funding, the catalyst, that allowed people to think bigger."

A vessel for learning: developing the Melosira

UVM's first research vessel, also named the Melosira, was a 47-foot former fishing boat the university acquired in the late 1960s from a charter operator in Brooklyn, New York's Sheepshead Bay. Before she and Phil Lintilhac were married, Crea Sopher worked on the vessel as a graduate student in the late '70s, with the late geology professor Allen Hunt.

"We were describing the extent of the Champlain Sea," Crea recalled. "My job was to identify foraminifera, the one-celled organisms that only live in a marine environment. You take sediment cores, examine them, and pick out the foraminifera.

"That really got me launched in a career in oceanography. I worked on some projects at the Graduate School of Oceanography at the University of Rhode Island, then I moved back to Vermont when Phil and I got married. I got involved with the Geology Department again — taught paleontology labs with Allen Hunt for a bit.

"But what shocked me, when I came back and got involved with the foundation, was that there was no research vessel on Lake Champlain."

By then the first Melosira had been retired for safety reasons, after its captain, Richard Furbush, found that its aging steel hull was no longer sound. "In the spring, I'd be scraping, chipping paint," Furbush said, "and all of a sudden I put a chip hammer through the bottom. So a big red flag went up, and in '81 we tied it up."

For a couple of seasons, the university used a state vessel to continue some fisheries research. "Then I heard a rumor that we had an unnamed, potential donor to replace our vessel," said Furbush. "We were directed to start putting together some details for a replacement vessel. We thought, 'What an opportunity!'"

The university announced that the Lintilhacs would support the building of a new research boat. Furbush and fisheries biologist George LaBar began to visit the John Williams Boat Company in Hall Quarry, Maine, where the well-known boat builder had recently produced a research vessel for the University of Maine.

For scientific research, "there's no such thing as an off-the-shelf boat," Furbush said. "You start with the shell and you build it."

The new Melosira was a larger adaptation of a Maine lobster boat. "They were called 'lobster yachts,'" Furbush said with a chuckle. After an overland transport to the lakeshore, he said, "It was launched in February of '87. Brutally cold. Crea and Phil came over, we put the boat in the water, Crea broke the champagne.

"I think of it as a work boat, with a larger open deck space," added Furbush, who would captain the new Melosira for the next 23 years. "A work boat gives you the ability to have reasonably good control over your vessel, and also to get out onto the work deck."

⇊

Fast-forward to autumn 2018: After more than three decades of steady service, the Melosira is still in almost daily use.

"It's everything," said Jason Stockwell, an aquatic ecologist who is the current director of UVM's Rubenstein Lab, where the now-iconic research vessel docks. "A week or so ago, I met with Steve Cluett, our captain, and he said, 'Of the next 31 workdays until the end of October, 29 of them have at least one trip.'

"It's a combination of laboratory classes: the fisheries class, the limnology class, the geology class," Stockwell continued. "They'll go out for multiple afternoons and do their teaching out there. We also have the Lake Champlain Sea Grant Watershed Alliance Program," which uses the boat to do education outreach with younger students and with teachers.

All UVM students in the Rubenstein School take NR1, the introductory natural history course. In a recent fall semester, a total of 180 NR1 students went out on the Melosira.

"So," Stockwell summed up, "we've got the classes, we've got teaching, we've got the outreach program to kids in the community,

UVM's present-day Melosira is a "work boat with a larger open deck space," said its first captain, Richard Furbush.

and we do our research," all making use of the Melosira.

Ellen Marsden and colleagues at the Rubenstein Lab have begun to envision an up-to-date replacement for the research vessel, one that would run on electric power with diesel backup, so researchers could move silently and cleanly around the lake.

"Imagine that for teaching," she said. "You wouldn't have to shout at students."

Shipwrecks as public treasures:
the origin of the Maritime Museum

Lake Champlain is the most historic body of water in the western hemisphere: a silver dagger from Canada to the heartland of the American colonies that forged the destiny of France and England in America, and of the United States. Liberated from war and the threat of war early in the nineteenth century, it became a thriving thoroughfare of trade and travel.

– Ralph Nading Hill, *Lake Champlain: Key to Liberty*
(Countryman Press, 1976)

There is no better way to honor the history of Lake Champlain than a rededication to its stewardship.

– U.S. Senator Patrick Leahy, foreword to *Lake Champlain:
An Illustrated History* (North Country Books, 2009), published with
support from the Lintilhac Foundation and others

Lake Champlain is 107 miles long, 12 miles across at its widest point and 399 feet at its deepest, and more than 300 sunken ships lie on its bottom. They include "intact wooden shipwrecks from every era of our history — Native American, British and French warships from before the Revolution, then from the Revolution and the War of 1812," said Art Cohn, co-founder of the Lake Champlain Maritime Museum in Ferrisburgh.

"There are early steamboats, the only known existing horse-powered ferry-boat, canal boats, sailing canal boats. We've got all these shipwrecks, and they're incredibly intact, in cold fresh water. The deeper the depth, the better the state of preservation."

Back in the early 1980s, when Cohn, an attorney and a professional diver, was running Northern Divers on the Burlington waterfront, "nobody ever talked about historic shipwrecks," he said. "Historic shipwrecks at that point were swashbuckling trophies that pirates cut up and sold to the highest bidder. It was a terrible situation — and that's what motivated me to want to define them as public, not private, resources."

On the Champlain shore in Vergennes, a half hour south of Burlington, sits the historic lakeside resort Basin Harbor. When Cohn brought a group of young nautical archeologists there in 1982, Bob Beach, the resort's owner and operator, told them about a wreck he had explored as a kid. Almost inside the club's marina, it still lay submerged in shallow water.

"Like many shipwrecks around the lake, it's passed-down information. We don't know much about it," said Beach, whose family has owned Basin Harbor for four generations. "So Art and I said, 'Hey, wouldn't it be great if someday there was a recipient of all this great Lake Champlain history?'"

That was the beginning of what would become the Lake Champlain Maritime Museum. But at the time, Cohn recalled, "I'm out there trying to be a voice of preservation for a class of objects that had never been viewed that way. People didn't understand what I was talking about.

"What the Lintilhacs did initially was, they had a couple of gatherings at their home, and they invited me to be the keynote presenter. It was a roomful of influence: decision-making, trend-setting community people. The Lintilhacs stood up and said, 'Hey, we've got a guy here we think you should listen to.'

"Now I had an audience. I said, 'Listen, this stuff is important. If we don't get a

Art Cohn, at left, with a dive team on Lake Champlain.

handle on managing and protecting our collection of public-resource shipwrecks on the bottom of Lake Champlain, we will not have a collection to give to our children.'

"The Lintilhacs were part of those initial few people who said, 'This is important, we get it, and we're going to give this guy a stage and some credibility.' Then all the specifics followed. We did create a museum, and very few people have been more generous than the Lintilhacs — but they helped me get started. They helped me get out of the gate."

The museum started small. Having secured a modest grant from the Vermont Council on the Humanities, Beach, Cohn and other volunteers put together a display of historical artifacts from 10,000 years of history in the Champlain Valley. They installed it in a historic, one-room stone schoolhouse on the Basin Harbor grounds.

Then, said Beach, "the person who helped us lay out that exhibit came forward and said, 'You know, you guys ought to build a boat.'"

So they did. On the lawn outside the tiny museum, a boat builder hired by the organizers began to replicate a *bateau*, a simply built carrier of cargo and people that was in daily use on the lake during the French and Indian War of 1754 to 1763, and the American Revolution.

"We said to the builder, 'Don't build this thing too fast — take the whole summer,'" Beach recalled. "Your project is not only to build the boat, it's to talk to people about it, about the history of the bateau and using old tools to do it."

"The Maritime Museum was in part created to help make that connection to

The Philadelphia II under sail. *Lake Champlain Maritime Museum photo.*

the public," noted Art Cohn. "There's got to be that connection."

"We launched that boat with great fanfare in 1987," Beach said. "Senator Leahy came; two thousand people came. We called it the Perseverance. And that led us to the next thought: We should continue to build historic replicas."

Their next boat project would be the first museum initiative supported by the Lintilhac Foundation.

And for it, Cohn and Beach had just the right vessel in mind.

The Philadelphia, relic of the Revolution

During the very perilous first year of the Revolution, Lake Champlain was the scene of a pivotal naval battle — one that played a key role in securing the new republic's independence.

On October 11, 1776, six months after the colonial uprising began in Massachusetts, a small flotilla of 15 colonial vessels, mostly cannon-armed sailing gondolas and row galleys, took up position in a deep channel of the lake near Plattsburgh, between the New York shore and Valcour Island. This first American naval force had been built in great haste under rebel general Benedict Arnold, at today's Whitehall, N.Y. at the south end of the lake. The flotilla now aimed to lure into the channel passage a group of some 28 British ships that had been pushing down the lake from Canada, with allied forces also moving on land.

The British had vastly superior firepower. They planned, after destroying the American vessels, to attack Fort Ticonderoga and take full control of the waterways from Champlain down the Hudson River, dividing and thereby defeating the young rebellion.

Their ships did turn into the Valcour channel, and in a close and ferocious afternoon firefight they inflicted heavy losses on Arnold's force. At dusk the British drew back out of cannon range, believing they had the rebels trapped and expecting to finish them off in the morning.

But in the dark, Arnold led his surviving ships and men in slipping between the British vessels and the shoreline, back onto the broad lake. The next day, as the British pursued in a fury and inflicted more damage, the rebels scuttled their five remaining vessels at what's now Arnold Bay on the Vermont side, and escaped on foot.

After the Battle of Valcour Island, the British commander, confronted by gathering colonial land forces and the oncoming cold weather, postponed his advance and returned to Canada for the winter. The next fall, the British sent a much more powerful force down the lake; but the year's delay had enabled the colonists to build up their strength as well.

At the Battle of Saratoga in October 1777, the Americans defeated the British and turned the tide of the Revolution. Historians have long credited the doomed stand by Arnold's ships at Valcour for making that victory possible.

Just off Valcour Island in 1934, a salvage engineer from New York named Lorenzo Hagglund found the burned and wrecked remains of a colonial gunship. Having closely studied accounts of the battle, he then searched for, and found, another gunboat from Arnold's little fleet.

This one was largely intact. It was the gondola Philadelphia, in 60 feet of water.

Hagglund raised the ship in 1935, and offered it to area museums. When none accepted, he placed the Philadelphia on a barge — and for 25 years, the rest of his life, he showed it in communities up and down the lake.

In 1961, after Hagglund's passing, the Philadelphia was transported to Washington, D.C. It's now on display in the Hall of Armed Forces History at the Smithsonian Institution's National Museum of American History, where it is surrounded by several hundred artifacts that were recovered along with the gunboat.

"When the Smithsonian got it, they did a full-scale blueprint drawing of the entire boat," Bob Beach recalled.

With those plans in hand, the Lake Champlain Maritime Museum launched its first capital campaign. The goal: to build and open to the public a full-sized, working replica of the Philadelphia.

"To share the rich history of the Champlain Valley"

The foundation gave significant grant support to the campaign, which raised enough money to launch the Philadelphia II project in 1989.

"We had four young boat-builders. Kids were coming to pound nails, it was great," said Beach. "It was all local oak and pine. We were out looking for oak trees that created the natural bend, what they call the knees of the boat. White oak for the frame. Doing natural logging with horses, we found what were called the King's Pines, these giant pine trees to cut the mast out of. We wanted to create our own metallurgy and nails, so we ended up building a blacksmith's shop.

"Our production date was the 200th anniversary of the founding of Vermont — so we launched that boat in 1991. We had a crowd of something like 5,000 people. Senators Leahy and [the late Robert] Stafford came."

Inspired by the project, area residents offered to donate their own vintage boats to the young museum. "Each boat had its own history, so we built our Small Boat Exhibit," Beach said. "And all the time we're doing this stuff, we're doing underwater archeology work. We found the great bridge, the [Revolutionary War] connector between Mount Independence and Fort Ticonderoga."

In summer 1777, as the British advanced toward the clash in Saratoga, they forced colonial forces to evacuate the fort. As the rebels crossed the bridge to Vermont, Beach said, "they were throwing stuff in the lake — so there were 900 artifacts that we found and raised. There was no place to conserve them, so we decided: We'll build a conservation lab. Also funded in part by the Lintilhac Foundation."

Young people had a hand in the building of the Philadelphia II.
Photo courtesy of the Lake Champlain Maritime Museum.

The Maritime Museum opened its Nautical Archeology Center in 1995. The lab has a two-fold purpose, said the museum's newsletter: "to house exhibits having to do with underwater archeology (read shipwrecks), and to provide temporary lab and dive support space for lake studies and artifact conservation." Acknowledging the foundation as the project's lead supporter, the museum said the new lab "will also serve as an active learning space to expose students and other museum visitors to the process of conservation."

Today, the Lake Champlain Maritime Museum occupies four acres provided by Basin Harbor next door. Its dozen buildings house a wide range of exhibits on underwater archeology, lake and Champlain Valley history, nautical technologies on the lake, Native American history and culture, and more.

The museum's approach is largely hands-on. Among its activities, young visitors build replica boats and kayaks, learn to paddle, interact with exhibits and museum educators, join in archeological digs, do metalwork, and explore shipwrecks with remote-operated vehicles.

"It's all about public participation," Bob Beach said. "Our primary goal has always been to share the rich history of the Champlain Valley with the public. We feel that we have given great value to the foundations that support us."

During just one recent year, 2017, the Maritime Museum:

- Engaged more than 2,500 elementary school students with museum exhibits and educators.
- Welcomed some 600 high schoolers from nine rowing clubs in the region, who practiced and competed in replicas of "pilot gig" longboats from the pre-steam era, all built by students.

- Hosted more than 1,200 young people in summer camps, where they explored snorkling, underwater archeology, kayak building, bronze casting, and the lake.
- Led graduate students in underwater archeology through three weeks of field school.
- Sent "content-rich multimedia exhibits" traveling to communities around the region — including the Lois McClure, the 88-foot replica of an 1862 canal schooner that the museum built and launched in 2004. Named for a prominent Vermont philanthropist and supporter of the replica project, the Lois McClure has traveled from Quebec to New York City and Buffalo, and has welcomed over 100,000 visitors so far.

On a cloudy summer afternoon in a quiet cove below the Maritime Museum, the Philadelphia II sits creaking at anchor. A volunteer guide is explaining how the colonists built eight gunboats like this one.

"They knew they were fighting the Royal Navy, the most powerful navy in the world," he tells a visitor as they stand on the vessel. "So these boats were made as simply as possible, specifically to carry cannon."

Alongside the Philadelphia at a museum dock are four pilot gigs. Those are replicas, built by area high schoolers, of 32-foot longboats that were used in the 18th and 19th centuries to transport pilot and crew to large sailing vessels. Each year a new pilot boat is built from white oak that students harvest in the Champlain Valley.

"Kids mark the harvest and mill it, and it dries for next year's boat," says Elizabeth Lee, the museum's education coordinator. "Place-based education is real, and human history has everything to do with the environment it takes place in. That's what we're trying to convey to the schoolkids. We tell them all the time, 'We're telling you this so you can tell the next part of the story. What happens next? You tell us.'"

On this summer day in the museum's conservation lab, six Vermont middle and high school teachers are working with Harry Chaucer, an education professor at Castleton University, on a weeklong course in inquiry-based learning.

"How to connect with the landscape is a big challenge, and

Aboard the Philadelphia II. *Lake Champlain Maritime Museum photo.*

the process of discovery is best going to occur when kids are invested," says Charlie Wanzer, a science teacher from Twinfield Union School in Marshfield, as he peers into a microscope. "I want them to experience the wonderment I've had."

"We've explored a sunken boat, we've ventured out to Abenaki historic sites, we've used a lot of primary resources," adds David Praamsma, an English teacher at Otter Valley Union High School in Brandon. "We're examining artifacts from a number of different fields, and making inferences from there.

"It's from the artifact up, and it's about authentic learning that honors kids' sense of self-discovery. Instead of being students of archeology, they'll be archeologists. Instead of studying biology, they'll be biologists."

"This is the first time this course is being taught, and it's a small group," he says.

"I don't think it will ever be this small again."

New work, new science, and a new threat

In the same year, 1990, that the foundation was starting to support the building of the Philadelphia II, it also began to make grants for direct scientific research on Lake Champlain. The initial grant went in support of a broad survey of lake plankton, including cyanobacteria or blue-green algae, led by Al McIntosh, then chair of the university's Vermont Water Resources Center.

"That was very intensive, in terms of the use of the Melosira," McIntosh recalled. "We took samples from many different areas of the lake — open waters, near shore. We provided information that really had been missing. It served as a baseline, so ten years later the state could go in and say, 'Well, back in '91 to '92, we had these numbers, and now the blue-green algae is much more.'

"We also discovered a species of zooplankton that had never before been seen in North America. *Thermocyclops crassus* was the name; it has a large red eye that allowed it to be identified. We were able to identify, for the first time, several unusual species occurring in the lake."

The year 1990 was pivotal for the lake in a larger way: With passage of the federal Lake Champlain Special Designation Act, the U.S. Congress named it a resource of national significance.

The legislation was sponsored by the U.S. senators from both sides of the lake: Leahy and Jim Jeffords of Vermont, and Pat Moynihan and Alfonse D'Amato of New York. "Its goal was to bring together people with diverse interests in the lake to create a comprehensive pollution prevention, control, and restoration plan for protecting the future of the Lake Champlain Basin," said the website of the Lake Champlain Basin Program, which was created under the legislation's mandate along with the Lake Champlain Research Consortium.

Under the consortium's umbrella, a number of research initiatives were carried out in the 1990s in support of the lake's new comprehensive management plan, which the Lake Champlain Steering Committee began to implement in 1996. The research cast new light on the "linkages within and between the lake's ecosystem and cultural, social and economic pressures," said the preface to *Lake Champlain in Transition: From Research to Restoration*, a 1999 volume, supported in part by the foundation, that collected papers on the recent research.

Chapters in the volume focused on McIntosh's plankton survey; on mercury deposition in the lake; on sediment toxicities, and their impacts on aquatic species; on phosphorus loading, its impacts and options for better management; and on new understanding of how large-scale, underwater standing waves dominate water circulation in the main lake.

Also in the 1990s, a new threat became evident to both scientific researchers and underwater archeologists. That was the alarmingly rapid advance along the bottom, and all over submerged artifacts, of an invasive freshwater mussel species.

"Art Cohn was finding a lot of shipwrecks on the bottom of the lake. But as he was doing that, we were seeing the spread across the lake of zebra mussels," recalled Mary Watzin, who was then directing UVM's lake research.

Zebra mussels had most likely come to the U.S. in about 1987, in ship ballast from eastern European waters. "The question that first emerged," Watzin said, "was 'What are zebra mussels going to do to these historic shipwrecks?'"

The Maritime Museum worked with Watzin, the Vermont Department of Environmental Conservation and others to issue a detailed report on the zebra mussel infestation in 1996. Even though five years earlier "hardly anyone in this region had heard of zebra mussels," Cohn wrote in the report, by this point the shellfish had "appeared in significant numbers on many of Lake Champlain's shallow water shipwrecks."

The mussels were multiplying exponentially. There was no cost-effective technology to contain their spread. "Zebra mussels in Lake Champlain will have significant impacts," the report predicted. It cited the clogging of intake pipes for power and water systems, the fouling of boat hulls, docks and beaches — and the probable encrusting of shipwrecks in shallow water.

"So we created an experimental program," said Watzin. "We put experimental substrates out in six locations, near shipwrecks on the bottom of the lake, and followed the colonization and looked at what happened to the surface of the wood and the wrought iron, and even the more modern steel." Down to about 50 feet, the mussels were completely blanketing both the test surfaces and the nearby shipwrecks.

And although zebra mussels can't live at the deeper depths where many Champlain wrecks lie, a related invasive, the quagga mussel, can spread into the lowest parts of the lake bottom. Quagga mussels haven't yet been found in Champlain; but they're in the Great Lakes, and scientists fear that an infestation here is inevitable. If and when it comes, it could have an even more severe impact than the zebra mussel on the lake and its ecosystem.

"We recommend the accelerated, systematic survey and inventory of Lake Champlain," Cohn wrote in the '96 report. "This remains our primary action item: to insure that valuable information about our submerged cultural resources is not lost. This lakewide survey will provide baseline imaging of Lake Champlain prior to full zebra mussel infestation, and track the changes in the lake over time.

"The Maritime Museum is willing and able to be the coordinating institution for this survey," Cohn added. "However, funding is an issue."

For the ambitious, multi-year Whole Lake Survey that resulted, the museum was able to bring in funding from a wide range of public, private and nonprofit sources, including substantial grants from the Lintilhac Foundation. To help carry out the project, Cohn turned to a pair of environmental scientists at Middlebury College — a married couple who had begun to play a lead role in Champlain scientific research.

Birth of a big idea: the Whole Lake Survey

Tom and Pat Manley came to Middlebury College in 1989 as oceanographic researchers. "I was Arctic Ocean; Pat was Atlantic, southern Arctic and Antarctic," Tom Manley said.

Pat Manley is a geologist whose specialty is marine sedimentology. She began teaching full-time at the college while Tom was busy completing work in the Arctic for the U.S. Navy.

At UVM, Al McIntosh knew the lake needed a new physical limnologist, or lake scientist. He approached Tom Manley, who at first declined. He declined a second time. But McIntosh was persistent.

"So I finally said, 'All right, I'll write a three-page proposal on Lake Champlain,'" Tom recalled. "I did my due diligence and came up with a plan for adapting large-scale deep-ocean technology into Lake Champlain."

The proposal was funded by UVM's Vermont Water Resources Center. Tom began to gather data on the lake's internal seiche, or standing waves, using sophisticated instrumentation borrowed from researchers on the Great Lakes.

"How the Lintilhacs came into this was, after the first year we started presenting results," Pat said. "Tom gave a report to the Vermont Water Resources Center. And Crea goes to all these talks, it's incredible. After listening to what my students do and what Tom was doing, she and Phil came to Middlebury."

"I'm wandering the halls of the old science center," said Tom, "and this couple comes up and says, 'We're looking for Pat Manley.' Oh, okay, just go in that door."

Recalled Pat: "They just said, 'We really like the work you're doing, and what is it you need? We understand equipment's a problem. We would like to fund you for five years, so you can buy equipment to continue understanding the hydrodynamics and bottom sediment structure of the lake.' This was about 1994."

"So I wander back in and talk to Pat," Tom added. "I said, 'Who was that?' She said, 'We've just been funded for five years.'"

As the push for lake research followed the Special Designation Act, that support made it possible for the Manleys to begin securing larger federal grants.

"Lake Champlain is very important to us," Pat said — "but when you write a grant to the National Science Foundation, it's a puddle, it's your little lake. Getting funding to do this kind of research is difficult, especially for the work Tom and I do, which is very costly because of the equipment we have to use. The Lintilhacs were one of the key movers in getting all of this started."

At the time, Middlebury College had only a small, outdated research vessel, the R/V Baldwin. But it did have side-scan sonar equipment, which could potentially be used to produce a detailed digital map of the lake bottom. Such a map would be far superior to the 19th century lead-line measurements that had been guiding Champlain sailors for decades.

So Art Cohn and the Manleys began talking about mapping the lake bottom, including its hundreds of shipwrecks, before zebra mussel infestations changed everything.

Said Tom: "When Art Cohn, who at the time was executive director of the Maritime Museum, heard that Pat was [at the college], he shows up and says, 'I've got this great idea!'"

Added Pat: "I said, 'I'm not just going to give you this piece of equipment. But if you'll allow my students to go out with you, and we can use this piece of equipment to look at the bottom geology of the lake, then yes.'

"That started in '94. We did several projects prior to the first major whole-lake mapping. That was a systematic mapping of the entire bottom of Lake Champlain."

Gathering a "priceless body of information"

"A systematic project to survey the entire lake bottom within the next five years has the potential to save a priceless body of information," the Maritime Museum declared in a 1995 newsletter.

"We believe there are dozens — perhaps hundreds — of unlocated shipwreck sites scattered throughout the lake," the museum said. "... Once [zebra mussels] colonize a shipwreck they will provide an effective barrier to extracting information from the site. The proposed project has the potential not only to document currently unlocated wrecks, it will simultaneously capture important geological and hydrological information and provide baseline imaging of the lake bottom as it is pre-zebra mussel colonization."

That five-year timeline turned out to be optimistic. The Lake Champlain Underwater Cultural Resources Survey, later renamed the Whole Lake Survey, began in 1996, led by Art Cohn from the museum working closely with Tom and Pat Manley of Middlebury College. It was late 2005 when the final, eight-foot-wide map of the entire lake bottom was unveiled in a college ceremony.

"When researchers began the survey, less than 10 percent of the bottom of Lake Champlain had been examined," the college reported. "When the survey was complete, they had collected images of more than 95 percent of the lake bottom using state-of-the-art marine survey technology. More than 70 new shipwrecks" — 85, in the end — "had been discovered as well." The foundation helped support the project with grants made from 1996 into the early 2000s.

"The principal survey tool was side-scan sonar, a torpedo-shaped device towed behind the primary research vessel, the R/V Neptune," said a college news article. "The development of two new technologies also contributed to the survey results: differential Global Positioning Systems (DGPS), a series of satellites that continuously and accurately plot the boat's position, and computers that collect, process and store vast quantities of sonar, positioning and depth information."

Laura Pergolizzi remembers how unlikely-looking the research vessel was. Because the college's own Baldwin was so limited in capacity, each summer the researchers towed the college's side-scan sonar equipment behind a privately owned vessel, the 40-foot R/V Neptune, captained by Fred Fayette out of Burlington.

"It kind of looked like a gray lobster shanty," said Pergolizzi, who was then Laura Kelly, a Middlebury student in the class of 2006 who worked on the Whole Lake Survey during three of her four college summers. "It had this big gray box, a

Middlebury College intern Laura Kelly and Professor Tom Manley work on the Lake Survey.

winch on the back; it was a sight for sore eyes! But you'd walk down into the hull of the boat, and inside there was this maze of computers, wires and equipment, literally all hand-tacked and tied by Tom and Fred to make this into a research vessel."

"We'd be out there for hours and hours every day," she said. "For the most part I looked at a computer, to make sure that the data from the side-scan sonar was tracking from the equipment to the vessel. If something of note was uncovered, we'd flag it, we'd document and talk about it. We might do another pass on it.

"The technology that we were able to use got better and better each year," Pergolizzi said. "Every single tree limb that fell into the lake, you'd have to measure it: the size, the depth. Is this a possible canal boat? Let's do another pass, let's look at it from different angles to try to figure out if it's something of historical significance."

Along with shipwrecks from a wide range of historical eras, Pergolizzi said the survey also found "some automobiles, and planes, and things you would never have expected would be in the lake. It's a reflection of the history of the lake, and all the commerce that happened on it."

By its end, the Whole Lake Survey had discovered and mapped the remains of several sunken vessels: the British sloop Boscawen from the French and Indian War, a 1759-era French sloop and French gunboat, and a U.S. row galley and two British brigs from the Battle of Plattsburgh in the War of 1812. It also found many 19th century canal boats, a canal schooner sunk in 1825, a sidewheel steamer, 19th century steam-powered tug and towboats, an 1870-era railroad drawboat (a heavy barge with rail tracks along the center), an 1880s lake schooner, two 1920s ferries, a U.S. Army aircraft rescue boat from World War II, modern sail and powerboats, a modern pontoon boat, a houseboat, and various wood and steel barges.

Taking bottom mapping to a new height

Before the survey, mariners on the lake had to rely on charts marked with data from an 1879 U.S. government survey that used lead-weighted lines for depth soundings. That laborious project produced about 10,000 depth measurements. In contrast, the side-scan sonar survey, with some additional technologies, produced 735,000 depth measures.

Among the Whole Lake Survey's key participants were Fred Fayette, a lifelong Champlain mariner who had been exploring the lake with underwater camera technology since the 1960s, and Peter Barranco, Jr., who had worked as a teenager for Lorenzo Hagglund, discoverer of the Philadelphia.

For four decades, Barranco had been gathering facts, legends and detailed information on the lake's history. He was "the chief survey strategist, and from the very beginning has plotted every solar line run by the survey," said a 1997-98 project report.

"Peter would join us often," Pergolizzi recalled — "and he had this notebook that had a compilation of his own and his father's newspaper clippings, as well as handwritten notes that had everything to do with the history of Lake Champlain that he had compiled from books, from newspapers, and from local folklore.

At Middlebury College's 2005 unveiling of the new Lake Champlain bottom map, Art Cohn of the Lake Champlain Maritime Museum talks with U.S. Sen. Patrick Leahy, at right. Sen. Leahy, a longtime supporter of Champlain research, secured key federal funding for the Whole Lake Survey, a project of the college and the museum, also supported by the Lintilhac Foundation, that produced the new map. *Photo by Tad Merrick.*

"We'd be going in the boat and Peter would say things like 'Oh I remember, right around this corner is where there was an old floating railroad trestle. On the next pass, see if you can see anything that looks like a train, or coal.' It was just fascinating to have Peter bringing in these historical references."

When the sonar mapped what appeared to be a shipwreck, data would be gathered for a dive team to go down and learn more.

"We would go back to make sure I was accurately plotting the boat's position, the depth readings, and any other information we had," said Pergolizzi, "because when the dive team went down to actually look at the shipwreck, visibility was often poor. Sometimes zero. It was also a little bit dangerous, because of the heavy currents. And there's a lot of fishing lines and things you could get caught up on when you're diving blind.

"Later, we got some remote-operated vehicles that we could send down and take videography with," she added. "And for a week or two we had a gradiometer, which is like a giant metal detector." That instrument helped divers map the debris field from the Battle of Valcour Island, giving new information on where the colonial and British ships had lined up for the engagement.

"I was mainly in the lab, working on the data," said Burch Fisher, Middlebury '03, who worked on the survey for a year after graduation. "The nice thing was that every oceanography class and every marine geology class contributed points to the final map. Every time they went out, they saved all those points. All kinds of students had a hand in it."

The survey mapped the whole main lake, along with every bay and cove. That meant a vast amount of data, all of which had to be reviewed and cleaned up.

"Say you hit a fish" with the sonar scan, Fisher said. "You'd still get a data point for that — and there were millions of points. So it took a pretty good effort between Tom and me to go through all the lake."

When the eight-foot map was finally unveiled in October 2005, a college news story noted that it "reveals the presence of several new features, such as shoals, rises, plateaus and faults. The map also offers insight into the increased extent and alignment of some of the already known features, including Juniper Ridge, located off Burlington Bay."

The college quoted Sen. Leahy, who had secured "essential federal funding" for the lake survey and attended the unveiling ceremony: "'Not only is Lake Champlain among our nation's most precious resources, but historically it may be the most significant body of water in North America. The survey results clearly document the lake's extraordinary collection of shipwrecks. This new map, with its new insights into the bottom topography of the lake, will also prove to be an invaluable aid to researchers in understanding the role of hydrodynamics in the lake's living ecology.'"

"We consumed more Peanut M&Ms on that ship! I mean giant, bulk-sized bags," Laura Pergolizzi remembered with a happy laugh. "And there was a trampoline. It was no more than two by two feet, but sometimes you just needed to stretch the legs and get some fresh air off the bow. It was the kookiest boat."

But, she added more seriously, "the work we did over those years is continuing. A lot of the work Tom is doing now uses the understanding of how the lake is mapped to impact pollutant flows into the lake, and their models. That has a lot of real-time implications for agriculture, and for treatment methods. So I feel like it's continuing to live on."

◇

Project GULP: studying a strange feature

Lake scientists from Middlebury College and UVM came together in 1999 for a foundation-sponsored investigation into some unexplained divots, or pockmarks, that the Whole Lake Study had found in the lake bed. The researchers called their work Project GULP: Groundwater Upwelling in Large Pockmarks.

"Large fields of pockmarks were identified in several locations in Lake Champlain," notably Burlington and Cumberland bays, said a paper on the project by investigators Tom and Pat Manley of Middlebury, Mary Watzin of UVM, and Josh Gutierrez, a Middlebury geology student.

Their findings were published in *Lake Champlain: Partnerships and Research in the New Millennium* (Kluwer, 2004), edited by the Manleys and Timothy Mihuc of Plattsburgh State University. The book was a collection of research papers that were presented at a symposium of the Lintilhac Foundation-supported Lake Champlain Research Consortium. Tom Manley was by now both teaching geology at the college and serving as executive director of the Research Consortium.

Project GULP focused on the largest pockmark in Burlington Bay, one wide and deep enough that the team named it "the General." About 40 meters across and four meters deep, the feature looks in the sonar image a bit like a doughnut of scattered dark sediment. In an echo-sounder profile, it shows up as a steep-sided divot in the lake bed.

The researchers gathered a year's worth of data from submerged instruments and cameras, trying to understand what had formed the General and what was keeping it there. Pockmarks on the lake bottom "may be manifestations of a significant source of upwelling gas or groundwater into the lake that was not previously defined," the scientists hypothesized.

Divers who investigated the General found that "the central portion of the pockmark was firm to the touch, sandy in nature, and contained clinkers (remains of coal combustion from 1800s steamboats)," the research paper said. But sediment cores found no evidence of gas expansion or cracks within the pockmark.

In the end, the researchers could only conjecture that the "most likely cause" was the release of groundwater.

"Several models were presented to explain observations and characteristics of this feature," they concluded. They added, intriguingly: "No single model accounts for all the observations."

$$\sqrt{}$$

Cyanobacteria: a "primordial soup" becomes a public-health issue

On a trail through woods to the water at the Maritime Museum, Angela Shambaugh was telling a group of elementary, middle and high school teachers about cyanobacteria.

"People call them algae, but in reality they're bacteria. They're a natural part of this community — you'll see them in any water, but they have an ecological advantage in warm, high-nutrient water," said Shambaugh, a senior environmental scientist with the Lakes and Ponds Program of the Vermont Department of Environmental Conservation's Watershed Management Division. "Climate change lets them bloom longer, adapt better."

Under a hot sun, she said, cyanobacteria in shallow water can rise to the surface and appear to bloom, looking like thick pea soup or a paint spill. Sometimes it even changes color.

"A bloom can be there in the afternoon, but not the morning. Toxins are contained within the cells; we don't understand what the toxins are for. We're trying to raise awareness of what cyanobacteria is, and people should avoid it. ... It's been called the poison ivy of the water.

"They're fascinating organisms," Shambaugh continued. "They've been around for millions and millions of years. They're believed to have been the first organisms to have figured out photosynthesis. To me, when they talk about primordial soup, it's cyanobacteria."

In late summer 1999, a pet dog died after drinking cyanobacteria-laden water on the Champlain shore. In 2000, a second dog died in the same way.

"I was called at home by the health department on Labor Day weekend, when they realized that there was potential data for this to be connected to cyanobacteria," recalled Shambaugh, who then was working with the UVM School of Natural Resources on a study of water quality in Burlington Bay.

Because of her previous, foundation-supported work with Al McIntosh on surveying lake plankton, including the phytoplankton called cyanobacteria, she said, "we had the data to say, 'Yeah, [cyanobacteria] microcystis are in the lake. We've been seeing it and yeah, the textbooks all say it can produce toxins.' So we had that background to be able to respond, when all that concern developed. If we hadn't had those studies — if we hadn't built off of that earlier work — we wouldn't have had that knowledge." (See the next chapter for more on cyanobacteria in Lake Champlain, and on the broad effort to build support for a state commitment to address the problem.)

Science in action: Middlebury's new Folger

From the mid-1990s into the early 2000s at Middlebury College, Tom and Pat Manley received several Lintilhac Foundation grants for research equipment, in large part to support the Whole Lake Survey. Also, Pat said, "when I had students who needed, say, $3,000 to analyze sediment cores, for getting long cores and stuff like that, I would write a small grant to the Lintilhac Foundation, and they would support that.

"Phil and Crea were pretty much instrumental," she said. "In fact, because of the support Crea has given, I nominated her to get an honorary degree at Middlebury College, which she did," in 1997.

By the late 2000s, the Manleys knew that the Baldwin, the college's outmoded research vessel, "was just running out of capacity," Tom said. "We put every piece of gear onto it that we could. Getting 10 students on there was like squeezing them in with Vaseline. It was a 32-foot lobster boat and it was one of a kind, a racing lobster boat. It had a huge V8 engine, but not a lot of room."

The couple spent a decade trying to convince the college leadership that Middlebury needed a new research platform.

"They would say, 'We just don't have the money right now.' Finally we just sort of gave up," Tom said. "We approached

Pat and Tom Manley, Middlebury College faculty members and Lake Champlain researchers.

the Lintilhacs and said, 'We just want to make a concerted effort, one last time, to get bids from marine contractors to actually build a vessel for Lake Champlain, so there's no question about what it's going to cost.'"

The foundation made a grant that enabled the development of project specifications, and the Manleys wrote a letter to the whole college. "Here's a universal boat, anybody could use it — chemistry, biology, show us what you would like and we'll incorporate it into the vessel," Tom said. "We got all these notes, and I wrote out something like ten RFPs [requests for proposals] to various manufacturers. Give us your best boat plans."

Federal funding became a possibility. The American Recovery and Reinvestment Act of 2009, enacted in response to the global financial crisis, made some new money available through the National Science Foundation.

"There was an NSF call that went out," Tom said. "I approached the program manager [at NSF] and said, 'This fund is to retrofit buildings or laboratories, and we've used the Baldwin as a laboratory during the school year.' He basically said, 'Yeah, I think that's a good idea.'"

"First, we had to get approval from the college. We wrote the proposal, and they said they could scrape the money together. It was a $1.7 million [NSF] grant; the college chipped in another quarter million."

The federal grant was announced in August 2010 — and by then, the Manleys and Richard Furbush, the longtime Melosira captain who had shifted to Middlebury College, had selected the college's new 45-foot catamaran-style research vessel.

"It reflects a new approach to research vessels with its twin hull, which will provide so much more stability," Pat said at the time. "We'll be able to extend our class and research time in weather we can't go out in with the Baldwin. At maximum cruising speed of 20-24 knots, we will be able to access distant regions of the lake that we have rarely been able to survey using our current boat."

On board Middlebury College's RMS Folger, Angus Warren '20 monitors progress of the recent bottom-mapping project using multibeam side-scan technology.

Launched at last on Lake Champlain in October 2012, the new vessel was christened the R/V David Folger. On board for the ceremony was its namesake, a retired oceanographer and Middlebury geology professor who had brought the Baldwin to the college a quarter century before.

"The 48-Foot R/V David Folger is equipped with state-of-the-art instruments to map the lake bottom, track currents, measure water chemistry and sample sediments," the *Environmental Monitor*, a national publication, reported in 2014. "It's at the forefront of the experiential, hands-on approach to learning in Middlebury's geology courses."

"We make sure we are out in the field every week and making sure students learn the whole process of how to collect data, how to interpret data and how to present that data," Pat Manley told the publication. "'In essence, it's the scientific method.

"Every time we do this — it's amazing — we find new things."

"An issue all over the world": learning more about cyanobacteria

Up and down the lake on the Vermont and New York sides throughout the warmer months, a citizen monitoring effort organized by the Lake Champlain Basin Program gauges the presence of cyanobacteria along the lakeshore. At UVM, the foundation has supported new cyanobacteria research with recent funding for three projects. One is a sophisticated data-gathering buoy on Shelburne Pond, which has an undeveloped shoreline and has become a living laboratory for cyanobacteria research.

The second was a worldwide review of research findings on cyanobacteria in water and in fish when those were measured simultaneously. That review found varying sensitivities among the different tests being used.

"This was a wakeup call," said Jason Stockwell, current director of the Rubenstein Lab. "This is an issue all over the world, and we're using different methods. How do we compare? In our paper, we call for the community to come up with some standardizations in terms of what we're measuring and how we are measuring it.

"The nice thing about being tuned into global research is that we can see where our place is, among the broader setting," he reflected. With cyanobacteria, "we think we're bad here — but you should see, for instance, in China." Along the lower Yangtze River Delta, he said, "Lake Taihu is of comparable size [to Champlain], but it has much worse blooms."

The New York Times reported about a major bloom on Lake Taihu in 2007: "Toxic cyanobacteria, commonly referred to as pond scum, turned the big lake fluorescent green. The stench of decay choked anyone who came within a mile of its shores. At least two million people who live amid the canals, rice paddies and chemical plants around the lake had to stop drinking or cooking with their main source of water."

The third current foundation-supported research at the Rubenstein Lab is Stockwell's collaboration with a Dartmouth Medical School physician. They're investigating whether a connection can be found between the presence of cyanobacteria in lakes and higher rates of neurodegenerative diseases, such as ALS, in neighboring communities.

"In the literature, there's some evidence that the toxins in cyanobacteria may get aerosolized, through wave and wind action," Stockwell explained. "We received funding from the Lintilhac Foundation to test this out, and around Shelburne Pond we've set up air samplers. The first is right at the shoreline; then we're going out 50, 100, 200, 400 and 800 meters. Are we catching anything?"

With foundation funding, Stockwell and his students have also placed air samplers around Shelburne Farms to look at whether cyanobacteria that grow in farm manure pits may be aerosolized when manure is sprayed on fields.

All the concern related to blue-green algae "is going to become more intense and more prevalent as things warm up," Stockwell summed up. "The lakes are going to be absorbing more runoff from increased [land] use, and the water is getting warmer. So it's highly relevant."

A hands-on approach to raising students' awareness

Out on the Melosira on a sharply windy October morning, Rubenstein School of Environment and Natural Resources student Kat Lewis '19 is exploring ecology with 21 bundled-up Burlington middle schoolers.

Lewis, an environmental sciences major, is one of eight Rubenstein School students who are paid watershed educators in the UVM Extension Watershed Alliance, part of the Lake Champlain Sea Grant program. She's telling the seventh and eighth graders from Edmunds Middle School that the ratio of land in the

On the R/V Melosira, UVM student Kat Lewis '19 explored the lake's ecology with a group of students from Edmunds Middle School in Burlington.

Champlain basin to water in the lake is 18 to 1.

"So thinking about how there's such a large amount of land draining into Lake Champlain," Lewis says, raising her voice above the wind, "what do you think some of the issues are?"

"There's a lot of runoff, like from farms," one student volunteers.

"And there's pesticides," offers another.

Lewis agrees — and moments later, the students are grabbing water-proof clipboards and markers and making notes on the weather, the geography around them, and the water clarity below. Guiding them together with Lewis is Ashley Eaton, the watershed and lake education coordinator for Lake Champlain Sea Grant, a cooperative program of the university and the State University of New York at Plattsburgh, with UVM Extension as a key partner.

Lake Champlain Sea Grant develops and shares science-based knowledge to benefit the communities and economies of the Champlain basin. As part of a network of 33 Sea Grant programs in important coastal areas around the country, it uses federal and state funding to blend research, education and outreach in a variety of ongoing projects.

Through the Watershed Alliance, elementary, middle and high school students and teachers up and down the Champlain basin are guided by watershed educators, all of them UVM undergrads, in hands-on lake sampling and stream monitoring.

"When I found this, I knew I needed to be a watershed educator," says Kat Lewis, who has watched the water quality deteriorate in a New Hampshire lake her family visits in the summer. "It's teaching the next generation how to conserve their water and improve water quality. Because I've seen what's happening."

New studies and the Spitfire: the work goes on

On the R/V Folger, Tom Manley has worked in recent summers with multibeam side-scan technology, a system for mapping the lake bottom that's more powerful than sonar. The multibeam emits 256 beams on either side of the boat; each beam produces a highly accurate depth reading. Manley secured three years of foundation funding to map as much of the lake as he can with this more accurate system.

"We're doing really significant stuff," said Angus Warren, Middlebury '20, who worked on the boat as a summer intern. His job was to keep adjusting the multibeam, overlapping each path and working with Furbush, the pilot, to make sure there were no gaps.

In the enclosed cabin, Warren stared at two monitors. As the boat moved through the water, the computers produced color maps of what the multibeam was finding, in real time.

"Our depth findings are as much as 20 meters away from what was measured" in the original lead-line soundings, Warren said. "So I'm aware that what we're

Spatial Coverage (as of Nov. 1 , 2020) of the Lake Champlain High-Resolution Multibeam Bathymetric Mapping Program
Funded by the Lintilhac Foundation, Vt EPSCoR BREE & Sea Grant

Produced by Middlebury College, the 2020 bottom map of Lake Champlain has added significantly to scientific knowledge of the lake. Employing multibeam side-scan technology and also supported by the foundation, the latest mapping work was led by Tom Manley of the college faculty.

The Missing Gunboat Found, an illustration of the discovery of the gunboat Spitfire, drawn from video and still images taken by a remote-operated dive vehicle.

finding has real applications."

At another workstation in the Folger's cabin, Tom Manley was looking at a computer screen on which colored lines showed water characteristics: temperature, density, turbidity, fluorescence. He explained how water moves in three layers within the lake, and how phytoplankton activity peaks in the thermocline, or middle layer.

The lake scientist pointed to a purple line that showed how deep sunlight was penetrating. That's information for biologists, he said. Chemists, he added, might be more interested in studying water samples — and on the rear deck was a cluster of plastic bottles, for taking samples at various depths.

At the college, various departments and programs — biochemistry, oceanography, marine geology, environmental science — have been making increasing use of the Folger. A young biology assistant professor and microbial ecologist, Erin Eggleston, is using the vessel with a student team to gather data that may help to build new understanding of how toxic viruses spread within and among various species of cyanobacteria.

But today, the mapping work is laborious. It's tedious. As the Folger "mows the lawn," traveling slowly along one track after another in a very deep part of the lake, Angus Warren brings up a digital photo on his monitor, just because it's so interesting.

In fact, it's an image of the Whole Lake Survey's most important finding: the intact wreck of the Spitfire.

Another of Benedict Arnold's gunboats from the Battle of Valcour Island, the Spitfire was damaged, out of ammunition and leaking on October 12, 1776, when she was scuttled and sunk by her crew. She was next spotted by the lake survey team, on June 6, 1997.

"Historians had long speculated that one gunboat of the eight known to have battled at Valcour Island was still unaccounted for, and possibly at the bottom of the lake," wrote Art Cohn and co-authors Philip Lundeberg and Jennifer Jones in the 2017 book *A Tale of Three Gunboats*. This account of the original Philadelphia, the replica Philadelphia II and the Spitfire was published by the Lake Champlain Maritime Museum and the Smithsonian National Museum of American History.

After the side-scan sonar detected "a gunboat-shaped target," a dive team went down to verify. When they surfaced, what they reported was electrifying.

> She rested properly on her bottom, as if she was still desperately trying to escape the British. The mast stood almost full-height, with about six feet of the very tip of the topmast hanging by a thin thread of wood. The big bow cannon, corresponding to the iron mass revealed on the sonar image, was still in its original carriage and on the special slide designed by one of Arnold's men. The cannon, in a forward firing position, looked as though it was still searching for the enemy.

With the threat looming of destruction by deep-water quagga mussels, Cohn and collaborators, including the U.S. Navy, have developed a 20-year, multi-million-dollar plan to manage, raise and restore the Spitfire.

"This boat is a direct connection to the formation of the country," Cohn said in an interview. "It's 1776. It doesn't get any more central to who we are as a people — and the archeological potential is off the charts. And the boat is under a death sentence.

"I've put out the management plan, and what I'm trying to do now is build consensus," he said. "If the plan is right, the money will show up. That's my experience.

"We can make the world a better place through this effort," Cohn reflected. "My philosophy, which came over the last 30 years, is that people with wealth want to spend their money wisely. They want to feel that their investment, in whatever it is, will be a good investment. And the preservation ethic that we've raised around this hidden class of resources is a very powerful way to help the planet.

"I just think it's incredibly valuable to future generations to preserve these connections to our past. To learn from them, and to build upon that knowledge."

A Maritime Museum guide enthralls a school group aboard the Philadelphia II.

STEPPING UP FOR THE STATE'S UNIVERSITY

S ince its creation in 1975, the Lintilhac Foundation has made many dozens of grants to the University of Vermont — none larger or more impactful to the university, its students and its pursuit of science and environmental studies than three commitments the foundation made in 2007.

During a UVM capital campaign that year, the foundation committed $1 million to the construction of James M. Jeffords Hall, UVM's new 97,000 square foot science building, which opened in 2010. It granted half a million dollars to the environmentally innovative renovation of the George D. Aiken Center, which reopened in 2012 as the home of the Rubenstein School of Environment and Natural Resources. Both those buildings earned high honors from the Leadership in Energy and Environmental Design (LEED) New Construction program of the Green Building Certification Institute.

The Old Mill on the UVM campus dates to 1825; its southwestern cornerstone was laid by the Marquis de Lafayette.

Also during the 2007 campaign, "in its third major commitment, which was very important, the foundation contributed just over a million dollars to what became known as the Lintilhac Scholarship Challenge," said Kathleen Kelleher, vice president for principal gifts at The UVM Foundation. The campaign's threshold for endowing a named scholarship fund was $100,000; the foundation pledged $33,000 to match any individual or family's commitment of $67,000.

"The Lintilhac Foundation contributed $1.033 million to encourage donors to create new scholarship endowments," Kelleher said. "Through this Lintilhac Challenge, donors created 26 new named endowments with commitments of over $2.3 million. Donors contributed an additional $923,000 to those endowments after the Lintilhac Challenge."

The foundation's initial commitment to the scholarship challenge was $1 million. But, said Kelleher, "There was one family who wanted to make a gift after the money from the Lintilhacs had been fully allocated. I went back to Crea, and the foundation made an extra $33,000 commitment so that family could be part of the challenge."

"Public universities have come into working with philanthropists later than private schools, but they rely very heavily on philanthropic support in this day and age," Kelleher explained. "Particularly the University of Vermont, because we're a major research university in a state with a population of a little over 630,000 people."

Both the Jeffords and Aiken buildings are standouts in environmental design. Jeffords Hall, home to the Departments of Plant Biology and Plant and Soil Science, has seven up-to-date teaching labs and three general classrooms, plus research labs and offices. It was designed to use more than a third less energy and half as much water as a conventionally designed building; the $56 million project was awarded LEED Gold certification in 2012.

The Rubenstein School's Aiken Center won LEED Platinum status, the highest "green building" certification. It's designed to be 62 percent more energy-efficient than the original Aiken building, built in 1982. The $13 million renovation features a nearly airtight, insulating "envelope" between its inner and outer walls, along with an "EcoMachine" system for treating wastewater, and 27,000 board feet of Forest Stewardship Council-certified wood paneling from UVM's Jericho Research Forest.

"Crea is a long-standing, dedicated member of the Rubenstein School Board of Advisors," Kathleen Kelleher noted. Overall, she added, the foundation's support "has been extraordinarily important to the university."

6

Waters in the Public Trust

Persistence in the battle for a
cleaner Lake Champlain

———— ⚘ ————

n 2008, the publishing company Rodale, which had lately had success with
Al Gore's climate-change warning *An Inconvenient Truth*, brought out a book
titled *Don't Go There!*

Compiled by Peter Greenberg, travel editor for NBC's Today show, *Don't Go
There!* billed itself as an "essential guide to the must-miss places of the world." It
had chapters such as "Toxic Places," "Worst Cruises" and "Highways of Death."
In its chapter on polluted waters, there was ... Lake Champlain.

> In 1999, two dogs died after ingesting Lake Champlain's blue-green
> algae-covered water. How bad is that?
>
> According to the Conservation Law Foundation, Lake Champlain has
> been polluted with an abundance of phosphorus for the past 30 years, and
> it's only getting worse in several parts of the lake. The water often looks
> cloudy and smells foul, due to algae blooms. ... Beaches along the lake are
> frequently closed in order to safeguard human and animal health. ...
>
> According to the Vermont Natural Resources Council, 126 rivers and
> lakes in Vermont don't meet the normal minimum water-quality standards,
> and stormwater runoff tarnishes the water quality of 26 streams.

"That was big. It made people look and say, 'What's going on here?'" said Eric
Wolinsky, who, as the longtime president of the St. Albans Watershed Association,
had spent years calling for action to clean up St. Albans Bay. About 20 miles north of

Burlington, the bay is one of the areas of the lake most heavily loaded with phosphorus, an algae-feeding nutrient that flows in from streams and surface runoff.

Tourism, boating and fishing on Lake Champlain and its shoreline altogether generate some $300 million in economic activity each year, and much of Vermont's economy depends on its almost mythic reputation as a clean and beautiful state. There was a spasm of indignation in the state over Greenberg's write-up, which had wrongly implied that the whole 107-mile lake was covered in blue-green algae.

In fact, the broad lake remained very largely clear. But what's more accurately called cyanobacteria were indeed producing scummy, foul-smelling, dangerous blooms during late summer and early fall in bays, coves and boat slips, mostly in the northern lake.

Cyanobacteria can produce several types of toxins that are dangerous to animals, and potentially to humans. Hot-weather blooms of cyanobacteria — a growing problem in lakes around the world — are fueled by excess levels of phosphorus, which had been building up in Champlain's bays and bottom sediment, largely through runoff from farm fields and paved areas, streambank erosion and rain-driven stormwater discharges. In St. Albans Bay especially, since at least the 1960s the problem had been growing very notably worse.

For at least half of those years, Eric Wolinsky kept showing up at public meetings and going to see public officials, demanding action to clean up his home bay. He finally wore out and gave up. Sitting for an interview by a deserted beach on a late summer day at his town's waterside Bay Park — a park that, a generation ago, was thronged on similar days, but no longer — he said his activism hadn't always made him popular.

"For years, I was the jerk," Wolinsky said. "I'll call it bearing witness, for somebody like me to go out and say, 'The water in front of my house is disgusting. My kids can't swim there.'

"I like to say I'm a bitter old man. I've put more work into this with less results than almost anything."

For a long time, he said, the general public wasn't aware that there was a problem, and "the government and the regulators had the attitude that if they just gave us happy talk and threw us a bone now and then, that would do it. Regulators would say, 'We need long-term solutions,' and that's great. But I need to swim tomorrow, not in ten years."

"Landowners have to make changes"

It wasn't that public officials and regulators had done nothing. They had, in fact, made strong progress on the most easily targeted source of phosphorus loading: discharges from wastewater treatment plants along the shore.

Harmful discharges through a specific pipe or channel, as from wastewater plants, are called point pollution, as they come from definable points. The federal Clean Water Act provided funds in the 1970s that enabled Vermont to make a very big investment in modern wastewater treatment plants — and in 1976, Vermont banned phosphorus in laundry detergents, which had been a major contributor of phosphorus to the water flowing into, and out of, those plants.

"That simple law, at really no cost to government, reduced the phosphorus input from wastewater by about 40 percent," said Eric Smeltzer, who was for many years a limnologist, or lake scientist, with the Vermont Department of Environmental Conservation. "You're never going to find anything easier than that, and we never have since. It gets harder and harder as you go on.

"So that was an obvious first step, and very effective," Smeltzer said. "Step two was to pass laws limiting the amount of phosphorus allowable in wastewater, requiring special treatment in the wastewater plants to remove phosphorus. Early '80s. That same law on detergents in Vermont was the beginning of wastewater limits on phosphorus. We kind of expanded on that through different legislation."

Those actions reduced phosphorus discharges from wastewater treatment by about 90 percent. And that, Smeltzer summed up, "has been the one shining success story on phosphorus in Lake Champlain."

The other sources of phosphorus loading are nonpoint. They flow into the lake and other state waters from diffuse sources that are much harder to manage or

Point-source water pollution flows from a specific point, such as a pipe, and is far simpler to regulate than non-point pollution — for example, phosphorus-laden runoff into Lake Champlain from farm fields spread with manure, as above. "Approximately 38% of the phosphorus load to the lake comes from agriculture (352 metric tons or 775,000 pounds each year)," according to the Lake Champlain Basin Program's 2018 *State of the Lake and Ecosystems Indicator Report*.

curb — primarily runoff from farm fields, eroding river banks and developed land, especially parking lots and other paved areas.

Under the federal Clean Water Act, nonpoint discharges were not regulated as were point sources. And despite significant investment of public funds and honest efforts by state agencies and officials, to date the total volume of nonpoint runoff — which today contributes about 94 percent of the phosphorus that goes into Lake Champlain — has not decreased at all.

"In fact," said Smeltzer, "the nonpoint side of the thing has grown while the point source, wastewater, has gone down over the decades." The nonpoint growth has happened, he explained, "for a variety of reasons: farming changes, we have different weather now, more storms, more impervious surface from development and stormwater. There's a lot of reasons.

"So at some point you've got to start going for these other sources, which are tougher, because they often involve activities on private land. Individual landowners have to make changes to address the problem. The sledding has gotten tougher and tougher with every step."

And just as *Don't Go There!* reported, since at least the early 1980s, cyanobacteria contamination in places along the lakeshore — feeding in hot, sunny weather on excess phosphorus in the water and lake bottom — has become steadily more of a visible, smellable mess.

"Listen. It's a fetid pool of disgusting," said Wolinsky of St. Albans Bay.

Along the way, in the late 1990s, Crea Lintilhac met Chris Kilian.

"What can you do for Lake Champlain?"

As an environmental litigator with the Vermont Natural Resources Council, Kilian had just won a high-profile battle with Citizens Utility, a giant utility holding company, over a planned expansion of a hydropower dam on the Clyde River in northern Vermont. With help from the U.S. Environmental Protection Agency, VNRC had halted the expansion project. Its efforts eventually led to the dam's removal and the restoration of the Clyde's historic salmon fishery.

"It was all extremely high-profile," Kilian recalled. "And shortly thereafter, I was at a conference at UVM, talking about this, and Crea, who I didn't know at the time, stood up and said, 'How are you doing this?'

"After I was done speaking, she came right up to the front of the room and introduced herself — and she immediately turned the discussion to, 'Okay, what can you do for Lake Champlain?'"

Soon after, in 1999, Kilian left VNRC and joined the Vermont staff of the Conservation Law Foundation. Headquartered in Boston with field offices in each New England state, CLF had built a reputation as an aggressive legal advocate for environmental action, in large part by pushing successfully in the courts, from 1983 into the 1990s, for action that substantially cleaned up Boston Harbor.

Looking at the Vermont non-profits then involved with water quality and Lake Champlain, Kilian said, "We observed that there really wasn't a hard-edged advocate that was just saying, 'Clean the damn lake up!' So I really started to gravitate to that. We saw a need there."

Chris Kilian of the Conservation Law Foundation in Vermont. *Image from the documentary* Bloom.

With the foundation's support, in 2000 Kilian and CLF began to file lawsuits.

"What we did for Boston Harbor, we have committed to doing for Lake Champlain," the organization said in a 2000 publication. "The lake ... is badly polluted by farms, sewage treatment plants, industry and overdevelopment throughout its watershed. The [CLF] Natural Resources Project is taking action to stop this pollution."

"We don't just show up in court; we persist year after year," said Francis W. Sargent, a former Massachusetts governor who was then CLF's board chair, in the organization's 40th anniversary publication in 2006.

Persisting year after year was exactly, with the foundation's support, what CLF in Vermont began to do.

Phosphorus and cyanobacteria: the nutrient connection

n 1999, the deaths of at least three dogs in the Point Au Roche region of Lake Champlain," on the New York side across from North Hero island, were "attributed to consumption of water containing toxic blue-green algae," wrote five environmental scientists from Vermont and New York in a paper published in 2004's *Lake Champlain: Partnerships and Research in the New Millennium.* The book collected materials presented at a 2002 conference supported by the Lintilhac Foundation.

"In addition to drinking the water, the dogs probably ingested significant amounts of cyanobacteria by cleaning their fur after contact with the bloom," the scientists wrote. "... The dogs died within hours with convulsions and respiratory paralysis, symptoms typical of anatoxin-a poisoning. Samples of the lake water and algal debris on the shore … confirmed the presence of elevated levels of anatoxin-a near this site."

In a study done after the poisonings, the scientists took water samples from 16 sites along the lake shore in 2000 and 2001, and from Burlington Bay and the outflow of five wastewater treatment plants. They found the bacteria had produced two types of toxins: hepatotoxins, which damage the liver, and neurotoxins, including the especially dangerous anatoxin-a. Toxicity levels were generally well below World Health Organization guidelines for human health; but when anatoxin-a "did occur," they wrote, "it sometimes reached levels that could potentially exceed threshold values affecting human health."

So what is cyanobacteria? What is its connection to phosphorus — and how did phosphorus, a naturally occurring element that is actually essential to sustaining life, become a big problem in waters like these?

"Long ago, humankind realized that by adding a little phosphorus (along with a few other key elements), one could grow a lot more biomass (i.e., food and fiber)," wrote William "Breck" Bowden, a UVM professor of watershed science and director of the university's Vermont Water Resources and Lake Studies Center, in a 2006 article for the "Lake Champlain Issue" of the *Vermont Journal of Environmental Law.*

The U.S. demand for phosphorus as fertilizer has grown so high, Bowden wrote, that "in 2014, we imported about 2.4 million metric tons of phosphate rock, largely from Morocco and Peru. … Eventually, this 'new' phosphorus introduced into the ecosystem found its way to downstream receiving waters."

In hot summer weather, cyanobacteria blooms have become all too common in bays, coves and boat slips, especially in northern sections of Lake Champlain. This is at Oakledge Park in Burlington. *Photo by Mary Watzin.*

Excess phosphorus accumulates in the bottom sediment of lakes, where it will rise toward the surface in warm, sunny weather and drive the growth of biomass. In this case, that biomass is "the pea-soup thick, bright green, and often smelly scums of plant matter that we see in quiet bays of Lake Champlain on some August days," Bowden wrote.

"Unfortunately, a large portion of these blooms are composed of a special group of organisms called cyanobacteria or 'blue-green algae.' ... These organisms are capable of producing species-specific toxins that can have serious human health impacts, including skin rashes, nervous system disruption, and liver damage."

Cyanobacteria were the first organisms on earth to develop the ability to photosynthesize. Today "these highly adaptable bacteria are found in all environments, aquatic and terrestrial, from the equator to the poles," wrote Angela Shambaugh, of the Vermont Dept. of Environmental Conservation, in a separate article in the law journal. And "though they vary in magnitude each year," Shambaugh wrote, "blooms on Champlain's nutrient-rich bays are present during much of August and into September."

In 2015, a citizen monitoring program for cyanobacteria, coordinated since 2003 by the Lake Champlain Committee, received more than 100 reports of algae blooms each week that July.

"Climate change has a lot to do with it; cyanobacteria are more adapted to warm water," Shambaugh told a group of Vermont teachers at the Lake Champlain Maritime Museum in summer 2018. But, she added, "for Lake Champlain in particular, nutrients are the key thing. Lake Champlain has a huge watershed — half of Vermont, and the Adirondacks on the other side. All of that material is working its way down to the lake, and it's carrying these nutrients with it."

The way to curb cyanobacteria blooms, she told the teachers, "is to limit the input of phosphorus in a lake. A surplus of it really stimulates algae growth."

That approach *sounds* straightforward. But it isn't — not with so many diverse nonpoint sources contributing phosphorus to the lake, and to the rivers and streams that feed it.

The reality is that phosphorus has been flowing into Lake Champlain since the advent of farming along its shores.

"For farmers, one of their main concerns is making sure their plants and their animals have enough of it," said Michael Wironen, an environmental scientist who focused his PhD research at UVM on phosphorus loading. "It's an essential input into agriculture."

Nor is farming the only supplier. According to the 2018 *State of the Lake and Ecosystems Indicator Report* by the Lake Champlain Basin Program, of the 218 metric tons of phosphorus that flowed into Champlain the previous year, 38 percent came from agriculture, 20 percent from forests, 20 percent from developed land, 18 percent from streambank erosion, and 6 percent from wastewater treatment plants.

Vermont has struggled in recent years to find ways of effectively reducing phosphorus runoff from virtually all the major nonpoint sources:

- *Dairy farms*, which have been importing more and more phosphorus in fertilizer and animal feed as Vermont dairy farms have grown larger, with more cows and more pressure to produce ever-larger amounts of milk;

- *Streambanks*, which receive and are eroded by runoff from fields, roads, and other sources, sometimes in very high volume as climate change brings intense weather events like 2011's Tropical Storm Irene; and

- *Developed areas* heavy in paved and impervious surfaces, whose runoff is channeled mainly through stormwater collection systems and can overwhelm wastewater plants during heavy storms.

In supporting and working with the Conservation Law Foundation, and with a number of other Vermont nonprofits focused in part or primarily on water quality, the foundation has helped to move the needle on each of these target areas. But the work hasn't been easy, and it hasn't come without controversy.

The foundation began in 1988 to make small grants to nonprofits working on water quality issues. It has continued to support work in this area by a number of organizations — primarily VNRC, the Lake Champlain Committee, the Vermont Public Interest Research Group, Vermont Conservation Voters, Lake Champlain International, Shelburne Farms, the Vermont River Conservancy, and the Connecticut River Watershed Council (now the Connecticut River Conservancy).

In 2000, the foundation's first in a long series of grants to the Conservation Law Foundation supported its Champlain Stormwater Project. CLF's Vermont Advocacy Center, based in Montpelier, headed for the courts.

"The most toxic recorded concentrations"

The first victory came quickly. In 2001, the Vermont Water Resources Board overruled a permit that the state's Agency of Natural Resources (ANR) had granted to Lowe's Home Center for a big-box store and parking lot on 13 acres in South Burlington beside Potash Brook, an already contaminated lake tributary.

"The Water Resources Board ... ruled that clean water laws are straightforward: No pollution may be added to already polluted waters until a cleanup plan is in place," reported CLF's newsletter, *Conservation Matters*.

"The water board's ruling will have a huge impact on Vermont's Agency of

Natural Resources," said CLF attorney Kilian. "It can no longer turn a blind eye to our serious water pollution problems."

But that, it turned out, was just the beginning. In January 2002, the Water Resources Board granted Lowe's permit, saying that although Potash Brook was polluted, the new development wouldn't make it worse. CLF appealed. Meanwhile, Gov. Howard Dean announced a new, two-year initiative to restore Vermont streams; and CLF started its Lake Champlain Lakekeeper Program, employing a full-time "lakekeeper" to monitor conditions, spot violations and build public support for cleanup.

In 2006, CLF and Lowe's

The Conservation Law Foundation's publication *Conservation Matters* devoted a number of articles, including this 2007 cover story, to CLF's efforts to bring about more aggressive pollution controls on Lake Champlain.

settled three lawsuits, resolving five years of litigation. The retailer committed to implementing state-of-the-art controls for stormwater runoff, to monitoring stream conditions for ten years, and to upgrading its current treatment system. "The Lowe's settlement is a model for how development can occur without making water quality problems worse," said Kilian, who had become director of CLF's Vermont Advocacy Program.

That same year, CLF began to broaden its campaign's focus. *Conservation Matters* reported that "last year's three major sewage and industrial wastewater spills into Lake Champlain and its watershed have caused CLF to take a harder look at the state's enforcement and cleanup policies." CLF had, the newsletter said, "begun to demand that the state's Clean Water Act enforcement program measure up to federal requirements."

"The summer of 2004 saw the most toxic recorded concentrations of blue-green algae," *Conservation Matters* reported in "Troubled Waters," a 2007 cover story. "In 2006, the lake sustained one of the longest bouts of the bloom."

Even so, CLF's tough tactics raised some big hackles. "All they do is make people mad!" said Gov. Dean, a moderately liberal Democrat, in a 2002 radio broadcast.

The Burlington Free Press reported that CLF had "evolved into the most contentious — and some say the most influential — green group in the state."

"CLF has helped people understand that they have a right to clean water," said Crea Lintilhac, who has chaired the organization's Vermont Advisory Board. "It hasn't been easy, but CLF's efforts to enforce the Clean Water Act and hold polluters and state agencies accountable are making a difference."

"We had to be more aggressive"

Succeeding Dean as Vermont's governor from 2003 to 2011 was business-friendly Republican Jim Douglas. And under Douglas, the state's relations with CLF became seriously contentious.

From 2003 to 2009, a series of court actions, state agency rulings, and petitions filed by CLF and allied environmental groups centered on a pivotal issue: to what extent the state can be obligated by the polluting of its waters to employ a little-known power called residual designation authority, or RDA. Under the federal Clean Water Act, RDA allows federal or state regulators to take action to curb discharges that harm water quality, even if those discharges are not specifically governed under environmental law.

During those years, "the Conservation Law Foundation, Vermont Natural Resources Council, ANR, and other stakeholders fought at the Water Resources Board, the Vermont Supreme Court, and Vermont's Environmental Court to determine the scope of the state's RDA as it applied to five impaired streams: Potash, Engleby, Morehouse, Centennial, and Bartlett Brooks," wrote Matt Chapman, then general counsel for the Vermont Department of Environmental Conservation, and Jen Duggan, then general counsel for the state Agency of Natural Resources, in the *Vermont Journal of Environmental Law.*

The RDA struggle took several turns. CLF and VNRC petitioned the Agency of Natural Resources in 2003, asking it to issue permits that would control discharges into several of those impaired streams. All feed into the lake, and the Water Resources Board had determined that all were being contaminated, largely by stormwater discharges from strip malls, parking lots and other development.

Eric Smeltzer was for many years a limnologist, or lake scientist, with the Vermont Department of Environmental Conservation. *Image from the documentary Bloom.*

ANR refused to take action. On appeal, the Water Resources Board ruled that it had to, saying "residual designation is not optional." ANR and others appealed to the Vermont Supreme Court, which reversed the board's decision. CLF and VNRC petitioned again. ANR again declined to act.

CLF appealed to the state Environmental Court, which "held that ANR was compelled to exercise its RDA authority, and ordered ANR to do so," Chapman and Duggan wrote. "In the aftermath of this litigation, Vermont has recognized the residual authority designation as an important tool in its toolbox to clean up and protect water quality in Lake Champlain and across the state."

Gov. Douglas was infuriated by CLF. "The group had impeded just about every major development in the state in the last few years. They try to stop everything," he wrote in his 2014 memoir *The Vermont Way: A Republican Governor Leads Vermont's Most Liberal State.* "... Because their focus is to harass and litigate, they've become quite proficient at it. They love to see themselves in the press, haughtily proclaiming victory for the public in some dispute, overlooking the fact that no one ever elected them to anything. ... I was once asked to identify the single greatest obstacle to prosperity in Vermont. Without hesitation I said, 'CLF.'"

But in the same chapter of his book, Douglas wrote of his concern for what, he noted, "is often called the Crown Jewel of Vermont.

"Lake Champlain is fed by many rivers and streams," Douglas wrote, "all of which carry stormwater runoff full of pollutants, and it's the ultimate repository of agricultural by-products of phosphorus-rich manure and fertilizer. The effects are often obvious to the naked eye. Despite some successful efforts to control the pollution, such as upgraded sewage treatment plants, it wasn't improving overall. At one event on the lakeshore, I was presented a glass jar of slimy green water collected nearby. I knew we had to be more aggressive."

In 2003, Gov. Douglas unveiled the Clean and Clear Action Plan. Developed but not implemented under the Dean administration, the multipart effort committed Vermont to spending $100 million over six years "to improve the quality of not only Lake Champlain, but all impaired waterways in the state," Douglas wrote. "Even as the economy slowed, this remained a priority for me: I felt that it was essential to our environmental future and prosperity."

"There was a tremendous ramping up of the efforts at ANR and the Agency of Agriculture," said Eric Smeltzer, the state limnologist. "Huge budget and staff increases; it was a big thing at the time. We were working our butts off to accelerate the phosphorus reduction efforts — but the CLF and parts of the [Democratic majority] Legislature started attacking it. Rightfully, they could also point out that the lake wasn't clean yet."

In 2008, CLF filed a new lawsuit. It charged that the "pollution budget" for phosphorus entering the lake — which Vermont and New York regulators had together set in 2002, under authority given to states by the federal Clean Water Act — "was based on inaccurate and incomplete data that overestimated how much phosphorus could be safely discharged, dooming the lake to further degradation," said *Conservation Matters*.

In spring 2010, the U.S. EPA announced that it had settled CLF's lawsuit. In light of current data on Champlain's water quality, EPA would reconsider the 2002 pollution budget — specifically its Total Maximum Daily Load, or TMDL, for phosphorus.

The Vermont ANR sought to block the settlement, but failed in federal court. Then, in July 2010, CLF filed a supplemental petition, this time asking the federal EPA to take over the regulation of water quality in Vermont.

In November 2010, two things happened that did much to build strong new momentum and public support for cleaning up the lake. Almost two years into Barack Obama's presidency, Vermonters elected a liberal Democratic governor, Peter Shumlin. Later that same month, a little-known video production company supported by the Lintilhac Foundation released a short documentary. It was called *Bloom*.

"Lake Champlain is running out of time"

J on Erickson is a professor of sustainability science and policy at the University of Vermont. He has published widely on topics related to the environment, economics, public health and climate change; and in 2008 he ventured in a new direction, cofounding a Vermont company called Bright Blue EcoMedia.

"I got into filmmaking as an outlet for our work on ecological economics — to tell stories of transition in the economy and society toward sustainable systems," Erickson said. "So I struck up a friendship with a fellow Vermonter, Vic Guadagno. I got to know him through Vermont PBS; he had done a series for them called *Emerging Science*. We founded this film company."

Bloom, the video documentary produced by Bright Blue EcoMedia in 2010 with financial support from the foundation, "does not mince words," wrote Candace Page of the *Burlington Free Press*.

"Crea was the first person who approached us. She said, 'I can't get any traction on this Lake Champlain stuff. I need to get the public's attention.'

"This would have been in 2009 — and we did our first film in three months," said Erickson,

During the filming of *Bloom*, cameraman Robert Killila, at left, and director Victor Guadagno, at right, interview Ben Falk of Whole System Design.

who was its executive producer. "It was a 30-minute special for PBS called *Bloom: The Plight of Lake Champlain*, funded by the Lintilhac Foundation."

The filmmakers did the final editing in a spare room at the Lintilhacs' home in Shelburne. "A key member of the team was Mike Rapacz, former Lake Champlain Lakekeeper and staff scientist for the Conservation Law Foundation," Crea Lintilhac noted — "and thanks to Mike, Chris Cooper," an Academy Award-winning actor, "agreed to narrate the film."

Bloom premiered on November 29, 2010, at the Palace 9 theater in South Burlington.

"This army of people showed up," Erickson said, "from the environmental advocates on one side to the farming community on the other, all ready to rumble. There's this tension in Vermont between the right-to-farm state, with this idyllic vision of rolling fields of grass and red barns and cows, and the reality of a farming system that has become quite industrial, that externalizes its waste. Crea has been right in the middle of this for years.

"This was in the midst of the transition between the Douglas and the Shumlin administration," he added. "So we made this film that was largely focused on the problem."

"*Bloom* does not mince words," wrote Candace Page of the *Burlington Free Press* on the day of the film's debut.

Opening with color panoramas of iridescent green scum covering the water along Champlain's shores, *Bloom* showed Jim Tierney, assistant commissioner of the New York State Department of Environmental Conservation, saying the blooms are "an indicator of gross failure."

"Blue-green algae's a threat everywhere. Everybody's involved in this," said Paul Madden, chair of the Business Alliance for a Clean Lake, recently formed by several prominent business organizations in the Burlington area. "Everybody's got to start paying attention."

"The political will to enforce existing law is very difficult," noted David Deen, a Vermont state representative from Westminster who was the longtime chair of the House Committee on Natural Resources, Fish and Wildlife.

Turning to the impacts of large-herd dairy farms along the lake, *Bloom* pointed to polluting runoff from stored and spread manure, and from fields left bare in the months between harvest and planting. In recent years, as many Champlain Valley dairy farmers, under huge pressure to compete in a merciless commodity market, greatly expanded their herds and boosted milk production per cow, they were importing more and more feed and producing ever-larger volumes of phosphorus-laden manure.

A dairy farmer countered on camera that the true culprit is the price of milk, kept cripplingly low for farmers by the federal pricing structure. "It's pretty hard to get motivated to start looking at a potential water quality issue when you can't even feed your kids," said Roger Rainville, an Alburgh dairyman who chaired the Farmer's Watershed Alliance in Franklin and Grand Isle counties.

On screen came Julie Moore, then director of the Douglas administration's Clean and Clear initiative. "Over the last seven years, we've invested upwards of $100 million in state and federal resources" in the effort to improve water quality, she said. Clean and Clear had funded a diversity of projects to improve water quality. But, she acknowledged, "the fact of the matter is, there's still algae blooms."

The 2002 TMDL for total annual discharges of phosphorus into the lake was 427 metric tons, Moore noted in *Bloom*. "Currently ... the load is anywhere from 600 to as high as 1,200 tons per year."

"Advocates are awakening an apathetic public"

The Vermont Legislature had asked for an audit of Clean and Clear, *Bloom* reported, to find out if its funds were being used effectively. "What we found was, they weren't," said Virginia Lyons, a state senator from Chittenden County who had chaired the Senate Natural Resources and Energy Committee. Initiatives were disconnected, she said in the film; standards and goals were not adequately set.

Chris Kilian of CLF had been reluctant to appear in *Bloom* at all. "He had taken such a beating from the press," said Erickson. "It took Crea to intervene and say, 'Chris, we are trying to make a film that's an honest assessment of the problem, and how all of us — urban, ag, stormwater — have to contribute to the solution.'"

Eric Wolinsky, longtime advocate for cleaning up St. Albans Bay, in the documentary *Bloom*.

Kilian went on camera. "The lake's getting worse," he said, and noted that under the federal Clean Water Act, "the EPA has the obligation to approve TMDLs."

With CLF's lawsuit in the mix, "the Environmental Protection Agency may take away the state's control of the Clean Water Act," said Erickson, appearing in the film. "If that happens, we will be the first state that has their TMDL opened up and given a second look."

"The scale of this problem is enormous," said *Bloom*'s narrator, Chris Cooper, as the documentary concluded. "Our current model has exceeded the ecological limits. Lake Champlain is running out of time. ... There is a point where these eco-systems become unrecoverable. And advocates are awakening an apathetic public."

"We're trying to get that voice heard by the legislators," affirmed Eric Wolinsky, the longtime advocate for St. Albans Bay.

Bloom finished as it had started, with Tierney of the New York Department of Environmental Conservation.

"In my experience," he said, "the way pollution goes down in a water body is comprehensive, effectively implemented regulatory programs based on the science. But it's whether or not society wants to put the human and fiscal resources into making it happen."

"Your film put us on the hot seat"

B*loom* had a widening impact. At the premiere, officials from both the Douglas and incoming Shumlin administrations joined farmers and environmentalists in the audience — and afterward came an often-heated discussion, one of several that would follow showings of the film around Vermont.

"It was this wonderful, dynamic conversation," said Erickson. It came, he noted, "right at a moment where both sides — people who say there's too much regulation, and people who say we're not regulating enough — were saying to the Shumlin administration: 'You've inherited a mess. It's time to take action.'

"Then it showed on PBS, and got the broader public engaged. It must have been 16 or 20 different press outlets that picked it up," he said. "We screened the film for the public all over the state. It became an opportunity to bring people together; it's only a 30-minute film, so you watch it and then we would assemble these panel discussions. We would bring different sides."

Not everyone, of course, was happy.

"My own dean at the time [at the Rubenstein School] was Mary Watzin, whose nickname was Queen of the Lake because she had done all the pollution and algae-bloom research," said Erickson. "Her science was top-notch on this, but she in public meetings was quite critical of me and the film. To me, that always felt like a badge of honor. If I've stirred up my own boss, then I'm probably doing something right here!"

Watzin, now dean of the College of Natural Resources at North Carolina State University, said she felt that as a scientist, Erickson had crossed a line to advocacy.

"You're most effective when you don't blur the line between honestly presenting the information you have, and what you think it means, to advocating for something," she said. "What I thought *Bloom* did was blur that line. Now, did it raise public awareness about the fact that there was a problem, and that nonpoint source pollution was a big part of that problem? Absolutely."

Bloom won a 2011 New England Emmy for best environmental program. Having spotlighted the problem, Bright Blue EcoMedia followed up with a three-part, 2012 series that focused on solutions: ecological wastewater treatment, sustainable local agriculture, and landscape design to minimize stormwater runoff and flood damage. The new-farming episode won a second regional Emmy.

Still, said Erickson, "It was the 'problems' film that stirred things up. When Peter Shumlin came in as governor, because of *Bloom* and Crea's foresight that led to the film, they had an agitated public that they had to deal with."

Erickson said people in Shumlin's administration told him, "'You know, off the record, your film put us on the hot seat.' They had to raise consciousness, especially within the farming community. They had to deal with the threat of the EPA delegating authority. It wasn't going to get swept under the rug anymore."

"This is a problem that we've all created and we all need to address," said Shumlin's secretary of agriculture, Chuck Ross, in Middlebury's Town Hall Theater

Mary Watzin was dean of UVM's Rubenstein School of Environment and Natural Resources from 2009 to 2012. *Image from the documentary Bloom.*

after a May 2011 screening of the first *Bloom*.

At that showing, "a sea of more than 100 citizens, lawmakers and public officials debated how to fix Lake Champlain's pollution problems," the *Addison Independent* reported.

"We're all a part of this very complicated ecosystem, and a very complicated economy that ties us all together to the lake," the paper quoted Ross saying. "There's not a silver bullet here. This is a problem that did not begin yesterday."

↓

"Upping the regulatory approach"

In January 2011, the EPA struck down the 2002 phosphorus TMDL.

"When they do that, the EPA is required to write the new rules," said Eric Smeltzer.

"We see opportunities to ultimately build and further strengthen the restoration work underway in the Lake Champlain basin," EPA Regional Administrator Curtis Spalding wrote to ANR Secretary Deborah Markowitz. And with that, EPA and state officials began a long process of working together to develop a new, more effective TMDL.

"The Shumlin approach to the EPA was to cooperate with them, stop fighting," Smeltzer said. "So I spent the next five years of my career working on the technical side with EPA. Also there was a real effort among all the different state agencies — ANR, Ag, Transportation especially — to look harder at programs, and to propose better ways to address water quality in each of those areas: river, agriculture, highways."

The TMDL work wasn't done in isolation.

"EPA and Vermont state agencies met with people representing a wide array of perspectives from across the watershed," recalled David Mears and Trey Martin, who respectively were Shumlin's commissioner of the Department of Environmental Conservation and deputy secretary of ANR, in the *Vermont Journal of Environmental Law*.

"The common theme that emerged from those conversations," they continued, "was that Vermonters love Lake Champlain, they grasp the environmental significance, economic cost, and health risks associated with allowing its continuing decline, and they have many good, some competing, ideas for protecting the lake. Working within this context, state and federal officials worked to develop an approach that was based in science and data, [and] targeted the most significant sources of pollution, in order to produce measurable results and a healthier Lake Champlain."

The EPA issued a new, stronger TMDL in 2015, and the state rolled out a new Lake Champlain TMDL implementation plan.

"It was upping the regulatory approach to a whole new level," Smeltzer said.

"And the funding: We revised those cost estimates to $500 million, $800 million, now over $1 billion over a period of time. So more realistic funding needs were identified."

"There's no question that if the CLF doesn't file that lawsuit, there isn't the 2015 TMDL," Trey Martin said in an interview. The 2002 TMDL "didn't have the kind of intensive focus on the nonpoint source reductions, and the kind of public-private partnerships that are meant under this TMDL to drive results."

Reflected Smeltzer, now retired as a state lake scientist: "I think you could say, looking back, that as painful and miserable as that contentious process was, and the huge amount of effort that it took just to write a new plan, let alone implement it, we've got a much stronger water quality footing in Vermont now than we ever had. So I guess you'd have to give CLF credit for having kicked that process off."

There was a need for new legal frameworks that would support and reinforce the complex weave of planned actions aimed at cleaning up the lake. A growing number of Vermont legislators knew they needed to act.

Then, in August 2011, came Tropical Storm Irene.

Devastation, then legislation

When they move northward along the Atlantic coast, tropical storms and hurricanes usually move out to sea off the mid-Atlantic region — but Irene didn't. The storm veered instead up the Hudson River Valley, turned east and struck Vermont very hard.

In a single day, on Sunday, August 28, 2011, Irene dumped some 11 inches of rain all across the state. Six people died; 13 communities were temporarily cut off. According to a report by the Vermont Long-Term Disaster Recovery Group, "Over 3,500 homes, including some 500 mobile homes, were damaged or destroyed, along with over 300 bridges and more than 500 miles of highways. In all, 225 Vermont municipalities reported storm damage."

The worst flooding since 1927 struck 10 of Vermont's 17 major river basins, inundating 20,000 acres of farmland, scouring streambanks and pushing huge volumes of nutrient-laden mud out into Lake Champlain. Overwhelmed waste-water plants discharged some 10 million gallons of raw or partly treated sewage.

"In too many Vermont towns and watersheds, Irene illustrated the risks of development without regard to 'natural watershed storage' capable of capturing water, sediment, and woody material during heavy rainfall events," wrote Trey Martin, then ANR's deputy secretary, in the *Journal of Environmental Law.* "The resulting devastation demanded a strong response. Almost as soon as the flood waters began to recede, the Vermont General Assembly, Shumlin Administration, and municipal and private stakeholders worked together to bolster existing flood resilience policies, create new laws and policies, and prepare for the inevitable next storm."

In the four years that followed Irene, Martin noted, "the Vermont General Assembly passed three critical pieces of legislation aimed at improving surface water quality through land use regulation":

- **Act 138 of 2012** created "new regulations to promote and enhance the function of natural floodplains and to decrease reliance on engineered structures to protect against flood hazards," Martin wrote.

- **Act 172 of 2014, the Shoreline Protection Act,** set up a state permitting program to impose new standards on the creation of new cleared or paved areas that are within 100 feet of lakes and larger ponds.

- **Act 64 of 2015, the Vermont Clean Water Act,** was the most ambitious, complex and far-reaching of the new laws. Eleven different State House committees worked on it, and it passed with broad bipartisan support.

Algae blooms had been widespread in summer 2014 — and as the 2015 legislative session opened that January, Gov. Shumlin called for strong new action, coupled with more resources. "The State of Vermont continued to face pressure from EPA, clean-water advocates, and stakeholders around Vermont to take strong action to protect Lake Champlain," Martin wrote.

Act 64, passed that session, requires the Agency of Agriculture, Food & Markets to change its "accepted agricultural practices" to "required agricultural

August 28, 2011: the center of Wilmington, Vermont during Tropical Storm Irene.

practices" that are aimed at better storing and managing nutrients, and at protecting rivers and streams from livestock and field runoff. [For more on farming and water quality, see pages 132-155.]

The law also gives the state new power to "regulate runoff from municipal roads, and to require redevelopment and retrofits" to developed lots with more than three acres of paved surface, Trey Martin wrote. "Developed lands will require improved practices, such as stormwater retention ponds. ... Natural infrastructure like floodplains, wetlands, and forests will be conserved and protected as perhaps the state's best defense against stormwater pollution."

That last is especially important, he added, "as Vermont's climate changes and the intensity and frequency of rainfall and snowmelt events increase."

These challenges are huge. Meeting them, and sustaining the needed changes, will require long-term effort by everyone from private landowners to towns, cities, organizations and regional planning groups up and down the Champlain Valley.

There also remained one big, unresolved issue: Money.

Act 64, the Vermont Clean Water Act, created a new Clean Water Fund to support compliance work by cities and towns, farmers and watershed groups. But how to *fund* the fund, through the years of hard, collaborative work that was envisioned — that was left up in the air. Act 64 only set up a three-year surcharge on the property transfer tax, which would raise about $5 million per year. That was nowhere near enough.

"Our back roads in Vermont: We'd like to see the road crews out there doing parabolic ditches, right-sizing the culverts, doing bridges correctly, and then maintain them," Martin said. "To make it a habit of local government to take care of the roads for water quality is a big ask.

"Then we have 6,000 to 8,000 farms. There are so many projects, there's so much need; it's again building routine practices, like cover cropping and fencing livestock away from the water sources. It's creating buffers that are bigger, better and more robust. So where does the money come from?"

Act 64 called on the state treasurer to look into funding options, and to report back by January 2017.

That was the beginning of a whole new struggle.

"Fasten your seatbelts"

State Treasurer Beth Pearce projected the long-term costs of meeting the EPA's cleanup requirements at $50 million per year, for 20 years. In 2016, she proposed that the state allot a two-year "bridge" totaling $50 million in capital funds, while the Legislature developed and committed to a plan for long-term funding.

"In preparing her 2016 recommendations," said a report by *Seven Days* columnist John Walters, "Pearce examined '60 to 70 revenue sources,' she says. 'We vetted and modeled each one. We ended up with a per-parcel fee tied to the amount of pollution. Polluters pay.'"

Lawmakers approved the interim $50 million — and they created a working group on water quality funding, charged with recommending a long-term funding mechanism focused on the per-parcel approach. Republican Gov. Phil Scott assigned administration staff to the group, even though in his first term in the 2016 election he had committed to no tax increases of any kind.

In September 2017, cyanobacteria blooms hit high-alert conditions on dozens of Lake Champlain beaches, and on Lake Carmi in northern Vermont. But when the working group delivered its report in October, it took no stand on where or how to find the 20-year funding. Instead, its report said that for the next six years, the group "recommends existing revenue sources to fund clean water investments." It suggested that lawmakers in the coming session start studying other funding options.

Environmental groups were disappointed, as were leaders of the Democratic-majority Legislature. "We are struggling to see how we're going to meet the goal with existing money," said Tim Ashe, a Democrat/Progressive from Chittenden who was president pro tem of the State Senate.

"The working group was charged to find a long-term funding solution," said Jared Carpenter, water policy advocate with the nonprofit Lake Champlain Committee. "It misses that mark by a wide margin, offering no solutions and no legislation."

In total, *Seven Days* reported, "Vermont is spending $78 million a year on water quality efforts, including $25 million in state money, $25 million from local municipalities, $16 million from the federal government and $11 million in private contributions. Of that, $22 million is coming from the state capital budget this year."

"We're not putting off action," Julie Moore, now secretary of the Agency of Natural Resources, assured the public. "We're actively engaged in really significant work. It's full speed ahead."

"The working group has backhanded the ball into the Legislature's court," wrote Walters in *Seven Days*. "Lawmakers will be working not only to appease a variety of constituencies, but under threat of a gubernatorial veto.

"Fasten your seatbelts, good people," Walters concluded.

"This is a giant mess"

As the 2018 legislative session got underway in January, a new clean water working group was meeting regularly in the State House, bringing key legislators together with academics, activists and environmental groups supported by the Lintilhac Foundation.

"There's a sense of urgency, and a need to move forward," said State Sen. Christopher Bray of Addison, chair of the Senate Committee on Natural Resources and Energy, at a session of the group in February.

With interim cleanup funding set to expire after 2020, Bray assured the group that legislators were working on a budget that would invest more money in clean water than ever before in Vermont. The state would face new lawsuits, he warned, if "diligent action were not taken."

"We also asked the Agency of Agriculture," Bray said, "to deliver a report on building healthy soils, reducing agricultural pollution, and how to provide financial support for transitioning out of dairy to less polluting practices." With curbing nutrient runoff from farms clearly the most sensitive issue politically, Bray called the request "a question we're putting out to the ag community: Let's evolve in a more ecologically friendly fashion."

"One of my biggest concerns is the proximity of dairies to the waterways," said Crea Lintilhac in the same meeting of the working group. "Maybe some of that land needs to return to woodland, and to wildlife."

But by March, the proposed funding legislation had been chewed up in conflict between the Senate Natural Resources and Agriculture committees. Bray's bill was "shredded" by the Ag Committee and its chairman, Essex-Orleans Sen. Robert Starr, said Jared Carpenter of the Lake Champlain Committee at a March meeting of the Water Caucus, a convening of nonprofit advocacy groups.

"This is a mess. This is a giant mess," Jon Groveman of the Vermont Natural Resources Council told the Water Caucus. "Things are in a very political place right now. We'll get back to the policy when we get [the bill] into the House."

"We hope they move forward with a source of funding," urged Crea Lintilhac, a regular Water Caucus attendee. "We recommend a per-parcel fee. Nobody should be able to pollute the water — it's a public trust."

"More study committees are a waste of time and tax money," she declared. "We need to take action now."

But that didn't happen — not in 2018. As the State House session wound down in late spring, the House passed an increase in the state's rooms and meals tax to help fund water cleanup. But the Senate then stripped the bill clean of funding mechanisms.

The Legislature adjourned. "The state still has no plan to pay for clean water," *Seven Days* reported.

"This is what happens. This is what's been happening for three years on this," lamented VNRC's Groveman. "All the hotel and hospitality industry people complained. We were hoping this would be resolved, but we need to continue to work to identify a long-term stable funding source that creates enough money. The gap funding that the treasurer recommended and the Legislature implemented expires on July 1, 2019."

"Back to political will"

That summer, with the Legislature between its annual convenings, longtime Westminster Rep. David Deen, chair of House Natural Resources, Fish and Wildlife, took time to stop in at the Hartland Diner in Hartland Four Corners, to reflect in an interview on the long journey toward real cleanup of Vermont's lakes and rivers.

"I've been at this since the '70s," said Deen, a professional fishing guide who served for 20 years as a river steward for the Connecticut River Conservancy. "Back in the '90s, we knew that agriculture was a big part of what was going on, and that towns were a big part of what was going on, in terms of the degradation of water. We, the society, through the [federal] Clean Water Act, had built those treatment plants and were taking care of straight discharges. But we weren't taking care of surface runoff."

In the early 2000s, as chair of what was then House Fish and Wildlife, Deen began working on water quality with Groveman and VNRC, which began receiving Lintilhac grants for the work in 2004. "Chris Kilian was with VNRC then. He became a pusher" on the issue, Deen said. "Both I and VNRC were willing to compromise, because we were getting small progress, but Chris couldn't stand it. So he went off to a place where an absolute was an absolute, and he's done wonderfully well in terms of doing that.

"Back in the 2000s, classifying groundwater as a public-trust resource was a major victory. That gave government an affirmative responsibility to protect groundwater," Deen recounted. In the State House, "Crea starts showing up at my committee meetings, asking questions. And I need help, because I'm in the middle of a fight with Vermont Yankee," the nuclear power plant in Vernon. "They are discharging hot water, some of it 100 degrees, into the Connecticut River."

That period of hot-water discharges saw plummeting numbers of Atlantic Ocean shad, a popular sport fish, migrating up the river to spawn. The foundation began making modest grants to what was then the Connecticut River Watershed Council, now the Connecticut River Conservancy.

David Deen, longtime chair of the Committee on Natural Resources, Fish and Wildlife in the Vermont House of Representatives, retired from the Legislature in 2018 after serving in the State Senate from 1987 to 1988, and in the House from 1990 to 2018. *Image from the documentary Bloom.*

"We needed a lot of staff and consultant help, and the foundation helped out with that," Deen said. "Not big grants, but on a consistent basis, so that we had unrestricted funds to go out and pursue other funds, which I did. It paid my salary to do that."

After Vermont Yankee shut down in 2014, the River Conservancy began more broadly applying its Lintilhac funding to its work on water quality and river cleanup. In Montpelier, "in the meantime," Deen said, "Crea was continuing to attend my committee meetings."

"That personal involvement is very, very different from what you would expect from a CEO of a foundation," he observed. "They're all nice, they come, they look, they read your annual report, they meet two or three people, and they either give you a grant or they don't. Crea's sitting in the room, pushing on water quality."

By now the foundation had extended its support on water quality to other groups working on aspects of the issue: Vermont Conservation Voters, Lake Champlain International, the Lake Champlain Committee, the Vermont Public Interest Research Group. Then, Deen recalled, came "the really big turning point": 2011, the year of Irene. Passage of the key pieces of water-quality legislation, culminated by the state's Clean Water Act, followed the storm and the state's recovery.

"It all started moving in the right direction. With leadership from the [Shumlin] administration, and the Lintilhac Foundation behind the scenes pushing the political will and giving to organizations that had a clean water agenda, we were able to get it done."

But the story, Deen cautioned, is not finished. Along with finding long-term funding, more needs to be done on required farm practices to protect the state's waters. The per-parcel fee approach to funding was dead politically, he said — but even so, "I think we're in pretty good shape. This no-new-taxes [Scott] administration ponied up $25 million each year for two years, out of unused capital dollars, in an era when there are shortfalls in the budget."

The state treasurer's 2016 report, he noted, identified more than 45 potential funding sources for the long-term work. "We know the spectrum of what's out there. Again, we're back to political will."

"That circles back to funding"

Phil Scott was re-elected governor in November 2018. While campaigning for his second term, Scott had signaled he'd be open to raising new revenue.

"So it seems like there's more opportunity," Lauren Hierl of Vermont Conservation Voters said that autumn. "There's a lot of work happening; the secretary of natural resources and some others are exploring ways of collecting the money and distributing it. That's encouraging. It all comes down to, as we've consistently seen, that the House and Senate often have very different views on what needs to be done."

Water Caucus members had been talking to State House leaders. "They are going to be a little bit up against the wall this coming year," Hierl said, "because the two-year capital funds are going to run out in July. If we don't put something in place, it's all grinding to a halt."

Under the state's Clean Water Act, new requirements, regulations and systems were rolling out across the state to better manage stormwater flow — and funding was going to be needed for implementing and maintaining all that work at the state and local levels.

"The devil's in the details, about how it's all implemented and rolled out," Hierl said, "but the structure is in place. We know what we need to do.

"With farming, I think there's less confidence that the policies we have in place will be adequate to what we need to be doing. Are the stream buffers wide enough, are the basics of the actual policy strong enough to actually get to clean water? Certainly there are farmers doing great work, and there are a lot more good practices on the ground than there were five years ago — and that circles back to funding, too. We should be helping farmers make these transitions."

By March, halfway through the 2019 session, things were looking dicey again.

"Democrats in the State House have yet to find a funding source for what they have signaled is a majority priority this session: long-term water cleanup efforts," *VTDigger* reported.

Chris Bray of Addison, the Senate Natural Resources chair, had included a per-parcel fee in a bill he introduced, tagged S.96; but that provision was stripped out while the bill was still in the Senate. No funding proposal had yet emerged from the House side. In early April, S.96 passed the Senate unanimously, but still without a funding mechanism. Now the customary late-spring adjournment was looming, and the public pressure to find a solution was strong.

Wildlife species that rely on clean water, like the common loon, the belted kingfisher and the brook trout, "would, if they could, demand stronger action to protect Vermont's lakes and ponds, rivers and streams," wrote David Mears, the former DEC commissioner who was now executive director of Audubon Vermont, in an April 3, 2019 *VTDigger* commentary. "Real questions have emerged about whether the Legislature will act on the imperative to establish long-term clean water funding. It is up to those of us who can write messages and letters, or make calls, to let our legislators know that we are waiting, impatiently, for them to act."

"Most of Vermont's beautiful streams, rivers and lakes are not healthy," declared Jen Duggan, now CLF's Vermont vice president, in her own online commentary. "This time of year, melting snow and rain carry pollution like chemicals, oils, salts, nutrients and animal waste into our waterways. ... Over this summer, we will once again be faced with cyanobacteria blooms.

"We have all the information we need to act," she said. "... Without long-term funds, projects to restore wetlands, retrofit roads, and implement best management practices on farms are in jeopardy. If we do not act now, costs will only increase over time."

On May 9, the House gave preliminary approval to a revised version of S.96, with a new, $6 million tax on cloud computing software. The bill would also take 4 percent of the rooms and meals tax from the state's Education Fund, about $7.6 million per year, and dedicate it to clean-water project funding.

At this, the Vermont Technology Alliance rose up in protest. The cloud tax would be a "disincentive to the growth of tech businesses and jobs in the state," wrote its executive director, Jeff Couture. Tim Ashe, president pro tem of the State Senate, said he also opposed a cloud tax.

That approach to finding the money was in trouble. And adjournment was nearing fast.

$$\sqrt{}$$

"This is a really important step forward"

Then on May 20, Democratic leaders in the House and Senate agreed on an idea that involved no new taxes. They would, instead, redirect 6 percent of the state's 9 percent rooms and meals tax from the General Fund into clean-water funding.

By 2021, that would "start to generate about $12 million for clean water each year," *VTDigger* reported. Because state tax collections in 2019 were running higher than projected, Democratic leaders were confident that the lost General Fund money would be replaced by increased revenues from the state's income and corporate taxes.

Both State House chambers voted yes. Not everyone was entirely sure about the approach, which counted on higher tax revenues continuing over years — but in the messy world of legislative sausage-making, it was a commitment.

On June 19, Gov. Scott signed the bill, which became Act 76. And in July, the EPA sent a letter to Julie Moore approving the strategy. "In combination with the other dedicated clean water funding sources enacted by the Vermont Legislature since 2015, Act 76 is expected to produce long-term funding levels in the ballpark of the needs identified by the ... Vermont State Treasurer's report," wrote EPA official Deborah Szaro.

With the funding in place, *VTDigger* reported, "Moore and the Agency of Natural Resources will focus more directly on implementation. Current and upcoming projects include conservation measures on farms, addressing stormwater runoff, and wetlands preservation."

Jen Duggan of CLF gave a thumbs-up. "We think that additional monies are needed to clean up Lake Champlain and waters in the state of Vermont," she said. "But we felt that this is a really important step forward."

In the 2021 session, the Legislature allocated a total of $225 million — including $115 million in federal Covid-relief funding through that year's American Rescue Plan Act — to projects and investments related to clean water. The money will "help modernize our drinking water and wastewater systems, address combined sewer overflows, remove toxic contaminants from water supplies, implement dam safety projects, and address other water infrastructure needs," said a news release from VNRC and the nonprofit Vermont Conservation Voters.

"Initially the Legislature was considering using the ARPA funds to replace the [state] Clean Water Funds," said Jon Groveman of VNRC. "We advocated to use both our state dedicated funds and the new ARPA money for clean water, because we need both — and the Legislature ultimately agreed."

Waters in the Public Trust

SPOTLIGHTS ON FARMING
AND WATER QUALITY

"AN ECONOMY AT STARK ODDS WITH THE ECOLOGY"

A conversation with Champlain advocate James Ehlers

James Ehlers is the founder and was the longtime executive director of Lake Champlain International, a nonprofit supported by the foundation that advocates to improve water quality. Currently a policy advisor for LCI, he recently had this conversation with the author.

James, how do you view the state of the lake today?

I'm going to tell you the unvarnished truth: I believe the state of the lake right now is horrid, relative to what it should be from an ecological standpoint. From a public health standpoint, it's dismal. Politicians who have other interests besides ecological ones, interests rooted in an economy that benefits from extraction and pollution, try to frame it in a different light. But when the survival of humans and wildlife is jeopardized by the lack of quality of the water, I don't know how to be honest and express it in any other terms.

So how would you relate the efforts of recent years, Act 64 and the related legislation, and the effort to fully fund a cleanup of the lake? Does it go far enough?

Not even close. Act 64 is such a broad piece of legislation, it's hard for me to comment with a general observation. I think it's been a very useful tool in raising awareness with respect to nutrient pollution. My one regret was my inability, during the crafting of that legislation, to have included other pollutants that I think Act 64 overlooks — for example, industrial agriculture and its reliance on pesticides. I felt strongly then, as I still do, that Act 64 should have included regulation for pesticide application. It wasn't an accident, in my view, that that was excluded.

Act 64 was a political response, I believe, not to solve the pollution issues but to give the politically interested an opportunity to suggest that they were doing something. I know people find that to be a very harsh criticism, to be over the top — but I just point to the state of the lake.

What would it take to really make an impact on nutrient loading in the lake, from farms, from development, from all the contributors to this complex problem?

Well, I think describing it as a complex problem is part of the problem. It gives people an opportunity to not address it, or to befuddle the public — distract, obfuscate, by saying "Oh, these are extremely complex problems." I don't really believe that's the case.

It's a pretty simple situation: We continue to operate an economy that is at stark odds with the ecology. The social aspects of that, I will concede, are complex, but the scientific realities are not. I'll use an example. Pizza tastes good, a slice now and then is satisfying; but if you eat too much pizza, you're going to have serious health implications. It's the same with the landscape. We're continuing to feed the lake, and all of our water bodies, more nutrients than are required. And when you do that, it puts us in a state of unhealthiness.

Ecologically, the system is always going to find equilibrium. In some cases, equilibrium is what we describe as death. And there are sociological implications of that; there are people who don't want their property values compromised, with the death of St. Albans Bay for example. The particulars of Act 64, "Oh we've reduced 16 million tons" — that's like saying, "We were eating two pizzas a day, now we're only eating one." It's still gonna kill you! We need to totally overhaul our diet.

It still gets back to the question, what can be done that would make the kind of difference that needs to be made?

Oh, it's the easiest thing of all, and it's the most unpopular. What's the best way to prevent a heart attack? Exercise, get yourself back in shape. It's no different here: It's regulation. The whole notion that we're going to continue to use technology to solve the problems created by technology, I think is a fool's errand. That we're somehow going to treat the lake with more chemicals, to alter the impacts of prior chemicals, is foolhardy, because we don't know what we don't know. The simplest answer is to control, and regulate, the amount of inputs.

I don't think these things are complicated, I think they're harsh. They're hard. No, there's never going to be enough money. I think that's a distraction, requiring the taxpayers to underwrite developers and commercial agricultural interests. Regulation, which would cost these enterprises up-front money, is extremely unpopular. But that is the solution, in my view. If you want to cure someone of their problem with alcohol, you don't continue to feed them alcohol. You regulate, you put in structure. You eliminate the practices that are contributing to the phosphorus in Lake Champlain.

This goes back to the Lintilhac Foundation, and why I have great respect for them. These messages are very unpopular. Nobody likes the idea of having to quit eating all of their ice cream and chocolate chip cookies, and drinking all their alcohol, until they've had a couple heart attacks and the doctor says, "Change your lifestyle or you're not going to see your grandkids at Christmas." I feel like that's where we are, on the landscape. I believe nature will heal itself — but what are going to be the costs to this generation, and future generations, because of the short-term greed, the gluttony, that is currently driving the system?

"Our programs give people an array of options to join the team and fight for a swimmable, drinkable, fishable Lake Champlain," says the website of Lake Champlain International, which James Ehlers founded. Along with running annual fishing derbies for all ages on the lake, LCI works toward restoring its fisheries, educating the public about lake pollution, and helping young people and adults learn more. This photo tops the home page of www.mychamplain.net, LCI's website.

AT A "PIVOTAL TURNING POINT" FOR VERMONT DAIRY FARMING, THE PROSPECTS FOR CONVENTIONAL AND ORGANIC ARE DIVERGING

Up in Highgate Springs close to Canada, Guy Choiniere and his adult son Mathieu work a fourth-generation Vermont dairy farm beside the Rock River, a winding stream that has been classed as impaired, primarily by phosphorus-laden soil that runs off from the farms along its path to Lake Champlain. When he was a young man, Guy (pronounced "Ghee") joined his father Henry in running the farm, just as Matt has joined him today.

One day about 20 years ago, Guy and his dad were working on a piece of equipment when specialists from the USDA's Natural Resource Conservation Service stopped in. At that time, both the farm's barnyard and the riverbank across the road were brown and bare.

"They said, 'We have a program that can help you with your issues,'" Guy recalled. "My dad and I looked at each other and said, 'What issues?'

"What they saw was that we had mudslides every other year, and we were losing soil by the ton into the Rock River," he said. "We'd been seeing that for years. To us, it was normal."

Henry and Guy had been running the farm as a conventional modern dairy: They grew a lot of corn and high-energy forage, bought a lot of grain, and produced as much milk as their Holsteins could generate. "But everybody was doing the same, and the market became flooded," Guy recalled. "There was no stability, it was a roller coaster. I had a lot of changes I wanted to make."

As he took over the farm, Guy set out to learn all he could about organic agriculture, and by 2005 he was producing certified organic milk. Over the years since then, thanks to the substantially higher prices that organic milk brings, plus a lot of matching-fund assistance from the U.S. Department of Agriculture and the State of Vermont, "we have invested over $200,000 into preventing soil erosion into the Rock River along our property," the Choinieres say on their farm website.

"Between planting 5,000 trees, creating cattle lanes, utilizing buffer strips, building lined waterways, managing our water runoff and following a nutrient management plan," the family says, "we are doing our best to minimize our impact on the Lake Champlain watershed." Buffer plantings around the barnyard's edge and catch basins for water running off the barn roof now slow the drainage to a safe percolation; the trees and shrubs they've planted along the riverbank have grown so densely that Matt calls that green strip "the rainforest."

The Choinieres have also given up raising corn and buying grain, shifting their 80 cows successfully to a diet of 100 percent grasses and clovers that they grow on the farm. Their vet bills have dropped from some $6,000 per year to a third of that for preventive services, nearly nothing for illness treatment. And Guy and Matt have diversified their operation: In addition to organic milk, they now produce grass-fed beef along with pork, veal, chicken, free-range eggs and honey, which they sell from their self-serve farm store.

These days farmers come here from all over Vermont, and well beyond, to talk with Guy and Matt and learn how they've succeeded. And while six other farms along the Rock River have also gone organic, most of the Choiniere's neighbors are still conventional — yet

Matt (standing) and Guy Choiniere on their organic dairy farm in Highgate Springs. *Photo by Caleb Kenna.*

those farms too are often doing more with cover crops and no-till planting, to improve soil health and reduce runoff.

"That is helping. The river is a lot cleaner," Guy said. "They've seen the success, so now the neighbors aren't afraid to try new things. It's not necessarily strictly organic, but it's definitely conservation-minded."

"Historic farm losses"

Up and down the Champlain Valley, farming practices that affect water quality are generally changing for the better, spurred in part by the example of farms like the Choinieres', and by the shift from "accepted" to "required" agricultural practices put in place by Act 64, Vermont's Clean Water Act of 2015. There has been a notable increase in cover cropping and no-till planting — and more farmers, like Guy and Matt, are injecting liquid manure into their fields instead of spreading or spraying it, aiming to keep more nutrients in the soil that might have been lost to the water or the air. Younger farmers in particular are often modeling and promoting more eco-friendly practices like these.

But for non-organic dairies the big picture is dark, and has been for a while. About 90 percent of Vermont milk still comes from conventional farms, and for those farmers the pressure to make often-costly changes that protect water quality couldn't have come at a harder time. For five years in a row, from 2015 to 2019, a nationwide milk glut pushed the price paid for conventional milk down below the costs of production — so much that, according to a 2019 study conducted by two respected observers of the Vermont dairy industry, the total annual loss for Vermont's conventional dairy farms in those years amounted to $75 million.

"External costs, including water quality remediation, add at least another $30 million annually," wrote the authors, former state agriculture secretary Roger Allbee and Dan Smith, founder of the Northeast Dairy Compact Commission, in a proposal to the governor and Legislature that drew on their study, which was funded by the Lintilhac Foundation.

Allbee and Smith argued that Vermont dairies cannot keep on increasing production and expanding acreage, as many have, to keep up with national trends: "Chronically inadequate pay prices have caused the exits of two-thirds of Vermont's dairy farms since 2000. This is a pivotal turning point for the state's cultural and historic identity as a 'dairy state.' ... Without radical change in current trends, we forecast that the Vermont dairy industry could well include fewer than 100 conventional farms by 2030."

They were not the only experts raising the alarm.

"From State fiscal year (FY) 2010 to 2019, we estimate that Vermont spent more than $285 million on programs and policies that support the dairy industry and/or address detrimental environmental impacts of dairy farming," the office of the Vermont state auditor declared in a May 2021 investigative report. "In FY19, the most recent year of our analysis, spending totaled more than $35 million."

In spite of all that public investment, "Structural changes affecting the dairy industry are resulting in historic farm losses across the state, negative profit margins for many farms, and slow and steady declines in farm equity for many farm families," said *A 2018 Exploration of the Future of Vermont Agriculture*, a report by UVM Extension and the Vermont Housing & Conservation Board (VHCB). "The outcomes of this process are consolidation and farm closures."

The stakes here are very high. "Dairy farms still contribute close to 70% of Vermont's farm sales (about $1.3 billion annually), and manage over 80% of Vermont's open land," the Extension/VHCB report said. "... In our opinion, the magnitude of this issue may be historic: The marketplace has failed the farmer and in our lifetimes Vermont may lose the agricultural foundation of our working landscape, with all it means to our quality of life and the statewide value from agricultural exports ($776 million annually), the agricultural economy ($2.6 billion annually), the recreational economy ($1.51 billion annually), and the tourist economy (almost $3 billion annually)."

"We have too many cows, too close to the water"

In spring 2018, five relatively young dairy farmers walked into a State House meeting, organized by the Lintilhac Foundation, where Allbee and Smith had been discussing research they had done into the prospects for expanding organic dairying in Vermont.

The Choiniere farm from above, with the Rock River at left. Plantings of recent years have created a runoff-absorbing buffer around the barnyard; trees alongside the river now protect it from soil erosion. *Photo by Caleb Kenna.*

The five farmers all run conventional operations — but when a questioner asked how many were doing more no-tilling and cover cropping than five years ago, all five raised their hands. "We're pretty poor farmers if we're just blowing nutrients into the stream," said Andy Nolan of Panton.

Other farmers are noticing these conservation practices, Phil

Livingston of New Haven said. "They're driving by these fields and thinking, 'I wonder how that's going to work.' Come September, they're seeing the corn's just as high, it looks just as good. They're thinking, 'There might be something to that.'

"We're 100 percent go on that," he added. "But the biggest challenge we still have is trying to survive in these doom-and-gloom milk prices."

"I know water quality is a huge issue right now," said David Defreest of Warren, "and it's a good thing to focus on, because going forward I want my kids to be able to work the farm, like my father and me."

Chase Goodrich of Salisbury told the group he had spent much of 2015 putting Act 64's newly required farm practices in place, but "the lake didn't get polluted in a day, and it's not going to get fixed in a day. I get that it's an urgent situation, and we're all looking for an urgent answer. But fixing land practices takes time."

And in truth, not every conventional dairy is so progressive. In an in-depth February 2020 report, John Dillon of Vermont Public Radio said Vermonters continue to file reports and complaints about sometimes egregious discharges of farm waste into state waters.

"Since 2017, the agriculture agency has referred 88 suspected cases of farm waste entering waterways to ANR [the Agency of Natural Resources]," Dillon reported. "Twenty-nine cases — about a third — are still open at ANR.

"... Farm regulation is divided between two state agencies," Dillon noted. "The Agency of Agriculture inspects and permits farms, and it can also help farms find funding. But if water pollution leaves the land and runs directly into a ditch or stream, the Agency of Natural Resources takes over. But it's hardly a perfect partnership.

"Records show that cases are tossed back and forth between the two bureaucracies, even when evidence seems to be compelling. Sometimes pollution can continue to flow for months. In some cases, despite repeated warnings and legal sanctions, the same violations repeatedly reoccur."

After the meeting in the State House, Crea Lintilhac wondered if the determination those five young farmers had expressed, to get through the current crisis and pass the farm on to their children, was truly realistic.

"I don't know what the future will look like," she said. "I don't think dairy will disappear, but we need to create an ag landscape that will allow for smaller herds, smaller farms. It's not just about nutrient runoff — we have too many cows, in this topography, too close to the water. We can have a dairy future, but it can't be what it is now."

Proposing a complete conversion

In mid-2021, 415 of Vermont's dairy farms were conventional operations, while 169 were certified organic. In recent years for a conventional dairy, the break-even price on bulk milk has been roughly $17 per hundred pounds (a "hundredweight," or cwt). Between 2014 and 2018, the price paid to farmers, set under the bewildering complexities of the Northeast Federal Milk Marketing Order, ran between $15.25 and $16.78, according to the Vermont Milk Commission. After such a long run of red ink for farmers, in early 2018 the large milk-buying coop Agrimark sent its members "a list of suicide and mental health hotlines — along with the news that milk prices would drop even lower this year," reported *The New York Times*.

In 2019, the average price was better, at $17.46, and at the year's end it rose to $19.28, lifting farmers' hopes. But as news of the novel coronavirus spread in February 2020 the price began dropping again, and by May it had sagged below $15. With schools and restaurants closed amid the pandemic isolation, the average bulk price in 2020 was $16.45, slipping to $15.42 in early 2021. Some farmers began dumping milk that they had nowhere to ship.

The prospects for organic dairies have been brighter, though the market has been up and down. During years of strong growth in demand, the cwt prices paid to Vermont farmers for organic milk ranged from $32.89 in 2010 to $38.58 in 2016, according to an analysis by the late Bob Parsons of UVM. Those prices drew more farmers into organic milk, and the number of organic Vermont dairies reached 203 in 2016 — but then demand seemed to have peaked. As sales of organic milk sagged from 2017 to 2019, the bulk price

Figure 2. Number of dairy farms in Vermont,
Average number of milk cows per dairy farm

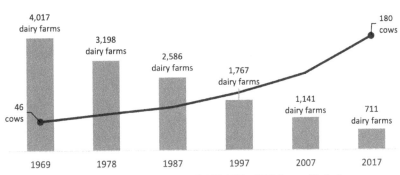

Source: USDA National Agricultural Statistics Service (NASS), 1969 to 2017 Census of Agriculture.

Figure 3. Distribution of cows in Vermont by herd size

Herd size	1978	2017
1-49 cows	29% of cows	5% of cows
50-99 cows	44% of cows	14% of cows
100-499 cows	26% of cows	34% of cows
500+ cows	1% of cows	47% of cows
	Total: 187,424 cows	Total: 128,742 cows

Source: USDA NASS, 1978 and 2017 Census of Agriculture.

Graphics from *Examining Vermont State Spending on the Dairy Industry from 2010 to 2019: A Report from the Vermont State Auditor's Office*, May 10, 2021.

went down by as much as $5 per cwt, and the number of organic farms shrank to the present 169.

But organic sales again rose sharply during the pandemic year. "Demand for organic milk has gone up across the country by 11.3 % in the past 52 weeks," *VTDigger* reported at the end of 2020. "... Right now, organic milk in Vermont is sold for $30 to $35 a hundredweight, and there's an extra premium for grass-fed milk, which ranges from $35 to $40. Conventional dairy farmers get about half that much."

"We need quite a bit more milk," the news site quoted the New England manager of Organic Valley, the country's largest organic dairy cooperative — and the one to which the Choinieres ship their milk — as saying.

The numbers seem clear enough. So why don't all, or at least most, Vermont dairy farms go organic?

The first answer is that by and large, conventional dairying here has made a huge investment in going the opposite way: toward ever-larger herds, as farmers strain to turn a profit by producing ever-greater volumes of milk. As Figure 3 on the previous page shows, nearly half of all the milk cows in Vermont are on farms with herds of 500 or larger. Organic dairying relies on pasturing its cows, which isn't practical for herds that size — so for Vermont's very large dairy farms, going organic simply doesn't look possible.

A second reality working against a major shift to organic is that demand, while growing at present, isn't nearly high enough. It's a volatile situation, though: "The market for drinking milk in this country is in a real transformative period," Dan Smith, the Northeast Dairy Compact Commission founder, told the above-mentioned State House meeting in 2018. Whether the pandemic experience may generate a long-term boost in demand for organic and grass-fed milk isn't yet clear. The market has been self-regulating: To balance supply with demand, organic milk distributors have, in recent years, kept a tight rein on the number of farms they admit.

Despite all that, one vocal advocate has been pushing for a huge new state investment in organic farming. "I propose that the state ... pay its ... small and medium conventional dairy farmers to convert to organic," James Maroney of Leicester, author of the 2009 book *The Political Economy of Milk*, wrote to Gov. Phil Scott in January 2019.

"I do not for a moment underestimate the difficulty of such a change," added Maroney, an art dealer who bought a Leicester dairy farm in 1986, converted it to organic, and ran it for nine years. But if "the state were to manage the conversion of Vermont's entire dairy industry to organic," he wrote in *VTDigger* in 2020, dairying could here could become "an industry making a taxable profit of $78 million/year."

Such a huge conversion would, he predicted, reduce phosphorus loading by farms "by half and at the same time reduce by half the taxpayers'... cost of myriad state programs, all intended on their faces to 'save agriculture and protect the lake' and all failing to do either."

Maroney has struggled to find allies for his bold proposal. "While many of us agree that moving to zero pesticides and organic fertilizers is needed," wrote Roger Allbee in an email, "where some of us differ from Jim Maroney is that it cannot be done overnight, as the markets are not there currently. And it would take a major change in the major buyers, like Cabot and Ben and Jerry's, too."

Crea Lintilhac has been advocating strategies that would at least push toward a major shift. "How do we enable small dairies to transition to organic and increase the size of the state's organic dairy sector?" she asked. "How we can increase institutional purchases of Vermont organic milk, and increase demand for Vermont organic milk? Most importantly, how do we reduce synthetic pesticide and non-therapeutic antibiotic use and growth hormones in our food supply?"

But Maroney persists in arguing that only an extreme change will solve a problem that is itself growing steadily more extreme.

"If the State of Vermont were to ... convert dairy to organic, it would make front-page news all over the world, and bring people here in droves," Maroney wrote to Gov. Scott. "... Challenging conventional dairy farming would lower production, raise farm revenue and clean up the lake all in one fell swoop. We would be on the road to clean water and a vibrant new agricultural economy."

"We're stuck in this really difficult tradeoff"

An ecological imbalance is the key reason why dairy farming contributes some 38 percent of the phosphorus runoff that gives rise to cyanobacteria blooms in Lake Champlain. As conventional farms have taken on more and more cows to squeeze profit from razor-thin margins, their herds have needed more and more feed, beyond what the farm's corn and hay production can supply even if boosted with chemical fertilizers. As a result, the quantities of phosphorus imported onto farms have in many cases grown larger than the farms' ecosystems could absorb.

"Imagine a farm 100 years ago. They're basically just grazing the cows out back, and whatever doesn't turn into milk or meat ends up as manure and gets spread it back onto the field. It's kind of like an internal loop," explained Michael Wironen, who did in-depth research on this issue for his 2018 PhD thesis at UVM's Rubenstein School of Environment and Natural Resources. "But in the last 75 or 80 years, our research shows that our farmers are no longer relying on what they can grow out back — they actually buy a lot of corn and soybeans and grain, say from the Midwest and Quebec. And they import that and feed that to their cows, or other animals."

"Phosphorus is brought onto farms as fertilizer, animal feed (e.g., corn grain, soybean meal), and mineral supplements; some leaves as a marketable commodity, and the rest accumulates in the soil or runs off to water bodies," Wironen wrote in his thesis. "... Vermont's agricultural sector has consistently had a statewide annual P [phosphorus] surplus of 1,000 tonnes or more."

Although "fertilizer use peaked at 4,152 tonnes in 1950, declining to less than 800 tonnes in 2012," Wironen wrote, "feed imports increased, constituting the largest source of P entering Vermont's agricultural system since 1982."

What farm fields can't absorb of the phosphorus surplus tends to find its way, mostly through surface runoff, into nearby streams and rivers. In the Champlain Valley, those lead into the lake.

In recent years, as many conventional farms have either gone out of business or taken on ever more cows, the industry has seen "this concentration of animals into a smaller part of the state, mostly the Lake Champlain Basin and Orleans County," Wironen said in an interview. "So we've got fewer animals, but they are really well-fed, with a much more scientifically managed diet. A cow now might produce 25,000 to 30,000 pounds of milk in a year, where in 1940 they were producing 5,000. Which is staggering."

"When it comes to water quality, we could regulate very heavily the farms, but unfortunately our farms don't have the ability to pass that cost on to consumers. We're stuck in this really difficult tradeoff: We could fix water quality, in part by destroying agriculture, but not many people in Vermont want that. But also not many people in Vermont recognize that the cute little farms that are represented in the farmers' market are only maybe a couple percent, a few percent, of the overall state. Agriculture is on a road to ruin, both environmentally and economically."

"It's a whole different outlook"

On a summer afternoon in 2021, Guy and Matt Choiniere take a break from feeding animals to perch on wooden bench swings in their backyard, and talk.

"When we finally committed to going organic, a lot of regulations came down on us," Guy says. "The cows had to go out every day, year-round — and at the same time we had an environmental push of people watching what we were doing with our landscape and water runoff. It was great timing, because while the organic people were saying, 'Let your cows out,' the environmental people were saying, 'We can help you build these covered barnyards, so they can come out and not affect the environment and the water quality.'"

The Choinieres now put their cows outside every day they can. Guy and Matt send them up the cow paths they've built, shaded with trees they've planted, to the fields they've added to meet their need for full pasturing. When the weather doesn't permit outdoor grazing, the cows are turned loose inside three large, open-ended hoop barns, where they're fed a variety of farm-grown grasses. Manure from cows and other livestock mingles in the hoop barns with bedding of dried grasses and wood chips to create a compost that is spread on the fields.

Guy and Matt shifted their cows to an all-grass diet in 2014. For that to succeed, the farm needed a lot more pasture — so they added 300 acres, plus some rented land, to the farm Matt's great-grandfather started in 1945. The farm now includes about 600 total acres, with 300 acres managed for grass feed and 150 in pasture.

"We probably produce 20 percent more than we need for feed," Guy says, "but it carries us on the poor years, and on the good years we catch back up. We harvest our own feed and we make our own bedding, which is basically the same feed but drier. We're pulling 1,200 tons [a year] out of these barns, to return to the soil; you can create a compost at the same time you're housing animals."

Matt and Guy continue to learn, attending workshops through the Northeast Organic Farming Association. To listen to the father and son explain all the interconnections within what they're doing is to glimpse how deeply they've come to understand the natural systems they are nourishing.

Before going organic, Guy says, "We were feeding our crops conventional fertilizer — but conventional fertilizer is basically NPK: nitrogen, phosphorus and potassium. That grows a crop, but it doesn't fill the crop. It doesn't fill the stems. The only thing that can do that is strong, reaching- mature root systems that have access to all kinds of different microbial byproducts, fungi, and all the systems that are going on.

"When you're feeding the plant with NPK, the roots don't have a need to go search, because they're getting what they need to grow — but the root system is not getting what it needs to fill the stem full of the energy and minerals that support the strong immune system, and replace that grain scoop.

"It took some time," he continues. "It took first of all cleansing the soil from the chemicals, so the microbes would be able to survive. We're trying to house as many microbes as we can [in the soil], to digest and feed the hummus that feeds those root systems. That is why the cows started getting healthier. But it's also taking the stress off them — getting them out of the barn, better ventilation, more comfortable in the pasture. That is a huge factor in cow health as well."

It's not just the farm's livestock that is diversified; so are the grasses grown for feed. "I have a hundred different species of plants in that pasture, because they all benefit each other," Guy says. "On a dry year, my deep-rooted plants will supply; on a wet year my shallow-rooted plants will supply. You need diversification, and you need a lot of different foods."

"Organic farming works," he sums up. "You just need to learn Mother Nature a little better, how she operates. Mother Nature is ready to do the job if you allow her."

Asked whether more farmers should be pressed to convert, Matt is reflective. "Going organic isn't something you can necessarily force somebody to do," he says. "It's a mindset change. It's a whole different way of approaching problems, approaching health, a whole different outlook on how we produce food.

"Everyone who's made this transition, even if they were skeptical, they did it on their own," he says. "Everyone I've ever talked to who's transitioned, they're like, 'Oh my gosh, my cows are so much healthier, we love it.' Some of the biggest skeptics are some of the biggest advocates. But it was because they did it on their own.

"Providing opportunities and pathways for younger or next-generation and first-generation farmers to come into the market, I think is very important to the future success of the industry, and feeding the world," Matt concludes, "for one because we're losing farmers way faster than new farmers are coming in. But also, this next generation is coming with new ideas, new values. They're passionate about environmental health. They want to produce something that's meaningful."

"This is a conversation that can't end," Guy adds. "It has to be a constant conversation, because many farmers are pushing the nutrients so hard."

SUPPORTING FARMERS' FIGHT FOR THE MEANING OF "ORGANIC"

Davey Miskell and Dave Chapman are pioneering Vermont organic farmers who have taken on a large and challenging cause: preserving the integrity of the organic label on food.

That's not so simple as it sounds. This is an era when the production and marketing of what people regard as all-natural food has taken off, well beyond its roots on small farms like Miskell's and Chapman's, to become an ever-bigger business, with ever-larger players involved.

"The big farms, coming in and not following the rules, have changed the idea of what organic has always meant," said Miskell, who raised organic tomatoes for many years in

Charlotte. "We're trying to take that back."

In 2019, the foundation began supporting the nonprofit Real Organic Project, a nationwide initiative among farmers and others that Chapman and Miskell began to organize in about 2013. The focus of the growing campaign is to protect, and to apply in farm certification, the original definition of "organic" in agriculture.

That doesn't just mean food produced without chemical additives. It also, critically, means food grown or produced through farming practices that are rooted in naturally nurtured soil.

That's a vital element for traditional organic producers, "farmers who have spent years tending their soil so that it produces the nutrients plants need," said a *New York Times* report in 2016. "They argue that organic production is first and foremost about caring for the soil, which produces environmental benefits that go beyond growing plants."

But today a significant number of food producers, including growers outside the U.S. and some powerful American companies, are putting the U.S. Department of Agriculture's organic label on produce that was grown hydroponically, in nutrient- enriched water. Consumers generally can't tell whether the tomatoes, lettuce or berries they're buying as organic have ever seen soil at all.

At the same time, a growing volume of produce and grain from other countries is being called organic without having met the U.S. standards for the label. And a significant portion of the eggs sold as organic around the country are produced on factory farms with

concentrated animal feeding operations, far beyond an ecologically balanced approach to raising food and nurturing soil.

The USDA's National Organic Standards Board recommended in 2010 that hydroponic production be excluded from the organic label — and in 2017, large numbers of farmers who keep to the core standards called for that exclusion in 15 demonstrations organized by the Real Organic Project around the country.

Some two dozen other countries don't allow organic certification of hydroponically grown produce, the *Times* reported, but the USDA continues to permit it. The Real Organic Project (ROP) has responded by developing an add-on "Real Organic" label that it hopes can be placed on products from farms it has certified. In 2020 the label won approval from the U.S. Patent and Trademark Office.

Meanwhile, the project organizes symposia that

From left: Tom Beddard, owner of Lady Moon Farms, a large organic produce farm in Pennsylvania; organic farmer Dave Chapman of Thetford, Vt., executive director of the Real Organic Project; Eliot Coleman, organic farming pioneer and author of *The New Organic Grower* and other books; and Davey Miskell, who for many years grew organic tomatoes in Charlotte, Vt., and helped organize the Real Organic Project. Above is the project's new label for products from certified organic farmers.

bring together farmers, experts and others. It publishes a widely read weekly e-newsletter, and it has created its own farm certification program, developed by farmers, that by spring 2020 had approved about 600 organic farms across the nation.

"It's happening. It's growing quickly," said Dave Chapman, who raises organic tomatoes in Thetford while serving, as does Davey Miskell, on the ROP's Executive Board. "Our goal has been to get the word out, get people to understand what is happening, and really get the farmers involved."

"Integrity in the food supply chain"

The stakes involved here are very large. A growing movement that began in the early 1970s, as a hodgepodge of small organic producers around the country like Miskell and Chapman, has today become a multi-billion dollar industry. In 2016, there were more than 14,000 certified organic farms in the U.S. — 56 percent more than in 2011, according to the USDA.

"Organic is the fastest growing sector of the U.S. food industry," with sales that hit $47.9 billion in 2018, reported the Organic Trade Association. From 2009 to 2018, U.S. sales of organic food grew by an average of 8.95 percent per year. By comparison, total food sales rose in 2018 by just 2.3 percent.

"Organic fruits and vegetables make up close to 15 percent of all the produce sold in the U.S., and have nearly doubled their market share in the last 10 years," the association said.

The Organic Trade Association, a nationwide group, supports the USDA's organic label. It also warns, on its website, that "millennials are pushing for transparency and integrity in the food supply chain, and they are savvy to misleading marketing."

Can the Real Organic Project's push for a stricter add-on label make an impact on protecting that integrity? Will it be worth all the work and trouble involved?

"That is the question. My answer is, I don't know," said Will Lintilhac, the foundation trustee who is the second of Crea and Phil's three adult children.

Supporting projects in the farm sector is mostly a new direction for the foundation, but Will has focused his own career on agriculture. He has held full-time jobs on four farms, in Vermont and western Massachusetts, each of which had some portion of its operation in organic practice.

"I have enormous respect for them putting in the work," Will said of the Real Organic Project, "to try to understand how we can, in a lot of cases, even just get large organic producers to comply with the law and the standards. They are not a bureaucratic body that is making rules without the input of farmers; they're hearing from farmers what they would like to see changed. And farmers are going to be the determining factor in whether this is a feasible operation."

At the same time, Will said, "even some of their supporters, ourselves included, have questions. How many more rules do we really want to put on farmers?"

If the Real Organic label is approved, what sort of pushback or challenge will it generate? "The literal interpretation is, we are the real organic project and you are the fake organic project," Will observed. "It's clearly contentious. But at base, are they wrong, in using that name and calling out organic in that way? No. They're not."

It's not easy for farmers to participate in the Real Organic Project. They tend to work very long hours, "and they're a very tough group to organize," noted Dave Chapman. "But it's very important that they participate in this, both for their own survival and for all our survival."

THE INSECTICIDES THAT ARE KILLING BEES

"**H**oneybees and other pollinating insects are crucial helpers in putting food on American tables," the *New York Times* noted in 2019 — yet "beekeepers in the United States lost an estimated 40 percent of their managed honeybee colonies from April 2018 to April 2019."

What's often called colony collapse disorder had become a major worry as early as the mid-2000s, Vermont beekeeper and author Ross Conrad has written. In 2014, a report by the International Union for the Conservation of Nature made it clear what many beekeepers, in Vermont and around the world, were suspecting: A prime culprit in the unfolding calamity was neonicotinoids, a group of insecticides, chemically similar to nicotine, that have become the most widely used bug killers in the world.

First synthesized in 1970, "these chemicals are wreaking much more environmental havoc than previously thought," the *Times* declared in a 2014 editorial, "Risking Another Silent Spring."

"Industry stakeholders and some scientists reject the connection between neonicotinoids and bee deaths, arguing that these chemicals are safe," the editorial noted. "Yet most scientists believe that while multiple factors account for the die-offs, including loss of habitat and viruses, the connection to neonicotinoids is indisputable."

In Vermont, a group of nonprofits has formed a Pesticide Coalition, with Lintilhac Foundation support, that is working to achieve better control and accountability over the use of pesticides — and to ban "neonics," as the European Union did in 2018. Some 1,051 pounds of neonics were applied as an insecticide in Vermont in 2018, primarily on golf courses, *VTDigger* has reported.

Students at Essex Junction Technical Center in Essex, Vt. manage beehives. *Photo by Hugh Gibson.*

But that's only the simplest part of the problem. Neonics are also commonly used to coat agricultural seeds. And those "treated articles" are not subject to any pesticide regulation.

"They are commonly coated on seeds rather than sprayed on leaves, so they guard against soil pests; later, the seedlings take up the pesticide, protecting the plant from insects," said a 2017 article in *Science* magazine. "But neonicotinoids also find their way into pollen and nectar, posing a threat to pollinators."

"That's huge," said Ross Conrad, co-author of *The Land of Milk and Honey: A History of Beekeeping in Vermont* (Green Place Books, 2020). "That's when we started seeing all the problems with bees, when those seeds started to be used by a majority of farmers.

"These neonicotinoids work really well; they kill bugs like nobody's business," he said. "Really toxic. Supposedly people can handle it better, because we can metabolize nicotine better than insects. But of course, there's so many problems with the whole regulation system that we don't really know what it does to people."

The ongoing collapse of bee colonies may indeed be just the first indicator of neonics' ecological impacts. After an exhaustive survey of 529 bird species, *Science* reported in 2019 that the total number of birds in the U.S. has fallen by 2.9 billion, or 29 percent, over the past half century.

"Neonics kill birds both directly and indirectly," Conrad declared in a six-part series on the pesticides for *Bee Culture* magazine in 2017-18. "A single neonicotinoid-coated seed can kill a small songbird the size of a house sparrow. ... As early as 1998 French scientists were finding dead partridges with neonic-coated grain in the birds' crops."

More widely, he added, "the crash in farmland bird populations that has occurred wherever neonics have been used intensively, appears to be at least partially related to their insect food disappearing."

Banding together for action

Vermont has so far taken two first steps toward controlling or banning neonics, and advocates are hopeful for more far-reaching action soon. In 2016, the Legislature created a Pollinator Protection Committee, which includes two beekeepers. And the nonprofit Pesticide Coalition celebrated a victory in spring 2019 when the Legislature passed Act 35, restricting the sale of neonics to licensed pesticide applicators only.

"Act 35 passed with significant support, and there are strong legislative champions that want to build on this success to address the environmental and public health threats that neonicotinoids pose more broadly," said Jen Duggan, vice president of the Conservation Law Foundation and director of its Vermont office. "We now have more data that demonstrates the widespread harm caused by this class of pesticides, and public awareness and support for further regulation of neonics is growing."

CLF helped pull together the Pesticide Coalition, which also includes VPIRG, the Lake Champlain Committee, Rural Vermont, the Toxics Action Center, NOFA-VT (the organic farmers' nonprofit), and the Sierra Club.

Restricting the sale of neonics to pesticide professionals "did get some things off the shelf, but it was a little bit more of a symbolic victory. Treated seeds are the next step," said Kanika Gandhi, who was VPIRG's environmental advocate in 2019 before becoming agrichemical program director at the state Agency of Agriculture, Food and Markets.

"There's a push both from the agency side and the coalition of nonprofits to really make that happen," she said. "Crea and the foundation have been very helpful in gearing up the support and making sure we can keep doing what we're doing."

The coalition is also pushing for action that can make the state's Pesticide Advisory Council (VPAC) more effective in overseeing pesticides and reducing their use.

"VPAC was created about 20 years ago, and it has a very specific charge, in terms of reviewing pesticide use with the overall state goal of a decrease in use," said Jared Carpenter, water quality advocate for the Lake Champlain Committee. "But over the years, they have not done that."

"The Advisory Council has become just kind of a rubber-stamping body," agreed Kanika Gandhi.

The council is supposed to produce "an annual report to document progress," Judy Bellairs of Vermont's Sierra Club chapter has written. "There is no evidence that these annual reports were ever prepared or filed as required. Integrated Pest Management — the idea that we should minimize the use of pesticides and use them only as a last resort — has fallen by the wayside."

"These poisons are systemic"

Banning neonics outright in Vermont would be a huge step forward, "and for that reason, it's also going to be a heavy lift," said Carpenter. A bill that would have imposed the ban, starting in mid-2023, was among the measures that failed to see action in the pandemic-disrupted State House session of 2020. The Pesticide Coalition aims to push for strong action in the near future.

"I do think that next year, or in future years, it definitely will happen," Kanika Gandhi said.

Meanwhile, a working group created by the Legislature in 2019 is looking at whether the state could compensate farmers for "ecosystem services" — farm practices that improve soil health, curb runoff into rivers and streams, and potentially reduce the use of herbicides, fungicides and pesticides, including insecticides.

"We lobbied really hard and succeeded in getting a seat on that group for both NOFA and the Healthy Soils Coalition. So we got some strong voices on that group," said Andrea Stander, a policy consultant for Rural Vermont.

Beekeeper and author Bill Mares of Burlington, Vt., cuts a wild swarm.

"Farmers are all set up to work with chemical agriculture, and to get them to change is really hard," noted beekeeper Conrad, who serves on the state's Pollinator Protection Committee. "They don't have the equipment, they don't have the knowledge, and they may not even get a loan from the bank unless they do it in the chemical way."

But year after year, neonicotinoids are spreading from treated seeds into the ecosystem, Conrad noted in his *Bee Culture* series.

"These poisons are systemic," he

wrote. "Applied as a seed coating, they are absorbed in the water and are taken up by the roots. ... Neonics render every part of the plant toxic, from the roots to the flowers including the nectar, so that the plant in essence becomes a pesticide itself. ... Neonics are also water-soluble, so they leach into ditches and ponds, streams and rivers."

In bees, neonics "destroy the immune system at levels that are undetectable, leaving other culprits to take the blame for colony deaths," he wrote. Among those are the varoa mite, which the pesticide industry often cites as the key cause of colony collapse.

Reporting on the results of a global sampling of neonicotinoids in honey, a 2017 article in *Science* magazine said: "We found at least one of five tested compounds ... in 75 percent of all samples."

Two years later, *Science* reported that a 2017 study had "found the chemicals can poison bees, causing symptoms like paralysis, vomiting, or death when they eat contaminated nectar or pollen, or even crawl over sprayed surfaces. Yet neonicotinoids still account for more than 20% of the world's insecticide market."

∿

TILE DRAINS: A PHOSPHORUS-LOADING PROBLEM

Nobody knows how much Vermont farmland, especially in the Champlain Valley, is underlain with miles of buried plastic piping for better drainage — but it's a lot. Tile drains, as they are called, appear to be a major channel for the nutrient loading that causes cyanobacteria blooms in Lake Champlain.

"The reason they're called tile drains is because they used to be terra-cotta cylinders that got put into the ground. It's now giant spools of corrugated plastic pipe that are rolled out in trenches," explained Don Meals, a watershed environmental scientist who studied phosphorus loading from tile drainage in a St. Albans Bay watershed.

"They're quite common and they're growing in use," mainly under farmland, he said. "They're perforated pipes. They capture water in saturated soil and convey it away, so they have the effect of essentially lowering the water table to whatever depth they're installed at."

"As early as the 1830s, clay tiles were installed to drain surface and shallow subsurface water from particularly wet areas of farm fields," said a 2018 report on the issue by the state agencies of Agriculture and Natural Resources. Before federal wetland protections were put in place in the 1970s, the report said, "as many as half of the wetlands in the United States and 35% of the wetlands in Vermont were converted into agricultural fields or developed land uses."

A 2012 agricultural census estimated that just under 5 percent of Vermont's total cropland is tile-drained — but that may far underestimate the reality. The Agency of Agriculture, Food & Markets "has confirmed, based on aerial imagery, that some subwatersheds in the Lake Champlain Basin may have as much as 70% of the cropland in tile," the state report said.

The benefits to farmers of tile drainage "can be substantial," noted the state report. Land that was untillable can now support crops, fields can be much more productive, and tile drains can even help farmers cope with the intense rainfalls that have become more common as the climate changes. But scientists have recently started working to measure just how much phosphorus, the main nutrient that nourishes toxic cyanobacteria blooms, is being carried by tile systems into public waters, largely from fields treated with manure and chemical fertilizers.

The findings are worrisome.

"It's literally a straight pipeline to surface water," said Don Meals. "About 10, 15 years ago, researchers started wondering about phosphorus in tile drainage — and pretty much everywhere they looked, they started to see a lot more phosphorus than they expected. Nobody really thought about this in Vermont till probably five or six years ago, when people started to wonder if this was a problem."

The study that Meals conducted with Dave Braun, a water resources scientist with Stone Environmental of Montpelier, was the first effort to measure how much phosphorus tile drains are carrying into Vermont waters. Its results were published in 2019 by the Lake Champlain Basin Program.

"We monitored 12 tile drains on silage corn and hay land on commercial dairy farms in the Jewett Brook watershed, St. Albans, Vermont for a full year," said the study's final report. "... During the monitored year, approximately 26% of the total P [phosphorus] load exported by Jewett Brook was contributed by tile drains.

"These results demonstrate that tile drains have the potential to contribute substantial quantities of P to surface waters in the Lake Champlain Basin."

"We know enough to act now"

A group of environmental nonprofits has been pushing the state to more aggressively address this challenging issue. They're pointing out that Act 64, the multipart 2015 legislation aimed at improving water quality in Lake Champlain and elsewhere around Vermont, requires that the state's Required Agricultural Practices (RAPs), developed and overseen by the Agency of Agriculture, "include requirements for reducing nutrient contribution to waters of the State from subsurface tile drainage."

Solutions are clearly elusive. The pipes are underground, after all, and so far they're not even mapped. But even so, the environmental groups argue that Vermont's RAPs can, and should, be much stronger on tile drains.

"Managing subsurface tile drainage is critical to clean water," said a 2018 letter from the Conservation Law Foundation to the Legislature's Committee on Administrative Rules, urging the panel to object to a proposed amendment to the RAPs on tile drains. That measure, since adopted, bans new installations of surface inlets, which carry water from areas in fields where it collects directly into subsurface drainage. CLF argued that surface inlets already in the ground should also be banned.

In pushing with Lintilhac Foundation support for more action on tile drains, CLF has been joined by the Lake Champlain Committee, Vermont Natural Resources Council, Vermont Conservation Voters, Lewis Creek Association, and the Vermont chapters of Trout Unlimited and the Sierra Club. "We know enough to act now to develop and implement improved policies," the nonprofits declared in a 2016 joint letter to the secretaries of agriculture and natural resources.

"Modern technologies allow for the rapid installation of tile drains across vast areas of the state," the letter said. "Any person who has spent time in rural Vermont, particularly in Franklin County, can attest to the thousands of acres of new farmland drained by plastic tile drain tubing that has been laid across our state's farm fields in just the past decade."

State agencies have not, to date, proposed a ban on new subsurface tile drains. The new RAP amendments, adopted in 2018, "include the required installation of rodent guards" on new tile-drainage outlets, the prohibition on new surface inlets, "and other provisions" focused on reducing the loss of nutrients from farm fields through tile drainage, according to a state announcement.

It's not nearly enough, said Elena Mihaly, senior attorney for CLF in Vermont.

"We were asking for better monitoring, and mapping, and even prohibiting the tile drains in certain situations," she said. "At this point, we're focused on exploring what legal hooks we have. ... How can we get these rules reopened, or is there another lever we can pull to open the door, if you will, to better regulation of these practices?"

Making a real impact on this problem clearly will not be easy. But there are steps the state can take, said the 2016 letter by the environmental groups.

"Across the United States, agricultural and environmental agencies have been engaged in a robust conversation about ways to address the pollution from tile drains," they said. "A critical and necessary step ... is to map the locations of all existing tile drainage systems in Vermont.

"There will likely also be some new and innovative practices that the Agencies may want to propose for future study," the nonprofits predicted — "but there is no reason they cannot implement practices that are known to effectively reduce pollution from tile drains now."

AT SHELBURNE FARMS, TESTING WAYS TO CURB PHOSPHORUS RUNOFF

To the nearly 150,000 people who visit Shelburne Farms each year, the grand estate with its Gilded Age barns can seem like a passage back in time. Walkers and vehicles move on slow-travel paths through 3,800 acres of a finely designed pastoral landscape, gradually descending to a Vanderbilt mansion that's now a renovated inn on the Lake Champlain shore.

The farm is also an educational nonprofit, and a forward-looking model of sustainable agriculture. While guests stay and dine at the inn, about 150,000 visitors each year can also visit the modern barns, just above the lake shore, where milk from some 170 Brown Swiss cows is turned each year into 175,000 pounds of cheddar cheese. As a working dairy with the resources to experiment, Shelburne Farms has lately become a demonstration site for practical measures that can sharply cut a farm's phosphorus runoff.

"If we're not being good stewards of our manure resource, we're wasting money," farm manager Sam Dixon told a group of visitors in late 2019. "Those are nutrients we want to capture."

His listeners were scientists, teachers, lake managers and other members of the North American Lake Management Society, in nearby Burlington for an annual conference. They had arrived here in a UVM van, passing a sign at the gate that says "Education for a Sustainable Future." That's what Shelburne Farms is aiming to do as it hosts school and professional groups, tourists and many others.

The foundation has provided support for Shelburne Farms at key points since descendants of Dr. William Seward Webb and Eliza Vanderbilt Webb converted their 19th century model agricultural estate into a learning-oriented nonprofit in the 1970s. Lintilhac grants in the mid-1980s helped rebuild the roof of the Vanderbilt mansion, whose revenues as a hostelry and restaurant help support the nonprofit. Later funding went toward Shelburne Farms' land conservation, its educational programs, and the construction of its popular walking path.

From 2008 to 2009, as concern was building about phosphorus loading in Lake Champlain, water sampling and research carried out by a UVM team and backed by a foundation grant showed that "the barnyard area at Shelburne Farms is a significant source of phosphorus runoff," according to the 2009 study report.

A second grant supported efforts from 2008 to 2013 to reduce those levels. Drawing on the expertise of professionals, that work employed methods "known to be ecological, practical and cost-effective," said a 2011 report, but at a "scale and funding level appropriate for a private, commercial farm."

Standing beside the dairy barns on a frigid November morning, farm manager Dixon showed the visiting lake professionals what the farm had done. Along with fencing livestock well away from drainage ditches and the lakeshore, plus improving the compost operation and switching from a chopped-silage pile to wrapped round bales with virtually no leakage, the farm installed a natural water-treatment system alongside its dairy barns.

The system uses no pumps or electricity. Instead, a small inlet pond captures water draining from the barnyards. The water flows into a constructed wetland, then into a second small pond, and from there into a flat-bottomed ditch that meanders down toward the lake on a zigzag path.

The farm tests that water each week — and the system is working, said Dana Bishop, woodlands manager. Average phosphorus concentrations at the farm's main drainage point into Lake Champlain were reduced from 0.33 parts per million, during 2004-2008, to 0.03 ppm during 2013-2018.

"We're trying to take these big ideas of sustainability and break them down into something that's concrete," said Megan Camp, director of programs. "Lake Champlain is always part of the story here."

⅄

SPOTLIGHTING SALT STORAGE BY A PROTECTED WETLAND

Townspeople in Shelburne were none too happy when, in 2016, Vermont Railways pushed ahead with plans to build a storage and distribution yard, with two large sheds for road salt, on 32 acres just north of the village center between Rte. 7 and the LaPlatte River Marsh.

"Vermont Rail plans to bypass local and state Act 250 review under a federal exemption designed to preserve interstate commerce — a move that has set off alarms in Shelburne," *Seven Days* reported. "... While the parcel is zoned for industrial use, it's an area that lures walkers, birders and kayakers. It's surrounded by Vermont Nature Conservancy land and lazy, curving stretches of the LaPlatte River, which feeds into Lake Champlain's Shelburne Bay."

The town sued to stop the project, saying it should be subject to local zoning — but Vermont Railway went ahead with construction and, in four successive rulings, federal district and appeals courts dismissed the challenges. Acrimony over the project and the town's effort to block it bitterly divided local government, which finally ended its fight in 2019.

So the railroad yard is in place, with sheds holding up to 80,000 tons of road salt that are delivered by train, then loaded onto trucks for distribution around Vermont. Next door is the 270-acre marsh, owned and protected by The Nature Conservancy and home to some 60 species of birds, 20 species of mammals and 50 species of reptiles. Those include "rare and protected species of plants, fish and amphibians that may be particularly sensitive to increased salinity," noted Vermont water quality scientist Rebecca Tharp and Dana Allen, a water quality consultant, in a 2020 research report in the journal *Environmental Systems Research*.

In 2017, the Vermont Natural Resources Council successfully petitioned the state Agency of Natural Resources to declare the LaPlatte Marsh a Class I wetland, giving it the state's highest level of wetlands protection, one of just six Class I wetlands in Vermont.

"This ecosystem is essential to helping filter and clean the water that empties into our lake," The Nature Conservancy said, "and is part of our nature-based solutions for water quality progress in Lake Champlain."

So it could be a problem if water runoff from the railroad yard, containing sodium chloride from road salt, was damaging the marsh's sensitive ecology. With funding by the foundation, Tharp and Allen spent two years measuring the salinity of that runoff. Under the terms of a state permit, Vermont Railways had been testing water in the river almost a kilometer downstream from the yard — but the researchers took water, soil and vegetation samples from four locations much closer to the salt sheds.

At two locations, they found that average sodium chloride content in the water measured "above U.S. EPA standards for acute toxicity." Those findings, they added, were "in conflict with findings from annual permittee assessments" by the railroad. Soil cores

Paddling the LaPlatte River, whose 270-acre marsh, home to rare and protected species of plants, fish and amphibians, is adjacent to a pair of large distribution sheds for road salt.

taken close to the yard, they added, also "indicate elevated chloride in plant tissues." The findings, they concluded, pointed to the need for "a move away from reliance on self-reporting by permittees."

"There are impacts on the wetlands"

"What the data show is that if you measure closer to the point of discharge, you get a vastly different reading than if you measure out in the river," said David Grayck, a Montpelier attorney specializing in environmental land-use law whose work on the LaPlatte situation has been supported by the foundation.

"The other key issue," he said, "is that representations were made to the federal court that a stormwater collection system would assure water quality; but the point of the data is, Whatever you said about your system and its ability to cleanse the water doesn't seem to be accurate."

Two additional studies, also supported by the foundation, were looking at whether the salinization was in fact harming plant and animal species in the marsh — and if so, how a solution might be engineered. VNRC, meanwhile, was considering its options for taking action to protect the marsh.

"The data seems to show there are impacts on the wetland, and ANR [the state Agency of Natural Resources] needs to use its authority to stop the discharges that are having these impacts," said Jon Groveman, VNRC's policy and water programs director. "What the legal mechanism for that is, we're trying to figure out."

Across the northern U.S. states, some 22.7 metric tons of road salt are stored and then scattered on roads and other paved areas each year. Road salt has had a hugely positive impact on reducing winter road accidents — but in the Midwest and Northeast, "many streams are at risk of becoming toxic to aquatic life within the next 100 years as a result of deicing salt inputs," Tharp and Allen wrote. And although the impacts on streams from salted road runoff have been closely studied, they added, those from salt storage sheds have not.

"In the snowy and cold northern regions of the United States, there are hundreds of deicing salt storage facilities," they wrote. "Without consistent and scientifically defensible standards for regulating these facilities, their water quality impacts will continue without oversight or appropriate control."

"It takes a commitment to environmental quality, and it takes funding to ensure that developments actually adhere to the predictions which developers make," said attorney Grayck. In this case, "the real significance of the Lintilhac Foundation involvement is, we're talking to a lot of experts. When you add that up, it's a lot of services."

BANNING PRODUCTS WITH TOXIC "FOREVER CHEMICALS"

Backed by diverse nonprofits, Vermont's action leads the nation

More than a decade after the Vermont Legislature first began to debate the dangers of a widely used family of toxic chemicals called PFAS, lawmakers in 2021 unanimously approved the nation's most inclusive ban on the sale of consumer products containing the toxins. "This step removes hidden 'forever chemicals' from human exposure," said Chittenden County Sen. Virginia Lyons, chair of the Senate Committee on Health & Welfare.

Commonly found in plastic food packaging and a wide range of other products, PFAS (per- and polyfluoroalkyl substances) have been shown to migrate into and accumulate within the human body. They "are a family of thousands of chemicals" that "do not break down naturally in the environment," wrote Seamus McAvoy in *VTDigger*. "PFAS are linked to several health effects, including cancer, behavioral and developmental problems in infants and children, fertility and pregnancy problems, and immune system problems."

The new law restricts the chemicals "in four main areas: fire-extinguishing foam, food packaging, rugs and carpets, and ski wax," Ellie French reported in *Digger*. "It also includes restrictions of phthalates and bisphenols, which are commonly used in plastic products." Other states have also banned PFAS products; Vermont's measure was the first to include ski wax along with those proscribed in other states.

"It is rare to find an emerging environmental health issue that is so universal, that contaminates both the water we drink, the air we breathe, and the food we eat," Rep. Dane Whitman of Bennington, a member of the House Committee on Human Services, told *Digger* after the committee took several weeks of testimony on the bill.

"Whitman said PFAS can be found in more than 100 public water supplies in Vermont ... but also in the blood of almost every person in the United States," French reported. "A large PFAS problem in the Bennington area required an expensive cleanup that will continue for years."

Along with the environmental advocates VPIRG, the Conservation Law Foundation, Vermont Conservation Voters and the Vermont Natural Resources Group, the ban was supported by the nonprofits Planned Parenthood, the National Education Association, Voices for Vermont's Children, the Professional Fire Fighters of Vermont, and Vermont Businesses for Social Responsibility. The measure passed 30-0 in the Senate, and 145-0 in the House.

"Your sandwich doesn't need to be coated in chemicals," said Marcie Gallagher of VPIRG after the Legislature took action. "Your carpeting shouldn't be a health threat to toddlers. Your skis should not leave a toxic trail in the snow ... Vermont just became the first state to ban PFAS in all these products."

"Passage of this bill ensures our members will not be exposed to cancer-causing chemicals in the equipment and extinguishing agents we use to fight fires," said Bradley Reed, president of the Professional Firefighters of Vermont, quoted in a news release from Vermont Conservation Voters

"My first recollection of talking about these chemicals on the [State House] floor was about a dozen years ago, and that debate was very contentious, shall we say," Rep. George Till of Jericho told *Digger*. "... Support for these desperately needed measures has grown and become virtually universal in this body."

Home to an unusual confluence of hiking trails, the Rolston Rest conserved property is just five miles from **Rutland City.** *Photo by Kurt Budinger.*

7

Conservation for a Critical Time

Protecting land to strengthen communities
as they adapt to climate change

Millstone Hill in Barre Town is a most unusual place.

Forested all over when Vermont was first settled, the hill became the birthplace of Barre's quarrying industry during the 1800s. By the 1920s, some 74 independent quarries were gouging holes in the hillside to extract the stone that made nearby Barre City a boomtown. But then the granite industry shifted to larger quarries nearby, and by the mid-20th century Millstone Hill had become a wasteland, cratered and treeless, piled with scrap granite and abandoned.

No longer.

"Today this landscape is dense with stands of sugar maple shading 30-foot-high granite-block walls; birch trees grow out of sloping rubble fields," wrote environmental journalist Joshua Brown in *Land & People*, the magazine of the nonprofit Trust for Public Land, in 2012. "... The hill is coming to life with birds, moose, bears and other wildlife, and also with cross-country skiers, snowmobilers from the local Thunder Chickens snowmobile club, kids with fishing poles — and especially mountain bikers bewitched by the vertiginous cliff-edge views and gnarly singletrack."

The story of how Barre Town, the Millstone Trails Association and the Trust for Public Land brought about the transformation of Millstone Hill, with support from town voters and an array of sources including the Lintilhac Foundation, is a bright example of how some Vermont communities are combining land protection with visionary planning. The goal, often, is to nurture a community's natural resources while also becoming a magnet for those Vermont-friendly forms of outdoor recreation that can keep thriving, and benefiting their communities, as the climate changes: winter sports that don't need the facilities of a ski resort, plus mountain biking, hiking and more in the warmer months.

In Barre Town, Pierre Couture was one who saw new possibilities for Millstone Hill. The owner of a local general store and inn, he grew up on a nearby farm, exploring the quarry ruins, fishing and swimming and skating in there. He left Vermont as a young man, but came back at 50. In about 2003, he started cutting the first recreation trails on the hill.

By the 1920s, Millstone Hill in Barre Town was home to some 74 independent granite quarries. *Photo by O.J. Dodge, courtesy of Vermont Granite Museum.*

"From the beginning, I thought: If I can just get people back there," he recalled. "They'd drive around the main roads and see the big industrial quarries — but the older ones, that were a lot more scenic, nobody really realized they were all buried back there. My feeling was, whether it's on skis or bikes or whatever, let me just get people back there and they'll get it."

Couture bought some property on Millstone Hill, but most of the trails he cut were on land owned by Rock of Ages, Barre Town's one large remaining quarry firm. The company was generous about allowing the trail use, and before long Pierre had recruited other local and area residents to form the nonprofit Millstone Trails Association.

In 2009, the *Boston Globe* named Millstone Hill one of New England's top ten mountain-biking destinations. Cyclists were coming here from all over to ride it. But then Couture got some two-sided news.

The bad news was that Rock of Ages was putting its Millstone land up for sale. The good news was that he'd have the first option to buy it.

"All sorts of people are coming here"

This was a daunting challenge, but Couture and the Millstone Trails Association decided to try. They worked with local officials and the Trust for Public Land (TPL) to put together a package of federal, state, private and foundation funding, including a Lintilhac Foundation grant, with a singular goal: buy and conserve this and several adjoining properties as the new town forest.

"Not only was this a preservation project, it was an economic development project, a cultural heritage project," Couture said. "It had components that no other town forest project ever offered."

The town's financial contribution was the final piece needed to make the project work. When completed, the project would make much of Millstone Hill into the Barre Town Forest, protected by a permanent conservation easement.

TPL, the Trails Association and local officials worked energetically to persuade residents to vote yes. Townspeople who worried about losing access were assured that longtime uses of the old quarry hill — hunting, fishing, snowmobiling, pretty much everything save (in nearly all cases) for motorized all-terrain vehicles — would still be permitted, without charge. In 2010, town voters approved a proposal that the town borrow $100,000 for its contribution to the $1.378 million project. The vote was 63 percent in favor.

Even though Millstone Hill's trails have since hosted elite mountain-bike racing events, the resource is not just for the extremely committed. On a warm sunny Saturday, while cyclists were off pushing themselves through the landscape's more challenging trails like Crossfire, Indian Trail, Boulder Dash or Sidewinder, other local folks and visitors were also there on the wider and easier trails. They were hiking, walking dogs, pushing off-road strollers, or enjoying the town forest's popular disc-golf circuit.

A 2012 UVM study estimated that "approximately $480,000 is currently spent by mountain bike and winter use visitors to the Millstone Trail Network."

Mountain biking on Millstone Hill today. *Photo by Jerry Monkman.*

"You'll see the parking lot packed full of people, doing all kinds of things," noted Marcy Christian, a Barre City resident who has served on the Trails Association board. "To me, that's the most exciting, coolest part of this whole project. It went from this very narrow-focused place," one mainly for mountain bikers, "to one where all sorts of people are coming here. And sharing this. I can't tell you how many people in Barre have told me, 'I didn't even know this was here!' Because it's sort of tucked away.

"One of the things that makes Millstone so special to me," she added, "is that my husband died suddenly, in 2007, and this was the place where I came, after that time, that sort of got me through. I would come here two or three times a day. So I have a deep, deep connection to this place."

"We try to make the most impact"

At about the same time the Millstone project was completed, the Lintilhac Foundation was beginning a generational shift that would expand its focus into conserving land for sustainable, human-powered recreation. Phil and Crea's three now-grown children, Louise, William and Paul, joined the board in 2012.

"We grew up as avid skiers, and that kind of transformed into general love for the outdoors," said Louise, a former managing editor of *Backcountry* magazine. "We look at the landscape as one of our most valuable resources.

"I personally feel that in order for people to really value its future, one of the most important things is getting them out in it, experiencing it — mountain biking, backcountry skiing, hiking, horseback riding. I believe all these different recreations can coexist, it just takes some forethought and strategic planning. The Trust for Public Land does an incredible job of integrating different interest groups into one landscape.

"Millstone is one great example," she said. "The Barre Town Forest is in an area that is economically depressed, with an incredible natural resource. The Trust for Public Land was able to help them create a recreational destination that not only gives townspeople a place to go hike, Frisbee golf, cross-country ski and mountain bike; there's also an incredible historical value. It also brings in a lot of people from out of state, and that's a big economic driver.

"One of the things I talk a lot about, with Mom and Dad and my brothers and others, is that if you are experiencing a healthy activity in a certain environment, you're going to care more about that environment. The health *is* the environment. So it's this positive feedback loop of creating healthy communities, that I see happening a lot with these areas where backcountry recreation is growing.

"We need to have a far better understanding of what the stakeholders in each location want from the conserved land — so you make sure you're drafting a management plan that reflects all the stakeholders from the get-go.

"We talk about being environmentally resilient in Vermont," Louise reflected. "And when you think about ways we can shape future economies in the state to be resilient in the face of global climate change, mountain biking is a perfect example of that. I love skiing, but if it stops snowing, a major part of the Vermont economy is going to disappear.

"Unlike traditional skiing, mountain biking is not resort-based. We don't need lifts, it's all human-powered — so it's a sport that can occur even if temperatures start to get warmer. We have an incredible resource for it in this state. The trails that are already here are incredible!

"So for us, it's more of an access thing — that's why we don't just preserve land. We try to make the most impact with any property that we can. How many stakeholders can we get involved, in terms of access, and in how many different ways? Is it recreation, or is it science? We will fund projects through organizations like Audubon, getting different stakeholders involved through the landscape. Sometimes it's mountain biking, sometimes it's hiking — and sometimes it's just data collection, to help people understand how to preserve the landscape."

From mountain huts to rail-bed trails

With this expanded focus, in recent years the foundation has worked with TPL to leverage some $5.2 million, outside of Lintilhac funding, in support of conservation projects with high-value trail networks. Along with Millstone Hill, those include Catamount Community Forest in Williston, Rolston Rest in central Vermont, and Ascutney Mountain, a former ski resort with 30 miles of trails that's now part of the West Windsor Town Forest, on the largest block of conserved land in the Connecticut River Valley. [See the articles on pages 174-178.]

Foundation grants have helped fund development of the Lamoille Valley Rail Trail, which when complete will cross all of northern Vermont on the old Lamoille Valley Railroad

The Vermont Huts Association is developing a network of heated overnight shelters along the state's growing network of multiuse trails.

trackbed. The foundation has also supported:

- The Vermont Backcountry Alliance, a growing collection of local groups that are creating and managing backcountry skiing and trail riding opportunities on publicly owned lands;

- The Vermont Huts Association, which is developing a network of heated overnight shelters along the state's growing network of multiuse trails; and

- The Vermont Mountain Bike Association, which is building a regional alliance of riders and promoting the economic benefits of trail riding.

The foundation also supports the conservation work of local land trusts. Among those is the Stowe Land Trust, which has received foundation funding for four projects that conserved a total of 861 acres.

"Their early and significant support for the Hunger Mountain Headwaters project, which will protect 2,000 acres of Vermont's wild and remote Worcester Range for people and wildlife alike, was especially helpful in getting this landscape-scale conservation effort started," said Kristen Sharpless, executive director of the Stowe Land Trust.

"I would talk to everybody in town"

Supporting land conservation with a focus on multiuse, human-powered recreation actually goes back to one of the very first projects the foundation supported. That was in Stowe, where the 5.3-mile Stowe Recreation Path, completed in 1989, was among the nation's first — possibly its very first — community-based, easement-protected recreation greenways.

Claire Lintilhac lived in Stowe from 1958 until her passing in 1984. For most of those years her home was on the upper part of the Mountain Road, which climbs from the town center up past restaurants, shops, lodging places and the Stowe Mountain Resort on the way to the Smugglers Notch mountain gap. In the 1960s and '70s, Claire saw traffic along the Mountain Road grow steadily busier, with virtually no sidewalks for pedestrians, bicyclists and the young mothers she saw walking with their children.

"My mom would be driving on the Mountain Road in her Chevy Impala in November, and it'd be dark and there would be people walking on the side of the road," Phil Lintilhac remembered. "She couldn't see them very well. The more she thought about it, the more she realized she wanted to see if she could help the town get people off the road.

"Her initial idea was to run almost like a sidewalk path that ran up the Mountain Road, not so much a recreation path as a safety path. But doing it that way involved so many rights of way and things like that, cutting across people's properties, that it wasn't really workable. So the recreation path was the eventual outcome."

In 1977, Claire asked local attorney Tom Amidon, who was serving on her new foundation's board, to put together a plan for a path. An engineer hired to do the planning work drew up a recreation path that would run near the Mountain Road and the West Branch River, which meanders curvingly close to the road. Though it would now run mostly behind Mountain Road businesses, the path would still largely cut across private land.

In the mid-1980s, Anne Lusk worked tirelessly to build the community support and landowner permissions needed to create the Stowe Recreation Path.

Facing such a complex challenge, the plan was essentially shelved until 1981. That year the Stowe Area Association, a nonprofit devoted to promoting the town and its region, proposed that the town hire a bike path coordinator for two years, to see if the project could be made to work. The salary would be $5,000 a year.

Anne Lusk was interested. A local mother of two who had just earned a master's degree in historic preservation at UVM, Lusk had lately chaired a project that restored the former Stowe High School, expanding it into today's landmark town library and Helen Day Art Center.

When the new opening came up, "I applied for the job," she said, "even though I had never built a bike path before. I knew I was competing against engineering firms, but it's a small town. The selectmen knew they'd get their money's worth from me, that I would just sink my heart into the project.

"There were other bike paths across the country, but they were primarily rail trails, long-distance ones that were more rural. So I said, 'Okay — if I do this, I will have to meet individually with property owners.'

"So I would have group meetings. The restaurants up and down the Mountain Road were good; people would organize a breakfast for me to come in and have coffee with people from that area. We'd sit down and figure out how to do this.

"I knew not to put a black Magic Marker over anybody's land. Instead, I would identify destinations along the Mountain Road, and I had the property owners identify where we could go on their land.

"I would talk to everybody in town, all the time — if I saw them at the grocery store, if they called me up. If they gave me good ideas, I put them in the *Stowe Reporter*. I wrote an article a week about this project: This is what we're doing, this was a good idea, this was a meeting that I had.

"It was a big project. Seven days a week. Claire provided the funding to build it, to construct it."

"Showing that the community wanted this"

I n 1983, the Lintilhac Foundation's board approved providing up to $84,000 to the Stowe Recreation Path, as a grant that would double-match the amount raised locally. It was the last significant grant the board approved during Claire's lifetime — and before she passed away in late 1984, she was able to see construction on the path begin.

"The year my mom died, I remember driving her through town to look at the installation of those very first bridges that crossed the river, here and there on the recreation path," Phil recalled. "She was pleased, although I think she was also a little bit disappointed that it wasn't able to be right alongside the road all the way. You still find people walking along the road at night."

Additional support for the project came from the town and the federal Land and Water Conservation Fund, and Anne Lusk invited personal contributions of any size, even the smallest.

"I made sure we had categories, so if you gave a dollar, you got your name in the book," she said. "We had different categories for distances: inches, rods, links. I wanted young children to be able to donate, to get in the habit of donating and to be acknowledged. I was taking pennies, and putting them in the bank account."

In the end she raised $300,000 toward the project's total cost of $680,000.

"I had to get deeds of easements from all the property owners. We were showing that the community wanted this, that we had the fundraising and everyone was behind it."

A bridge for walkers, runners and bicyclists on the Stowe Recreation Path.

At a Town Meeting shortly before construction began, Lusk recalled, "The town moderator asked if anybody had any objections to building the Stowe Recreation Path, for which I'd raised all the money, gotten all the permits and everything — and the audience laughed. Because there was no objection."

When construction began, local kids were so excited that they rode their bikes on just-laid asphalt, and the surface heat blew out one bicycle's tire. "The workmen loved building the path, because everybody was just egging them on all the time," Lusk said. "'Keep it going.' They got a lot of support."

"They knew the Stowe Path was theirs"

A parking lot down behind the Stowe Community Church is where the path, locally often known as the bike path, begins. On an autumn Saturday, its first stretch is peopled with hikers, walkers, strollers and riders. A huddle of young women, just down from the village, clutch containers of carryout coffee. More visitors take photos on the first little bridge over the West Branch, while a couple walks two dogs, serious walkers go pacing by, and bicyclists come the other way, pedaling down from a morning's ride.

The bike path isn't straight. It curves and rises and falls gently, crossing the river on a series of small bridges and moving through woods, past farm fields and alongside tall, tan stands of rushes by the river. Here and there, wooden staircases lead up to popular destinations: restaurants, cafes, ice-cream shops. Returning down the path, you can see the spire of the Community Church up ahead — and then you're back at the start, where a large placard tells the story of Anne Lusk and the community project.

A sign here says this little open area at the outset of the path is Lintilhac Park, "In memory of Claire Lintilhac, whose dreams helped launch this path for the town she loved."

The Stowe Recreation Path has won a number of honors, include a Point of Light Award from the George H.W. Bush administration. While the path was being built, in 1986 the President's Commission on Americans Outdoors released an influential report whose "vision for the future" was "a living network of greenways."

"Imagine walking out your front door, getting on a bicycle, a horse, or a trail bike, or simply donning your backpack and, within minutes of your home, setting off on a continuous network of recreation corridors which could lead across the country," the report suggested. "... Greenways are a way to provide open recreation spaces for every American, close to home. Greenways are our vision for the future.

"... Our concept is not to propose a federal initiative," the Commission added. "Greenways will be put in place by communities."

That's what happened in Stowe.

"What I like most is that it's free, and it has no social class to it," Anne Lusk said. "One time I went behind the Stowe Community Church to check on something, and I watched all these pickup trucks come in, with kids and their bikes. Parents were taking their kids' bikes out, it was a big gang. I asked, and they said the kids had voted, for their school spring picnic, to go to the Stowe Recreation Path. They were from Elmore, or Morrisville," nearby towns, "and that was what they wanted to do.

"I was so happy, because it meant they knew the Stowe Path was theirs."

"How could we do that?"

I t's not always easy to develop community support for a local conservation project. Lusk learned to cultivate the folks she called "the gas station grumblers."

"I knew the gas stations in town where everybody would gather at six, six-thirty in the morning — and I would go there at that hour and ask them: 'I'm going to do this, is this a good idea?' And they would, you know, grumble. But then I would go do what they told me to do, and I'd go back and say, 'Okay, I did this. What else should I do?' So they were guiding me all the way.

"You go to the people who are most likely to be upset, but also have good ideas. And it was a better project because of their ideas."

Over in Barre Town, Pierre Couture faced a lot of local grumbling when he first began cutting trails on Millstone Hill.

"Local people didn't get it," he said. "To them, [the hill properties] were just an industrial remnant. They didn't want the past, they wanted the future."

When mountain bikers began using the new trails, Couture said, "I remember getting accosted by somebody I went to high school with, saying, 'You're bringing all these strangers in here! All those people from Quebec and Connecticut, they're going to ruin everything!'"

What became key to turning the tide was the outreach Couture and the Millstone Trails Association made to the Trust for Public Land.

TPL is a nationwide organization, with offices in Vermont and 35 other states plus the District of Columbia. "Our mission is to protect land and create parks for the benefit of people," said Kate Wanner, project manager in the Montpelier office. "In some of our offices, we concentrate on urban projects: green schoolyards, rail trails, city parks. But in Vermont, as a rural state, our niche has been large forestland conservation.

"We've protected about 65,000 acres over the last 27 years. More than half of that has been additions to the Green Mountain National Forest, as well as additions to state parks and state forests — and community forests, like Barre Town's."

When Rock of Ages let Pierre Couture know it was putting its Millstone Hill land up for sale but he'd have the first purchase option, he said, "at first I was just kind of shaken. We're not going to buy that land, how could we do that? In my heart, I had always hoped that preservation would be the ultimate result — but this was way sooner than I thought I was ready, than the Millstone Trails Association was ready.

"But Mike Fraysier, who was on my board and worked for [Vermont] Forests, Parks and Recreation, had been involved in some projects with the Trust for Public Land, and he said, 'Let's see if they might be interested.' And they were all over it right away. Right away, Kate was the best partner.

"In order to make the town forest project work, Kate said, 'You need to get some local money,'" Couture recalled. "She suggested we ask for $100,000 from the town. Well, they were not interested at all."

"There was a public perception at the time that this place was only for mountain bikers," recalled former MTA board member Marcy Christian. "Barre Town is like the capital of ATV world, so it was sort of a cultural clash. But Kate was huge during that time, and Carl Rogers, the town manager, they really kept with it. Kate did this huge public relations campaign in the town, because they had to vote on the $100,000 bond to make it all work."

"The focus is engaging with people"

The project's $1,378,600 budget had a number of contributors. Top funding included $400,000 from the new federal Community Forest and Open Space Program, which had been championed by Sen. Leahy; $310,500 from the Vermont Housing and Conservation Board; and $200,000 in a Community Forest Grant from the Open Space Institute. Several nonprofits and foundations, including the Lintilhac Foundation, chipped in five-figure grants. The Millstone Trails Association itself raised $75,000, much of it from sales of properties that Pierre Couture had bought.

But the town funding was an essential piece, to demonstrate local commitment. It had to go through — "and it passed," Christian said. "Sixty-three percent, which never happens!"

"Because of the existing [trails] organization, people could see what it was, and could see that MTA was going to be able to maintain these trails," said Carl Rogers, the town manager. "I think that really was key."

"I'm an old mountain biker, and I think our trails are amazing," said Peter Kopsco, the MTA's current president. "When I got on the board, I learned very quickly that just maintaining what we have is enormously challenging.

"The focus of our efforts, and probably our biggest challenge," he added, "is engaging with people, and encouraging people to come out and volunteer — because it's a lot of work. Whether it's the bridges, or helping get rid of some of the roots and trying to figure out how to shore things up; just clearing brush and downed trees and branches from trails is a lot of work."

The Trails Association asks mountain bikers to pay a modest day-use fee, which goes toward equipment. All the upkeep work on the trails is done by volunteers. "People are respecting the trails and what has to go into them, so paying $10 to ride for a day is like giving back," said Kim Quinlan, a Vermont rider who was the Eastern States Cup's Enduro Series 2019 champion, Women's Open Pro Division.

"The trails have a great variety of old-school single track, most of which is technical because a large portion is covered in old root bed or chunky rocks that you need to maneuver through," she said. "There are also fun sections of man-made features like wooden bridges, jumps and drops.

"One of my favorite areas is Harrington Heights and Harrington Ridge. You climb up, run along narrow, natural rock slabs across the ridge and then descend after enjoying a great view (and snack) at the top. But what really makes these trails unique is riding by the amazing remains of granite quarries, some filled with vibrantly colored water, and stopping at the vistas to see the town below. Riding the Millstone trails is an experience not quite like any other."

"The potential is tremendous"

When TPL takes on a conservation project, "most of what we do is solve all the problems, tie it up in a neat little bow and then hand it over to a federal agency, the state, or a municipality," explained Kate Wanner. "Because of the relationship that we've built with the Lintilhac Foundation over the past 15 years, they know that once we start a project, and are sure we can do it and start applying for funding, that we will succeed.

"So they are often willing to put in the first grant — and that helps us a lot, because most of our projects last two, three or four years, and a lot of the funding we don't get until the very end. But we have expenses, significant expenses, starting in year one. So those early foundation grants are especially helpful to offset our expenses in the beginning of the project. Title work and legal and all that.

"I'd say 80 to 90 percent of our projects in Vermont involve federal funding — and when you involve federal funding, it's usually a minimum of a two-year process, the way those federal funding cycles work."

Take Rolston Rest. This one is a big project. Just northeast of Rutland in Chittenden, Mendon and Killington, the upland property includes "2,745 acres of important wildlife habitat, nationally significant hiking trails, and critical aquatic resources, and is the largest private unconserved inholding remaining within the Green Mountain National Forest," said TPL's application for foundation support. That application was approved in 2017. By late 2019, TPL was in the final stages of the project, acquiring Rolston Rest temporarily and planning to transfer it to the Green Mountain Forest in 2020.

If you go kayaking or fishing on the Chittenden Reservoir, a popular destination surrounded by the National Forest a few miles from Rutland, you'll see Rolston Rest as a high, slope-topped ridge that spreads broadly above the northern shore. You won't see any manmade structures up there at all. Home to an unusual high-elevation pond plus eight mountain summits, with spectacular views of the Adirondacks to the west and the White Mountains to the east, "the property supports more than 90 acres of wetlands, 11 miles of headwater streams and important breeding habitat for bear and moose," said a TPL publication. "This elevational diversity is critical to helping wildlife adapt to a changing climate."

Named for a hiker's shelter up on the ridgeline, Rolston Rest is also home to an unusual confluence of recreation trails. The Long Trail, America's oldest long-range hiking path, runs for three miles along those ridges. The Catamount Trail, a cross-country skiing path that also runs the length of Vermont, has followed a snowmachine trail below Rolston Rest, but will be rerouted to a more scenic, high-elevation path on the property. And the Velomont Trail, a planned single-track mountain-biking trail that when complete will also run the length of Vermont, is mapped to run through this property as well.

The Vermont Mountain Bike Association is raising funds to connect its various local chapters and their networks of trails up to the high-country Velomont Trail. The Vermont Huts Association is planning to build an all-season hut, to be

Kate Wanner, Vermont project manager for the Trust for Public Land.

named for Sen. Leahy, that can host 20 people, just behind the ridgeline and just out of view from the reservoir.

"It's a critical link for a lot of recreation," said Matt Williams, executive director of the Catamount Trail Association. "We're looking at a future where the Catamount Trail, the Long Trail and the proposed Velomont Trail all come together around a hut. So you have the three big human-powered recreation uses all coming to a confluence there, with significant ecological value up there as well.

"There's something to be said for sheer size, too," he added. "There just aren't more opportunities to buy big chunks of land like that in Vermont, particularly along the spine of the Greens and that close to some of the biggest ski areas in the state."

Rolston Rest had been the property of a private landowner who made a failed effort to develop Vermont's largest sugarmaking operation. TPL bought the land for the eventual transfer to the national forest.

"It's on a ridgeline — it's beautiful," said Shelley Lutz, an area resident and avid mountain biker who led the development of a trail network in Rutland City, five miles away. "The potential for what they want to do up there is tremendous. It's got northeast-facing access, so it's also perfect for glade skiing. There's a lot of potential up on that hillside."

"The deal provides a final link," the *Rutland Herald* reported, "that will guarantee not only public access but protection for the Long Trail, wildlife corridors and breeding habitat, research areas, and headwater streams that source public water supplies and hydropower downstream."

The view from Rolston Rest. *Photo by Kurt Budinger.*

"The setting couldn't be more ideal," said R. J. Thompson, executive director of the Vermont Huts Association. "You have a beautiful, high-elevation pond up there, quite unique for Vermont, and sweeping views. It just made sense to locate a hut up there. It's going to be a special place when it's finished."

A walk unlike any other

When Pierre Couture was wondering how he could raise money to help conserve Millstone Hill, he got an idea from WaterFire.

That's a stunning art event in Providence, Rhode Island, where 86 wood fires are kindled on anchored braziers that rise just above the surface of three rivers in the city. Started in 1994, WaterFire now draws some 40,000 people to the riverfronts each time it is staged, usually two Saturday evenings a month from May to November.

Why couldn't something like this be done, Couture wondered, on the trails up the old quarry hill?

That was the start of RockFire. When it was first staged on a summer weekend in 2012, RockFire raised close to $8,000 — and it continues today as an annual event organized by Couture, separately from the MTA, with more than 100 area volunteers.

RockFire starts on a broad, sloping meadow outside Couture's Millstone Hill Lodge. Musicians perform on a stage into the early evening, while visitors enjoy the music and grab dinner from food stalls and vendors. When dusk falls, organizers begin to lead groups across the road and upward onto the trails.

Along the trails as they steadily rise are some 40 campfires. They've been lit beside individual performers and groups, mostly folk and traditional musicians, who've been set up to play in clearings, under simple awnings suspended between poles of white birch. At one station is a fire organ, a large and striking instrument of vertical steel tubes that each sound a different unearthly note when a flaming torch is held beneath the bottom opening.

As you continue on up, you pass old quarries that are now filled with water, their calm surfaces glimmering tonight with reflections from drifting floats that hold little fires. Here and there, historical placards at key points tell the story of old Millstone Hill.

Then you come to the big bonfires. There are about a dozen of them, each at a tall, clifflike pile of quarried blocks; at some spots, small fires lit behind the blocks glow through crevices between them. The various fires illuminate artwork that's been carved by Barre's expert granite sculptors into the big blocks: gargoyle faces, animals, fanciful creatures, even a pair of claw-like hands that seem to be reaching from behind a stone slab.

An illuminated sculpture at RockFire.

"Barre sculptors are the finest in America," said Couture, "but nobody knows they exist! So I approached the granite sculptors. We called it graffiti art: something you're inspired to do that won't take a ton of time, but will leave a lasting mark on the terrain. They just loved it, because they got to work outside and do fun things, and the connection to the source was all stimulating to them. They were great."

In the fire-glowing dark, this is a walk like no other. At the trail's very top you come to the Grand Lookout, where the biggest bonfire of all roars up amid granite columns that loom like a ruined ancient temple in the night. There's music up here too, and awestruck people, their faces warmed by the flames.

"Unless you've seen it, you just can't get it," Couture said — "and even if you've seen it, it's hard to explain. It's something you've got to experience.

"One of the things people have said to me about RockFire is that it's a shared human experience. It's a huge group of people, but there's also an intimacy about it. I've got volunteers who've been there for seven years. That's something about that event; people really find satisfaction in playing a part in it."

All this on a hill that once was dead and abandoned.

Not anymore.

Conservation for a Critical Time

SPOTLIGHTS ON
CONSERVATION PROJECTS

"IT'S A DIFFERENT WORLD AROUND HERE"

Turning a bankrupt ski mountain into a "recreation destination"

Local volunteers first set up rope tows in 1946 on the lower slopes of Mt. Ascutney, which rises as a backdrop to the tidy village of Brownsville in the town of West Windsor. Skiing grew into the economic engine of this east-central Vermont community in the 1950s and 1960s, when the development of Ascutney Mountain Resort brought chairlifts and more trails to the mountainside, plus a hotel and condos below.

Then the ski town fell on hard times.

Standing east of the main spine of the Green Mountains, the Ascutney resort couldn't count on reliable snow. By 2010, Select Board member Glenn Seward, who'd been Ascutney Mountain's general manager, had worked for five different owners of the resort. That year, he and fellow townspeople watched with dismay as the final owners declared bankruptcy. In 2012, a heavy-duty helicopter lifted away the towers from the high-speed quad chairlift, for transport to a New Hampshire resort. Flatbed trucks carted off the rest of Ascutney Mountain's abandoned equipment.

"We're very much a second-home community, and it was just a devastating effect," Seward said. "We, the Select Board, felt we really needed to come up with a solution to bring the town back to life."

As they talked things through in a number of meetings and conversations, town leaders came up with an audacious idea. What if West Windsor itself bought the former resort's 469 acres?

The trails on Mount Ascutney rise as a backdrop to West Windsor village. *Photo by Jerry Monkman.*

With some 30 to 40 miles of networked trails, the mountain property could be joined to the nearby West Windsor Town Forest. With careful planning and stewardship, it might just possibly become a destination point for a more viable mix of outdoor recreation: snow sports in winter, then mountain biking and hiking in the warmer months.

"My whole focus was to develop something that would be sustainable long-term," said Seward, who became a key driver of the project. "Clearly a ski area doesn't work here, for a whole host of reasons. So I essentially came up with the idea that we should consider forming a nonprofit, to manage the recreational activities on the mountain as well as and in the town forest. Thankfully, the Trust for Public Land was willing to help."

Kate Wanner of TPL's Vermont office began working with the town and local volunteers to put together a conservation project. Meanwhile, community members were organizing Ascutney Outdoors, a new nonprofit.

"In 2015, Laura Farrell, one of the founders of Ascutney Outdoors, and a group of people with the support of the Select Board put up a small rope tow," Seward said. "Lo and behold, we had skiing back. Local skiing. At Ascutney."

Then that year the empty base lodge from the old resort burned. "It was just an awful site," Seward said. "We had a decrepit old chairlift that was left behind and the burned-out base lodge full of asbestos, right adjacent to the rope tow. It was a daunting project to say the least."

But support for Ascutney Outdoors was growing in the community. The three-person Select Board, led by Steve Crihfield, decided it was time to call a town vote on whether to acquire the property.

"It was the largest town meeting in history," Seward said — "and the article passed by a two-thirds majority. It was unbelievable."

"We do not want to relive the past"

"The development and improvement of a trail network with guaranteed public access less than a mile away from the village center will help establish the site as a recreation destination and provide a desperately needed boost to the local economy," said a Trust for Public Land message to potential funders of the Ascutney project. Along with TPL, the town worked on the initiative with the Upper Valley Land Trust, Ascutney Outdoors, and the volunteer group Sport Trails of Ascutney Basin. Funding came from the Vermont Housing and Conservation Board, the Open Space Institute, The Conservation Alliance, the Outdoor Gear Exchange, the Mascoma Savings Bank and several private foundations, including the Lintilhac Foundation.

In December 2015, the town closed on the Ascutney Mountain property. Ascutney Outdoors purchased the burned- out base lodge, demolished it and built a new multiuse operations center. Executing a five-year plan, the community group installed a new T-bar lift and a tubing lift, so a wide variety of users could enjoy the winter slopes.

"We wanted this to be something accessible to everybody in the community," Seward said. "We've had people on the tubing lift as young as three years old, all the way up to 90.

"Everything we do at Ascutney Outdoors is with an eye toward sustainability — because we do not want to relive the past. It nearly destroyed the community," said Seward, who now serves as the organization's pro bono executive director. "Now, along with with the new center, the T-bar, the mountain biking trails and the tubing lift, we work closely with

At a packed Town Meeting, Ascutney residents approved by a three-to-one margin the proposal to acquire the former Ascutney Mountain Resort property. *Photo by Kate Wanner.*

the local elementary school for what is called place-based curriculum. Kids are on the mountain every day, learning about their environment and conservation. We offer the Ascutney Outdoors center for open mike nights, for local musicians to come in. That has been extremely successful."

"I hope and expect to do more of these projects throughout Vermont," said Kate Wanner of TPL, "as communities realize the benefits of local control and local ownership of their most well-loved trail networks — or to create those from scratch themselves. We're working with towns to help conserve whatever is most important to them, whether it's a mountain bike network, a drinking water supply, or hiking trails."

For a West Windsor community that not so long ago was staring at financial devastation, the impacts of the Mount Ascutney project are looking more and more long-term.

"When the ski area was foreclosed on, property values within the resort decreased by over 40 percent," Glenn Seward said. "There were hundreds of homes and condominiums here, and as their value dropped, so did the taxes. So all of a sudden the town was in a financial pinch."

Today, "lo and behold, property values are starting to go up," Seward said. "Young people are moving into town because of what we offer. Many of the condominiums that were put up for sale at very low prices are now in demand as full-time residences.

"It's just remarkable, if you look at where we started in 2010. Here we are in 2020 and it's a different world, literally, around here."

CONSERVING A COMMUNITY GEM IN WILLISTON

Jim and Lucy McCullough live in a brick home in Williston, near Burlington, that was built in the late 1700s by Vermont's first governor, Thomas Chittenden. The 400-acre property had been in Jim's family since 1873 when they opened it, in the 1970s, to the public for cross-country skiing. "By 1990 their small experiment in the outdoor industry had become a wildly successful four-season operation that is still open for hiking, biking, skiing, and educational opportunities," said a Trust for Public Lands publication. "It is a regional icon that attracts more than 20,000 visitors per year."

But in this Chittenden County town with high property values and strong pressures for development, rising costs and expenses made it impossible in recent years for the McCulloughs to make ends meet. A buildout survey estimated that 150 to 200 new homes could be built on their land. "Developers had worn the shellac off our door knocking to buy the place," Jim told TPL's *Land & People* magazine.

Their property could have sold for $2.3 million — but the McCulloughs offered to discount it by $700,000, if the land could be bought by the town and conserved as the new Catamount Community Forest.

The Trust for Public Land worked with the family and the town to secure the property and raise a total of $1.9 million for its purchase. The funding was assembled from public sources, including the town, the Vermont Housing and Conservation Board and the Federal Community Forest Program; from several Vermont businesses and private donors; and from more than half a dozen philanthropic organizations, including the Lintilhac Foundation. In March 2019, 393 acres of the property became the new town forest, with a permanent conservation easement co-held by the Vermont Land Trust and the Vermont Housing and Conservation Board.

The conservation protects seven "wildlife habitat units," identified by UVM as blocks of land with little or no development that provide habitat for a large number of species — in this case, black bear, otter, bobcat, bald eagle and some 136 identified bird species. Twenty miles of trails weave through an ecologically diverse landscape, "a microcosm of Vermont's wild backcountry within the fastest-growing town in the fastest-growing county in the state," said TPL.

Also safeguarded is a healthy, happy tradition of human-powered recreation. Since the 1980s, the McCulloughs have been hosting weekly mountain-biking races for all ages and skill levels on their ski trails. Special Olympics has trained its athletes here for three decades, and Vermont Adaptive Ski and Sports makes good use of 2.5 miles of accessible trails for wheelchair hiking in summer and sit-skiing in winter.

Sliding at Catamount Community Forest. *Photo courtesy of Catamount Outdoor Family Center.*

In 2007, Olympian mountain biker Lea Davison and her sister Sabra, who grew up riding the Catamount trails, created Little Bellas, a biking program for girls from seven to 16 years old. It has since spread to some 16 states.

"Since the transfer to town ownership, the place — with its steady, laughing flow of summer campers, weekly racers, and day users — feels much the same," said an article in the fall-winter 2019 issue of TLP's magazine, *Land & People*. "These days there are more people enjoying it than ever."

PROTECTING UNFRAGMENTED WILDLIFE CORRIDORS

When the state Public Utility Commission (PUC) denied an application by Verizon Wireless to build an 88-foot cell phone tower in a parcel of forested land off Rte. 100 in Waterbury, it was careful to clarify that the 2017 ruling applied only here. It was not issuing "a blanket prohibition" of new cell towers in Vermont forests.

Even so, the ruling had a meaningful impact on efforts to preserve the corridors of forested land that are essential to certain wildlife species, notably black bears.

"The real issue is, where do we stand on the issue of development within wildlife corridors," said David Grayck, a Montpelier attorney specializing in environmental land-use law who appeared in the PUC case on behalf of several area landowners who were interested parties, including Phil and Crea Lintilhac. "The significance of the decision was to show that when the state Agency of Natural Resources invests its resources in identifying wildlife corridors — and when it commits to protection of those corridors — existing law is there to address the issue."

With its tower, Verizon Wireless aimed to fill in gaps in 4G cell coverage along the Route 100 corridor between Waterbury and Stowe. But the parcel where it proposed to build a tower "is one of only nine regionally significant linkages for providing landscape scale connectivity in the northeast region," said the PUC ruling, based on evidence provided by the Agency of Natural Resources.

"Forest fragmentation within highest-priority connectivity blocks will reduce the ecological integrity of the natural communities within the block and alter ecological processes," the ruling continued. "The effects of the fragmentation caused by the Project would radiate beyond the Project's relatively small footprint and into the forest block ... leading to the demise of its function as a critically important linkage for landscape connectivity."

"What the Lintilhac Foundation did in this case was to be out front on that issue," said attorney Grayck, whose work on the case was supported by the foundation. The PUC ruling, he noted, shows an important evolution in state efforts to protect natural areas that are key wildlife corridors.

"You can go back and find Act 250 decisions from the 1970s and 1980s where there was an issue about development, usually a ski area trying to develop in a high-altitude location where it was known that there would be particular wildlife, for example bears," Grayck said. "And the analysis that was being done was very focused on that particular location, the stand of trees and the bears.

"What really comes out in the PUC decision is an acknowledgment that we exist in a territorial range that goes from the Canadian Maritimes to the very edge of western New York, with mountainous undeveloped terrain in the Maritimes, in Maine, New Hampshire, Vermont and into the Adirondacks," Grayck said. "And it's not that individual animals are traversing that entire range; it's that the species rely upon that entire range for overall health. And that's why the PUC decision was significant.

"What we're looking at is, how do we facilitate development, which is a necessity of economic activity, but on the other hand maintain species and habitat — which is significant to our economic activity? It's not one or the other," Grayck concluded. "How we use our land is very significant to our economy."

PRESERVING THE BIRTHPLACE OF AN AMERICAN COLLECTION

When Hope Alswang became executive director of the Shelburne Museum in 1997, her challenge, as *Vermont Woman* described it in a 2004 article, was to "restore the institution to its rightful place as a major player in the museum world.

"Over the past seven years, Alswang and her staff have done exactly that — begun to reestablish the museum as the cultural jewel that it is," wrote Heather Michon in *Vermont Woman*. "With the help of a grant from the National Endowment for the Humanities, six of the oldest buildings on the grounds were selected for face-lifts, both to improve their safety and to reinterpret their holdings."

There was also a unique "cultural jewel," Alswang learned, that the museum would soon own. Deep in nearby Shelburne Farms stands the Brick House, where Electra Havemeyer Webb, the wealthy daughter of an American sugar magnate, and her husband J. Watson Webb, Jr., of the Vanderbilt family, lived, part-time and then full-time, from 1913 until their deaths in 1960. It was in the Brick House, on the Lake Champlain shore, where Electra first amassed and displayed the eclectic and voluminous aggregation of Americana art and decorative art that grew into what's now the Shelburne Museum collection.

"It looks out across rolling meadows to the lake and the Adirondacks; it's one of the most beautiful places," said Alswang, who led the museum until 2005. "What I was interested in was that it was a perfectly preserved, intra — by which I mean between World Wars I and II — colonial revival American country house. And these houses, fully furnished in the high-style taste of the time, were just disappearing hand over fist. Most of them were gone, and this house was like a fly in amber, it was so well-preserved."

For Electra Webb, the Brick House "provided an appropriate backdrop," *The Magazine Antiques* said in a 2003 article, "for her collections of American furniture, blown and pressed glass, pewter, quilts, dolls, and hooked rugs. ... It was her ingenuity and finesse in creating this whole new aesthetic that made her an original among collectors in her day."

With help from a New York architecture firm and a renowned landscape designer, the Webbs developed the Brick House from a modest brick cottage into "a 40-room masterpiece of the Colonial Revival style, with beautiful gardens and captivating views," says the museum's website. After their deaths in 1960, ownership of the home passed to their

Electra Havemeyer Webb's bedroom in the Brick House. *Photo courtesy of Shelburne Museum.*

son, J. Watson Webb III. After his passing in 2000, the Brick House became the property of the Shelburne Museum.

"It wasn't in any way horribly neglected," Alswang recalled, "but if we wanted to use it, it was going to need health and safety updates. My vision was that we would save the house, which was an incredible period piece, and use it for public programming of different kinds. So we had to go about convincing board members that it was worth the expense, because it was going to cost about $5 million."

Crea Lintilhac became a key ally. Serving then on the museum's Board of Trustees,

The Brick House. *Photo courtesy of Shelburne Museum.*

"she was, along with some other board members, a real advocate for saving the house," Alswang said. "That made a huge difference, in the beginning. Then the foundation made a pledge, which helped us get started."

The foundation awarded a five-year, $250,000 grant to the project, and a capital campaign successfully raised the remainder that was needed. The restoration work was completed in 2003.

"You can look at photographs of the way the house is now, and look at 1938 photographs, and it's virtually identical," Alswang said. "There's not many places where you can see that. This isn't typical conservation — here is a beautiful, human-made landscape, molded from the 1890s onward, preserved so that it remains that way. It maintains this wonderful sense of historic reality that would have been lost if someone had moved in there and torn it down."

Feb. 24, 2010: VPIRG volunteer activists Heidi Wilson, left, and Taryn Hallweather in Montpelier on the morning of the Senate vote.

8

Retiring Vermont Yankee

How a nonprofit coalition took on the nuclear establishment

———— \/ ————

This story starts with lightning striking twice.

In a thunderstorm close to midnight on June 15, 1991, lightning hit electrical equipment in two separate incidents, each of which would lead to a temporary shutdown of the fission reactor at an aging nuclear power plant. One of those plants was in southern Vermont; the other was 40 miles away, in western Massachusetts.

At 10:24 p.m., lightning damaged one of three transmission lines that carried power away from Vermont Yankee, the nuclear plant alongside the Connecticut River in Vernon, the state's southeasternmost town. Power was automatically routed to the other two transmission lines, but a faulty transistor shut one of those down, and the third line couldn't carry all that energy. So Vermont Yankee, which had been generating about a third of the state's electricity since 1972, was powered down for almost four days.

That was the lesser of the two mishaps. At 11:50 that Saturday night, just a few miles down the Deerfield River from the Vermont border, lightning struck a transformer at a nuclear power station in Rowe, Massachusetts.

Nearly two decades after that 1991 storm, the impact of the second strike would still be reverberating.

By that summer, the Massachusetts plant known as Yankee Rowe, or just Rowe, had been operating for slightly more than 30 years. It was the oldest commercial nuclear station in New England, third-oldest in the United States. The lightning started a small fire at the plant, knocked out its communication system, triggered an emergency alert, and prompted a multi-day shutdown of the reactor. Startled by the incident, local people in the rural area around Rowe began to come together to share their concerns.

The more they learned, the more alarmed the plant's neighbors became. The nonprofit organization they decided to form, called the Citizens Awareness Network or CAN, is still active today. Almost 20 years after those lighting strikes, CAN became part of a broad coalition of nonprofit groups whose persistent opposition to civilian nuclear power, specifically to the Vermont Yankee plant in Vernon, found its climax in a dramatic vote inside the Vermont State House on a snowy morning in February 2010.

On that day, following a potent and sophisticated advocacy campaign by the allied nonprofits — an effort that was supported in several ways by the foundation, along with other funders — the Vermont State Senate became the first legislative body in the United States to vote to shut down a nuclear power plant.

"In a small, ornate chamber packed with plant opponents," reported Matthew Wald in the *New York Times*, "the Vermont senators voiced frustration over recent leaks of radioactive tritium at the 38-year-old [Vermont Yankee] plant as well as the collapse of a cooling tower in 2007 and inaccurate testimony by the plant's owner, the Louisiana-based nuclear operator Entergy."

The Senate's vote that day in 2010 wasn't quite the end of the Vermont Yankee saga. But it was the most dramatic moment among many in the four-decade campaign by citizen groups and their supporters to close Vermont's only nuclear plant. The stance that the Vermont Senate took played a much-noticed part in the nuclear industry's fade from the forefront of American energy priorities and planning. It was also an important step in Vermont's ongoing effort to turn away from depending on large power-generation stations, nuclear and otherwise, toward a different kind of energy economy: one that relies to an important degree on efficiency and on decentralized, renewable sources of power such as solar, hydro and biomass.

This chapter and the one that follows trace these connected stories, of the campaign to close Vermont Yankee and the push for a clean-energy economy in Vermont. The focus is on the nonprofit organizations that have been working, with Lintilhac Foundation support, to help drive this fundamental change in how a small state — one that's often a looked-to laboratory for innovation and positive change — can respond to climate change and create a more sustainable future for itself.

The energy of resistance

E ven before the twin lightning strikes of 1991, the potential dangers of civilian nuclear power plants had been clear to a growing number of New Englanders. Back in 1971, a group of citizens and scientists in southern Vermont and western Massachusetts formed the New England Coalition on Nuclear Pollution, "to ask all relevant questions about design, construction, operation, public health and safety, and environmental effects before the Vermont Yankee nuclear plant received a license," says a history compiled by the group. In the years ahead, the New England Coalition would persist at highlighting safety issues at Vermont Yankee, concerns about its environmental impacts, and the plant's potential for a major accident.

"The New England Coalition on Nuclear Pollution engaged Vermont Yankee's owners in near-continuous litigation since its initial licensing phase of VY, years prior to it even being built," noted Clay Turnbull, who has served on the Coalition's small staff since 2005.

Much of the early energy of resistance to nuclear power in New England developed in and around the late-1970s protests against Seabrook, a nuclear station then proposed, and later built, in a community on the New Hampshire coast of the Atlantic Ocean. Some 1,400 protestors were arrested at the Seabrook site at a protest demonstration in 1977. Most refused bail, and instead spent two weeks in jail. They had been trained in protest tactics by the Clamshell Alliance, an antinuclear group formed in 1976 that would continue to battle the Seabrook project into the 1980s.

In 2010, the year the long campaign against Vermont Yankee finally came to a head, a "My Turn" guest op-ed in the *Burlington Free Press* by Philip Lintilhac, the foundation trustee who is a research

On the Connecticut River, protestors sail by the Vermont Yankee nuclear power plant.

assistant professor of plant biology at the University of Vermont, summed up the arguments against nuclear power and for energy conservation and renewable generation:

> A dollar spent on end-user conservation saves between three and 10 times the carbon from entering the atmosphere as the same dollar spent on nuclear, and saves it now. If one looks at reliability and distribution costs, green alternatives look even better because they can be produced on a regional if not a backyard scale, installed rapidly, repaired easily, returned to service quickly, and can be producing electricity much closer to the point of use. ...
>
> Why pin our future on a technology that is completely dependent on external sourcing, long-distance transmission and government subsidies when locally generated and distributed power could be generating wealth here at home? Would you invest your own personal money in an industry that cannot stand on its own without taxpayer-subsidized support, when it is constantly reminding us of its age with breakdowns and timeouts while exporting its profits to out-of-state holding companies that have no obligation to local energy independence?
>
> Lastly, the issue of storing highly radioactive materials on the surface of the Earth cannot be dismissed. These materials are inherently lethal. They cannot be incinerated, neutralized or rendered harmless by any chemical or biological means. They can only be left to smolder for many thousands of years. ... Like an earthquake, we don't know when disaster will occur but we know that it will.

That warning would soon come true. In March 2011, just over a year after the Vermont Senate voted against renewing Vermont Yankee's operating license, an earthquake and a resulting 14-meter tidal wave hit the Fukushima Daiichi Nuclear Power Plant on the east coast of Japan. In spite of frantic efforts at containment by the plant staff, the natural disaster escalated into three reactor meltdowns, three hydrogen explosions, and the release of radioactivity into the air and ocean near the plant.

Fukushima's self-destruction was not the first but the third public convulsion of a commercial nuclear station. It came after the partial meltdown in 1979 at Three Mile Island in Pennsylvania and, in 1986, the devastating explosion and massive radioactivity release at Chernobyl, in what was then the Soviet Union's Ukrainian SSR.

Vermont Yankee and the reactors at the Fukushima plant all came online in the early 1970s. They were all of essentially the same design.

"People began to meet"

n 1991, the lightning strike and its impacts at Yankee Rowe in Massachusetts were "a dangerous situation," recalled Deb Katz, a local resident who would become a leader of the new Citizens Awareness Network. A parent of two girls, Katz had moved up with her family from New York City in the late 1970s for a safer, more peaceful life in Rowe, four and a half miles from the power plant on the Deerfield River.

When the accident at Rowe happened, she said, "It started to rouse people in our community about what was going on at the nuke, and people began to meet. When we started, 100 people from the Deerfield River Valley were meeting every week."

The neighbors learned that in early June, just 11 days before the summer thunderstorm, the New England Coalition and the Union of Concerned Scientists had together filed a petition with the federal Nuclear Regulatory Commission. The petition called for Yankee Rowe to be shut down permanently, citing an NRC study which found that the steel vessel which contained the reactor core had become dangerously weakened — the term was "embrittled" — by 30 years of intense radiation.

"If there was the start of a meltdown, if they had to bring cold water in to cool it off, it could shatter like glass," Katz said. "We realized we had to form an organization, not just a group of people."

CAN learned that Rowe's owners were planning to apply for a 20-year extension to the plant's 40-year operating license. If that went through, Rowe would become the first — among dozens of U.S. nuclear plants that came online during the industry's boom years, in the late 1960s and early '70s — to extend its lifespan beyond the originally planned four decades.

CAN joined the effort to shut Yankee Rowe down for good. That July, nearly 1,000 people attended a public hearing at the Rowe Elementary School on the petition to extend the plant's license. Most called for closure. But the NRC denied the shutdown petition, saying the plant was safe.

But a few months later, the NRC said a closer inspection had found that Rowe might not be so safe after all. Its operators said the cost of the repairs now called for would be too great; they decided, instead, to shut down and dismantle the aging plant.

Yankee Rowe had been built for $39 million. The total cost of its decommissioning was $608 million, and the process took 15 years, from 1992 to 2007. The plant's most radioactive components, the spent fuel rods from its reactor core, were encased in 16 steel canisters inside reinforced concrete casks. Because the nation has still not settled on a disposal site for high-level nuclear waste, those casks remain on the ground at the old plant's otherwise empty site by the river. They're watched over by guards armed with automatic weapons.

Some 650 tons of Rowe's low-level radioactive waste, including piping, tubing, cable and the embrittled reactor vessel, were shipped to a landfill for low-level waste in rural Barnwell County, South Carolina. A 2007 investigation by *The State* newspaper of South Carolina found that groundwater beneath the landfill, near the Savannah River, had levels of tritium, a radioactive isotope, "exceeding the Environmental Protection Agency's standard for safe drinking water — in some cases by hundreds of times." By 2019, the landfill operator still had not stemmed the groundwater leaks.

After Rowe shut down in 1992, in the quiet communities around it "we were all going to get back to working in our gardens and forget about all this," Deb Katz recalled. But some of those who'd formed the Citizens Awareness Network continued to study and learn. They found out more about the potential health impacts of radioactive waste in their community, about the targeting of low-income regions like Barnwell County for long-term waste disposal, and about the vulnerability to terrorist attacks of the continuing storage of spent fuel rods in pools of water at still-active nuclear plants.

CAN's membership decided to stay together. With Katz as executive director, their numbers grew to include residents of southern Vermont, southwestern New Hampshire and western Massachusetts. In the years to come, CAN would focus more and more of its attention on Vermont Yankee, the plant that was continuing to generate power alongside the Connecticut River.

A fateful change

Vermont Yankee was under construction in 1971 when Diana Sidebotham moved to a farm in Putney, Vermont. When she learned that a nuclear plant was being built about a half hour's drive away in Vernon, she thought that sounded like a good thing, using atomic energy to make electricity rather than war. But soon she learned that even small amounts of radiation emitted by a nuclear plant could have worrying impacts on human genetics — and that "many questions regarding safety and engineering were left unanswered, swept under the rug," Sidebotham told Vermont Public Radio in a 2008 interview.

"Also," she said, "the public is aware that there is a huge problem with nuclear waste storage, both low-level and high-level."

Sidebotham became instrumental in the creation of the New England Coalition on Nuclear Pollution, later just the New England Coalition. She would serve as its executive director for the next 37 years.

In 1971, the Coalition intervened in the application for a 40-year operating license that had been filed by the eight utilities that owned and were building Vermont Yankee — principally the state's two largest utilities, Green Mountain Power and Central Vermont Public Service.

Yankee was a 620-megawatt boiling-water reactor. That design, one of two used in American reactors at the time — and the design used at Fukushima — called for water to circulate through the plant's nuclear core, which would boil it to make the steam driving the power-generating turbines. Yankee's heated water would then be cooled and returned to the Connecticut River, at temperatures that still were warmer than the water in the river. The Coalition's bid to block the plant from starting up was partly based on concerns, shared by scientists, environmentalists and citizens, that the heated water could destroy habitats and kill fish in the river.

The petition failed. The operating license was granted. But in responding to the heated water concerns, Yankee's builders made an addition that would, in time, prove fateful.

Near the building that housed the reactor, they installed a pair of elongated cooling towers, each one 60 feet tall and containing 11 cells where the heated water could be sprayed on corrugated metal to further cool it before it was returned to the river. Each cooling tower had a support structure built of wood. That wood softened over time, causing a breakdown at one tower that would become the very visible start to a series of public mishaps that gave potent new fuel to the campaign to close the nuclear plant.

The cooling towers also didn't solve the heated-water problem. The Lintilhac Foundation would in time support the Connecticut River Watershed Council, now the Connecticut River Conservancy, in its years-long, ultimately successful fight to prove that thermal pollution from the power plant was doing "irreparable damage," as the organization maintained, to the river's aquatic ecosystem.

VPIRG: "A force in the state"

Vermont Yankee came online in 1972, and so that year did the Vermont Public Interest Research Group. Over the decades to come, VPIRG would become in many ways the power plant's most formidable adversary.

VPIRG's roots trace back to a 1971 book co-authored by activist Ralph Nader, called *Action for a Change: A Student's Manual for Public Interest Organizing*. The paperback inspired students at campuses around the country to start up state-focused "public interest research groups," or PIRGs. Each participating college could allow students to direct a portion of their activity fees toward an ongoing stream of funding for their state's PIRG.

After Nader described his idea to some 3,000 listeners at the University of Vermont, UVM students created VPIRG in company with students at Goddard,

new england

news in brief

VPIRG Wants Plan For Closing Yankee

MONTPELIER (UPI) — The Vermont Public Interest Research Group today called on the state to set up a panel to plan for the eventual closing of the Vermont Yankee nuclear plant in Vernon.

The group also reiterated its belief Vermont Yankee should be made financially responsible for the costs of the permanent shutdown through written agreements with the state.

Vermont Yankee will be closed at the end of its useful life (decommissioned) some time after the turn of the century. The currently scheduled year is 2007

From the *Brattleboro Reformer* in 1975.

Castleton State and Johnson State colleges. They set up a funding stream for the new group from student fees at the colleges, then found an office in Montpelier and hired an executive director, the late Scott Skinner.

"In the 1970s VPIRG was a force in the state on environmental and consumer issues, organizing one of the first bottle bills in the country, legislation protecting drinking water, providing early opposition to nuclear power, and helping establish dental protection for kids," recalled a 2018 article in the *Burlington Free Press* by three co-authors, including Richard Watts, director of the Center for Research on Vermont at UVM.

In 1975, VPIRG "called on the state to set up a panel to plan for the eventual closing of the Vermont Yankee nuclear power plant," said a story in the *Brattleboro Reformer*. At the end of its 40-year license, the group argued, "it will be expensive to dismantle the plant in such a way that radioactivity does not endanger the environment."

Years later, as VPIRG led the final push for the Vermont Senate's 2010 shutdown vote, a photocopy of that old *Reformer* story would be pinned up prominently on a bulletin board at the nonprofit's office.

But back in those early years of the PIRG movement, powerful forces retaliated.

"You try to work the system"

"In the late 1970s, conservative student groups, with funding from the Koch brothers," oil-wealthy businessmen Charles and David Koch, "launched campaigns at campuses across the U.S. to defund PIRGs," recalled the *Free Press* article by Watts and others. "PIRG chapters were bounced from campuses across the U.S., defunding the organizations and limiting the activists. In Vermont, VPIRG lost its campus chapters in 1978 and by 1979 the budget was close to default. By 1982 the staff was down to one."

In mid-1982, the struggling group got a new executive director in George Hamilton, a personable, hard-working young organizer. Joining Hamilton as associate director the next year was Cort Richardson, an anti-nuclear activist who had moved to Vermont from New Hampshire after being involved for several years with the Seabrook protests and the Clamshell Alliance.

"I brought with me all this experience," Richardson recalled, "and we continued to focus on the problems at Yankee. The plant had a whole series of episodes: minor accidents, failed systems, unscheduled releases of radiation into the environment, problems with their cooling system. So we followed all that.

"This is the Ralph Nader approach: research," he explained. "You learn about the issue you're concerned about. You educate others, you organize them, and you take action. But that action is through the system — you intervene in legal proceedings, you petition for redress from authorities, you try to work the system to bring about positive change. And this is a hard row to hoe, when the system is so captured by big special interests."

Richardson had been one of those 1,414 Seabrook protesters who were arrested in 1977 and jailed after refusing bail. He and other Clamshell Alliance volunteers were carefully trained in nonviolent direct action, following the model developed by Mahatma Gandhi for India's

Paul Burns became executive director of the Vermont Public Interest Research Group in 2000.

independence struggle, and adapted for the American civil rights movement by Dr. Martin Luther King, Jr.

"That was a requirement for participation — the history, the principles, the tactics," Richardson said. "You had to know what you were doing, because things could get heated."

Richardson became VPIRG's executive director in 1985, after George Hamilton moved on to direct policy research for then-Gov. Madeleine Kunin. VPIRG began to raise awareness about an effort by the U.S. Energy Department to consider whether large rock formations around the country, including in northern Vermont, could be candidates for storing high-level nuclear waste.

"This was an enormous story," Richardson said. "People really identified with it, and VPIRG took a big step in terms of our resources, our membership. I became a speaker on tour, to talk about nuclear waste issues — and this sort of catapulted VPIRG into prominence, within the state and outside it."

Having lost its original funding stream from student fees, VPIRG had been patching together support from private donors, foundations and membership fees. Then in 1985, Joan Mulhern, a UVM student, came to Richardson with an idea.

Mulhern had been part of a national nonprofit's summer canvassing campaign. "She said, 'I've just spent the last two summers canvassing, and I think we could do that,'" Richardson said. "That created a whole new funding source that really worked well — but it was also consistent with our mission, which was to educate people.

"We brought information to people, we got names, and they became the base. When we were promoting legislation, we had this whole group of members that we could communicate with, and organize them and fire them up.

"That was the lead-in to the next step forward, which happened with the arrival of Paul Burns, and the Lintilhac Foundation and others getting involved," Richardson noted.

Burns, a talented and sophisticated PIRG organizer, became executive director in 2000. In the years that followed, Richardson said, "VPIRG took on a much broader mission as it built the resources to hire more staff and take on new challenges."

Crea Lintilhac joined VPIRG's board in 1998 (she serves on it still), and the next year the foundation became a steady supporter of the organization. Soon, all these elements — new VPIRG leadership, new funding support, even its summer canvass operation — would become key contributors to a whole new push to retire the Vermont Yankee power plant once and for all.

A big nuclear industry player moves north

As the new millenium began, a new player in this developing drama came to Vermont from New Orleans. It was a very large corporation, soon to be well-known to people all over this state, in name at least. It was called Entergy.

It was 2001, after the utilities that owned Vermont Yankee had applied for state permission to sell it, when Entergy stepped in. The Vermont utilities were observing the enormous costs still piling up for the decommissioning of Yankee Rowe — and for another plant now shut down in Maine — and "were becoming increasingly uncomfortable with the responsibility of owning and operating a nuclear power plant," said *Public Meltdown: The Story of the Vermont Yankee Nuclear Power Plant*, a thoroughly researched book by Richard Watts, director of UVM's Center for Research on Vermont.

Much of the country's utility industry had, since the late 1990s, been entering a new era. Many states (not including Vermont) had deregulated the production and sale of electric power — and that, Watts wrote, "had started to change the vertical utility model, wherein companies owned power plants and provided retail electricity services. ... Instead, companies formed solely to own power plants, selling the electricity directly into wholesale markets."

Entergy was a big player in this lucrative and fast-growing market. The company had been coming together and growing since the 1920s, through mergers and integration of electric utilities in Arkansas, Mississippi and Louisiana. By the time it put in a bid for Vermont Yankee, a subsidiary of Entergy Corp. called Entergy Nuclear was on a New England acquisition spree that also included its purchase of the Pilgrim nuclear plant in Massachusetts and the FitzPatrick and Indian Point Units 2 and 3 in New York. With 11 total plants in seven states, Entergy was becoming the nation's second-largest operator of nuclear generating stations.

But Entergy was not Yankee's first suitor. The plant's owners initially sought permission from the Vermont Public Service Board to sell it to AmerGen, another nuclear operator, for a price that started at $61 million, then plummeted to less than $10 million.

"Several groups in Vermont opposed the sale, most notably the Conservation Law Foundation," *Public Meltdown* related. CLF's Mark Sinclair "blasted the agreement for its fire-sale price, arguing the plant was worth much more. The Board agreed, requiring the Vermont utilities to competitively auction the plant."

Entergy won the bidding and, in 2002, bought Vermont Yankee for $180 million.

At that point, Yankee, which employed more than 600 people, had been operating for 30 years on a 40-year license. Throughout three decades it had reliably met 25 to 30 percent of Vermont's power needs. As part of its purchase agreement,

Entergy committed to selling Yankee's power to Vermont utilities "at less than they would have expected to pay had they retained ownership," Watts wrote, "thus reducing electric rates for most Vermonters."

Even so, CLF, VPIRG and the New England Coalition all called the sale a bad deal. "From now on," said CLF's Sinclair, "the future of the plant will be dictated by the bottom-line financials of an out-of-state company."

"I have lingering doubts"

n 2003, Entergy's first major move after its purchase of Yankee was to ask the federal Nuclear Regulatory Commission for permission to boost the plant's power output by 20 percent. This was part of a trend among the owners of the nation's aging nuclear stations.

"With new power plants increasingly difficult to build, the industry turned to increasing the operating capacity of the existing fleet," *Public Meltdown* said.

"... During the 1970s and 1980s, nuclear plants ran only 60 to 70 percent of the time. By the 1990s, the industry had increased this number to above 90 percent. ... These changes meant that nuclear power continued to contribute about 20 percent of total U.S. electricity."

Area residents and the New England Coalition energetically opposed the bid to boost Yankee's output. The NRC reviewed it more closely than it had any previous increase at any other nuclear plant — but in early 2006, the Commission granted approval.

"I have lingering doubts about the NRC's confidence that a 34-year-old reactor design can sustain increased power outputs," Crea Lintilhac wrote in a *Burlington Free Press* opinion piece at that time. "They simply don't have the data to make predictions, and nuclear power is an unforgiving industry."

"My opposition to nuclear power was spawned by my work on the Sub Seabed Disposal Program for Sandia Laboratories and the [U.S.] Department of Energy, at the Rhode Island Graduate School of Oceanography," she explained later. "This was an international consortium with members from France, Japan, Canada and the United States. My job was to find the most quiescent and geologically stable places on the Pacific sea floor for the safe disposal (deep burial) of processed high-level radioactive waste or

Veteran journalist John Dillon retired in 2021 as senior reporter and former news director for Vermont Public Radio. His career in news, first in print and then on radio, spanned some four decades.

spent reactor fuel.

"The program was later abandoned – mostly because the issues around transportation and containment of high-level radioactive waste were insurmountable. The conclusion, in my mind, is that there is no safe place on earth to dispose of high-level radioactive waste from the weapons industry or civilian reactors for the vast lengths of time necessary. We would have to bury canisters in the seabed that are supposed to last hundreds of thousands of years. I also believe that building civilian reactors leads to the proliferation of nuclear weapons."

An oil fire erupted within Vermont Yankee at 6:40 a.m. on Friday, June 18, 2004, while the plant was running at full power. The heat triggered an emergency sprinkler system, and within half an hour the Yankee and local Vernon fire departments had the blaze fully out. But Yankee was forced to shut down for more than two weeks, causing Vermont utilities to look elsewhere for power — and startling photos of the fire found their way to the New England Coalition.

"The blaze that started near a transformer caused cooling pumps that supply water to the reactor to stop working," Vermont Public Radio reported a few days after the incident. "The fire also caused the plant's circulation pumps to trip, or stop working," VPR's John Dillon said. He quoted Ray Shadis, of the New England Coalition, saying that those pumps "have a real safety significance."

The following week, a Nuclear Regulatory Commission spokesman told the press that a piece of an expansion joint, original equipment on the 32-year-old reactor, had broken off inside a pipe or duct that carried electricity to the plant's transformer.

"Part of an expansion joint just basically peeled off and, rattling around in the duct, it caused [electrical] shorts and faults," the spokesman said, according to a July 4 Associated Press report. "An oil pipe came loose and because of very high temperatures associated with the raw electricity, a fire started."

"The root causes of the event were determined to be inadequate preventative maintenance," the NRC said in its final report on the incident. "There was no release of radioactivity, or personnel injury during this event."

Entergy said the fire was unrelated to its bid to boost Yankee's power output by 20 percent, and the NRC accepted that. But the brief fire and resulting shutdown were, at least, a foreshadow of the alarming mishaps that would begin piling up at Yankee in the years not far ahead.

"Extending licenses became a critical issue"

long with the push to boost output, the nuclear power industry was also focused on extending operating licenses. Wrote Watts, in his 2012 book:

With the licenses of almost half the [civilian nuclear] fleet set to expire by 2015, extending licenses became a critical issue for the survival of the industry. The industry and the NRC discussed this ... leading to the creation of relicensing regulations in 1991.

... In 1995, the NRC amended the regulations to establish a more efficient, stable and predictable process. The new rule provided more credit for existing plant operator safety efforts, de-emphasized the plant's previous operating record, and restricted opposition groups' access to the process. Critics said the NRC had weakened the relicensing rules, because without the changes, older plants ... would not have been able to win license extensions.

Since 2000, the NRC has issued new licenses for all 71 of the reactors that have completed applications.

In March 2006, after thousands of hours of preparation, Entergy delivered to the NRC its application for a 20-year license extension. In spite of dogged opposition by the New England Coalition, its bid would be among those that won NRC approval.

Even so, "the only time owners of VY ever told a judge or regulators that public pressure or advocacy was having an impact on their operations ... was when NECNP [the New England Coalition on Nuclear Pollution] was challenging the license renewal to allow operations beyond 2012," said Clay Turnbull of the Coalition.

But something else happened in early 2006. It was an action by the Vermont Legislature that at the time did not seem terribly important, except to the nonprofits that were determined to keep Vermont Yankee from generating power and radioactivity for another two decades.

The Legislature had recently passed a bill that gave Entergy state approval to move some of its spent fuel rods, the plant's high-level radioactive waste, from pool storage into sealed casks at Yankee's site in Vernon, close to the local elementary school. Negotiations over that bill centered on the House Natural Resources and Energy Committee and its influential chair, Democrat Tony Klein of East Montpelier.

Openly skeptical of nuclear power, Klein had been an early promoter of renewable energy in Vermont. Before joining the Legislature in 2003, he had worked as a State House lobbyist for the Vermont Independent Power Producers Association and Renewable Energy Vermont (REV), two of the state's pioneering sustainable-energy advocates.

The legislation that would allow Entergy to move some spent fuel rods into dry casks was critical for the company. Without it, Klein said, "They didn't have enough room in their pool to complete their license run. So I went to REV, the [renewable energy] industry, and I said, 'How much money for how many years do you folks need to mature your industries?' And that's all you're going to get — there's not going to be any extensions, nothing.

"They said, 'Seven to ten years, $7 million to $10 million a year,'" Klein recalled. "We got eight years at $8 million a year — and that's what funded many of our renewable energy projects." In the end, Entergy would make payments totaling over $25 million into Vermont's Clean Energy Development Fund.

The negotiated bill was given the name Act 74 when Gov. Jim Douglas, a Republican who had been supportive of Vermont Yankee and Entergy, signed it into law in June 2005. The governor's approval opened the door for another legislative action, the following year. *Public Meltdown* picks up the story:

> As the plant increased its thermal output in January 2006, Entergy filed the 20-year license extension application with the NRC. In Montpelier, legislators gathered for the 2006 legislative session.
>
> ... As the session started, about four blocks from the Capitol in a run-down two-story office building, staffers at VPIRG kicked around ideas for the 2006 legislative session. Newly hired "energy advocate" James Moore joined the brainstorming. ... One idea the organizers came up with was to require that Entergy receive legislative approval, in addition to PSB approval, for their license extension.
>
> Giving the Legislature a voice seemed to be a natural extension of Entergy's 2002 commitment ... in line with the recent debate around Act 74. Vermont Yankee opposition groups and their allies in southern Vermont and the Legislature framed the issue as democratic, simply giving legislators a voice in this important decision.
>
> ... Entergy resisted the added level of approval, testifying in opposition, calling it "unnecessary" and pointing out the company was already committed to seeking PSB approval. Legislative leadership strongly endorsed the concept and the law passed the House by a margin of 130-0 and the Senate 18-5.
>
> "This is an important issue for Vermont," Gov. Douglas told a reporter. "I don't think it's at all unrealistic that elected officials should weigh in." Entergy put a positive face on the new law as well, with plant spokesman Robert Williams saying, "We commend the Legislature, especially the House Natural Resources [and Energy] Committee, for putting a lot of effort into drafting a bill that should serve the state well."

"I'm sort of leaning forward"

Duane Peterson is an experienced policy analyst and political organizer from California who managed 14 election campaigns there, including two gubernatorial efforts and the successful 1992 State Senate bid by activist

Tom Hayden. He came to Vermont in 1996, hired by Ben Cohen of Ben & Jerry's "to help him run the business as a force for social change," Peterson said. He would stay with the company as its "chief of stuff" for 12 years.

Looking to get involved in volunteer work in Vermont, "I kind of went shopping for a standup, aggressive environmental outfit, and chose VPIRG," Peterson said. "I joined the board in, I would guess, 1998.

"As a board member, my purpose was to actually contribute. So I sought out who I thought was the most dynamic staff person to engage, and that was James Moore. He was the Clean Energy Program director, and at that time clean energy was the most substantial of the campaigns at VPIRG. So I started hanging out with him."

Peterson had volunteered in California with the activist group that had successfully campaigned for the country's first shutdown of a nuclear power plant by citizen referendum, the Rancho Seco closure in 1989. That was the only time, so far, that a nuclear plant had been closed by a public vote. As he began serving with VPIRG, Peterson observed Entergy's nuclear plant-buying spree in New England.

"Utilities were happy to unload these aging industrial plants, and all the high-level radioactive waste that comes with them," he said. "So Entergy bought these things for pennies on the dollar, and figured they would come up to Vermont and these other little states and just have their way with these pissant little legislatures, the way they were accustomed to in the South.

"So in Vermont, their first act was to up-rate, to literally turn up the dial on this electricity factory and have it create more power. Well, power is revenue, so now they're printing money from this thing; and their next gambit was to get a 20-year license extension. Mind you, this thing was designed in the '60s — oddly, painfully, the same design as the ones that are still hemorrhaging radiation in Fukushima, Japan.

"So this is unfolding, and James, over beers, tells me that he and others had inserted a small clause into a Vermont statute that gave the Legislature a role in licensing large-scale power plants. So I'm sort of leaning forward in my chair.

"The federal government has so-called preemption authority over nuclear safety," Peterson noted — "but we still operate in a regulated utility environment in Vermont. State governments typically delegate that authority to some expert bureaucracy, like a public utilities commission. Those are the experts, and we rely on them to figure out this mind-numbingly complicated stuff.

"But that is done through statute — and just as a statute could delegate authority, it could retain some of that authority to the Legislature itself. That is exactly what James and some others had done."

The new law, enacted in 2006, was labeled Act 160. It required a positive vote, by both chambers of the Legislature, for Vermont to approve an extension of Yankee's license.

"We were trying to make a veto-proof legislation," explained Deb Katz of the Citizens Awareness Network, which worked with VPIRG to help shape the bill and advocate for it. "If it was a negative vote," thereby denying the extension, "the governor couldn't veto. That was a big process we went through, to make it impossible for the governor to stop Vermont Yankee from closure."

"We call this a focusing moment"

One hot afternoon — August 21, 2007 — as the temperature climbed into the 80s, plant technicians heard rubbing sounds coming from one of the cooling tower fans. ... Before they could act, a rotting wooden support beam carrying the water pipe in one of the towers dropped four inches. When the beam fell, the pipe burst and water then exploded through a hole in the side of the tower, cascading down in a torrent, carrying debris with it.

Plant technicians immediately reduced power as workers sought to understand and repair the damage. ... The cooling tower collapse was not considered a safety event because that particular tower was not essential to plant operation. Because of the "non-safety" categorization of the incident, local public officials were not immediately informed, in some cases learning about the incident first from a newspaper reporter. One of the workers at the site snapped a few photos.

— *Public Meltdown*

A photo that showed water gushing out from the ruptured cooling tower quickly found its way to the *Brattleboro Reformer*. The paper put the image on the top of page one, with the headline "VY cuts output after cooling failure." The same image was emailed (its photographer went unnamed) to Ray Shadis, an outspoken nuclear expert with the New England Coalition. Shadis passed it on to James Moore at VPIRG. Moore shared it with other media and other nonprofits — and soon after, Richard Watts wrote, the cooling tower photo "buzzed around the Internet.

August 21, 2007: Water explodes from a ruptured cooling tower at Vermont Yankee.

"A few days later the state's top regulator, DPS (Department of Public Service) Commissioner David O'Brien, visited the plant and announced that the cooling tower collapse was an 'isolated problem,'" said *Public Meltdown*. "Unfortunately for Entergy, as O'Brien left the plant, a faulty valve forced an automatic shutdown — or scram — spurring another round of internal and external investigations and an additional wave of media coverage."

"Vermont Yankee is slowly but surely falling apart," the *Brattleboro Reformer* declared in an editorial. "Incidents like last week's cooling tower collapse do not increase public confidence. ... Neither do emergency shutdowns. While the public was not in danger in either mishap, who's to say that we won't be as lucky the next time?"

"In the academic literature, we call things like this a focusing moment," said Richard Watts in an interview. "This was an enormously focusing moment."

Indeed, the cooling-tower mishap is "what turned public opinion in this state," said Tony Klein, the state legislator who in 2009 became the chair of the House Natural Resources and Energy Committee. "Nails and sticks, and you can't keep it together — and you expect us to have confidence in this?"

Until the coverage of the tower incident took hold, concern about Yankee and opposition to it had mostly been centered on the plant's home region around Brattleboro. "VPIRG was involved, but it wasn't really a statewide effort," Watts

In Montpelier in 2018, calling for safer disposal of high-level nuclear waste: from left, Leona Morgan, board member of Citizens Awareness Network; Chris Williams, Vermont CAN organizer; Kirsten Rudik, German anti-nuclear activist; Deborah Katz of CAN; and Tim Judson, president of CAN and executive director of the nonprofit Nuclear Information and Resource Service in Washington, D.C. *Photo courtesy of CAN.*

noted. "Why should someone in Burlington care about Vermont Yankee?"

But during the autumn after the mishaps, a poll by the Burlington TV station WPAX found that 58 percent of Vermonters who answered the survey were "concerned" or "very concerned" about safety at Yankee.

"VPIRG was able to raise some money around it," Watts said, "and then they did this communications thinking. 'How do we reframe this in a way that's going to make a difference everywhere in Vermont?'

"They did all the things that a strategic communications firm would do. What are the most powerful messages? What are the audiences that we need to reach, and how do we best reach them? What's an authentic message that builds on this 40-year effort?"

"From 2006 to 2010, there was a very intensive organizing and advocacy effort," said Paul Burns, who has been VPIRG's executive director since 2000. The collaborators were "a bunch of very citizen-based organizations," he said, "some of which had modest budgets, some of which had no budgets, just volunteer-based."

Notable among those was the Citizens Awareness Network, working in the power plant's home neighborhood.

"We changed the way people messaged the issue," said CAN's Katz. "We made it a positive campaign about what people could do, rather than a negative campaign about what was wrong with the reactor. VPIRG and CAN worked together on this, and the Sierra Club at the time.

"The job was about moving the middle," she said. "It didn't matter what the nuclear fanatics wanted to do; it didn't even matter what our own people wanted to do. We had to move the average working person who hardly spends time on this issue, and help them wake up to why it was bad for Vermont."

"This four-year effort to organize"

For Yankee to extend its operating license beyond 2012, "the Legislature needed to say 'yes' to a new certificate of public good," or CPG, said Paul Burns. "So we started meeting monthly, down at the house of one of the coalition members in Springfield. It was this four-year effort to organize, to actually get people to raise their voices and talk to their legislators, and urge them to ultimately deny the CPG."

"All those groups were good at the local fight," Richard Watts observed — "but it was really VPIRG that made it statewide. To win a vote in the State Legislature, which hadn't been done in any state, you had to make it matter to people up here."

The Lintilhac Foundation began supporting VPIRG in 1999 with modest general grants, plus a larger one for a "project investigating the early closing of Vermont Yankee." The foundation has continued to make grants to the nonprofit,

A 2012 march to the headquarters of Vermont Yankee, organized by the Citizens Awareness Network. *Photo courtesy of CAN.*

first for its Yankee campaign and then, starting in 2004, in support of VPIRG's efforts to promote clean and sustainable energy in Vermont.

Foundation grants also supported the Conservation Law Foundation's work on challenging Entergy's various regulatory filings. While VPIRG and its allies focused on public education, grassroots organizing, the media and the Legislature, "Sandy Levine at CLF was always thinking about the legal strategy — and that was really important," said Watts. "While VPIRG was running its political campaign, there were at the same time these ongoing regulatory processes."

Other nonprofits that the foundation supported during the Yankee campaign from 2006 to 2010 were the Nuclear Policy Research Institute, Vermonters for a Clean Environment, the Toxics Action Center, CAN, Greenpeace, the Consensus Building Institute, and Fairewinds Energy Education, a research-and-education nonprofit then based in Burlington.

Fairewinds had been co-founded by Maggie Gundersen, a journalist who had been a spokesperson in the nuclear power industry, and her husband, Arnold "Arnie" Gundersen. He was a knowledgeable and experienced nuclear engineer who had worked in the atomic power industry until the early '90s, when he appears to have been blacklisted by the industry for calling attention to radiation safety violations.

During the campaign to close Yankee, "Arnie was really important," said Watts. "He provided this credible nuclear scientist voice. People would attack him all the time, but he was never wrong — whereas Entergy, with all their lawyers, was wrong."

"We organized other groups, who got out and were doing walks," said Katz of CAN. "We wound up holding a rally with over 2,000 people in Brattleboro. We did all this lobbying work, we raised all of this money, and the Lintilhacs were really helpful.

"There are very few groups that will support anti-nuclear activities," she said. "It's usually family foundations that are concerned about the health consequences going on in their communities, or are concerned about how the nukes are eating up the ability to bring in sustainable energy. And these were the foundations that really helped us with this — because the big foundations wouldn't touch it."

"Crea and the foundation committed funds from the get-go," confirmed Duane Peterson, the VPIRG board member and activist.

"That's the craziest thing in the world"

"Starting in 2006, after James Moore was hired," wrote Watts in *Public Meltdown*, "VPIRG resources allocated to opposing Vermont Yankee increased sharply, growing more than five-fold and peaking in the two-month period leading up to the State Senate's 2010 vote. ... The Citizens Awareness Network also sharply stepped up its lobbying activities, hiring Bob Stannard as a full-time lobbyist."

Stannard is a colorfully blunt-spoken Vermonter who represented the Manchester area in the State House from 1983 to 1986 as a moderate Republican. He moved on to managing a local trash collection service ("I went from politics to garbage and saw it as a promotion," he told *VTDigger*), then became executive director of the Better Bennington Corporation. That, he said, was a good job.

Then in November 2007, Stannard agreed to meet with Katz and three other CAN activists. They pitched him on becoming CAN's lobbyist in the State House — a place to which, Stannard said, he had "pretty much no" desire to return.

"Her little band of advocates took me out to lunch, and there goes the good job," he said. "I didn't think nuclear power was all that bad; I didn't give a shit, I'm like everybody else. I said to them, 'You understand, there's like a 3 percent chance of doing this [shutting down Yankee].' And they're looking at me like, 'Yeah, well, so? That's better than 2 percent.' And I'm thinking they're nuts. You can't shut down a nuclear plant, that's the craziest thing in the world! So I said, 'Let me think about it.'"

Stannard, who was moonlighting as a blues harmonica player and bandleader, started reading all he could find about Yankee and Entergy. He came on the photo of the cooling-tower collapse. "It shows up on my computer screen and I'm like, 'Son of a bitch! If this company that owns this plant let it go into a state of disrepair to the degree that the cooling tower collapses, what else are they ignoring?'

"It sure was an indication that these guys aren't taking very good care of the plant. I said, 'God almighty, if there's something I can do to close this thing down, I owe it to my grandkids, who weren't even born at the time.'"

Stannard took the lobbying job.

"This was supposed to be a one- or two-year gig," he said. "It went on for seven years."

"Entergy also dialed up its legislative activities, increasing spending from $59,000 in 2007 to $361,000 in 2008, of which $244,000 was allocated to a paid media campaign," said *Public Meltdown*. The corporation added a second lobbying contractor in Montpelier, and a pro-nuclear group that called itself the Vermont Energy Partnership placed full-page ads in Vermont newspapers. The ads called nuclear power "Safe and Green," declaring: "Safe, clean, reliable and economically sound nuclear power is green power for the Green Mountain State."

In March 2008, Entergy applied to the state Public Service Board for the certificate of public good it needed to extend Yankee's operating license. The PSB was the regulating authority with the power to grant or deny the certificate, pending the needed approval from each chamber of the State House.

That summer, VPIRG canvassers visited with more than 30,000 Vermonters at their homes in some 111 towns. The young canvassers offered each one a brochure with the tower-collapse photo, along with a postcard that also showed the photo, with "UNSAFE AND UNRELIABLE" printed across the image.

"Closing Vermont Yankee as scheduled is the responsible thing to do," the post-card declared. "... Entergy's lobbyists are flooding our Statehouse. Go to VPIRG. org to contact your legislators and tell them to:

"Retire the reactor as planned."

"That fall," wrote Watts, "VPIRG delivered 12,000 postcards to Vermont legislators calling for Vermont Yankee to close."

CLOSING VERMONT YANKEE AS SCHEDULED IS THE RESPONSIBLE THING TO DO.

- The plant is too old to be safe or reliable.
- Entergy, the out-of-state corporate owners of Vermont Yankee, repeatedly lied about pipes leaking radioactive pollution into our groundwater.
- Keeping the reactor open past 2012 means risking more leaks and contamination, and Vermonters could get stuck with the billion dollar clean-up bill.

ACT NOW!
Entergy's lobbyists are flooding our Statehouse. Go to **VPIRG.ORG** to contact your legislators and tell them to

RETIRE THE REACTOR AS PLANNED.

Paid for by Vermont Public Interest Research Group (VPIRG). VPIRG is the largest nonprofit consumer and environmental advocacy organization in Vermont, promoting and protecting the health of Vermont's people, environment and locally-based economy by informing and mobilizing citizens statewide.

Vermont Yankee cooling tower collapse, 2007.

VPIRG canvassers distributed this postcard around the state in summer 2008.

Ammunition to the opposition

Gov. Douglas supported Yankee's bid to extend its license. "This is the cheapest power we have," he said, according to *Public Meltdown*, which also quoted Brad Ferland, president of the pro-nuclear Vermont Energy Partnership: "Because of Vermont Yankee's dependable and low-cost power, Vermonters have the lowest electric rates in New England."

Considerable economic leverage confronted the campaign to retire the reactor. "Originally purchased for $180 million in 2002, the plant had an estimated value of $239 million by 2006," *Public Meltdown* noted. "By 2009, Entergy was running the plant 93 percent of the time, on average ... the plant's gross sales averaged $200 million annually."

The plant continued to meet a third of Vermont's energy needs — and because of the favorable, 10-year power sales agreement that Entergy negotiated with Vermont utilities when it bought the plant, ratepayers in the state had access to Yankee's power for about 4 cents per kilowatt hour until 2012. Wholesale prices for power in the region were running from 4.3 cents to 8.8 cents per kWh.

"Economic value was a powerful message," Watts wrote, "and plant opponents knew they had to change the conversation." They focused on portraying Yankee as a deteriorating plant that should be retired on schedule, and Entergy as its "out-of-state corporate owner."

The out-of-state owner continued to give ammunition to its opposition. Shortly before submitting its state approval bid, Entergy said it would create a new subsidiary called Enexus that would own its nuclear plants, including Yankee, along with several billion dollars in related debt.

"Enexus is nothing more than a shell game," VPIRG's Colleen Halley declared in a statement from the group. Noting that the new entity had a "junk bond" credit rating, VPIRG charged that "Vermont Yankee has yet to answer how this will be good for Vermonters. With such a high level of debt, how will this spinoff company be financially viable?"

Entergy's estimate of the costs for decommissioning Yankee alone were well over $1 billion. The Vermont utilities that first owned the plant had built up a $310 million fund for its decommissioning. That fund's value continued to grow through earnings on investments; but Entergy, which had acquired the fund with its purchase of the plant, made no new contributions to it.

Entergy then declined to offer Vermont utilities a new power deal with favorable rates beyond 2012.

"The governor, the lawmakers, the utilities, the Department of Public Service and the Public Service Board have been waiting for Entergy to respond to requests for a power purchase agreement," Crea Lintilhac wrote in the *Burlington Free Press* in March 2009. "Meanwhile two deadlines have expired."

Entergy argued to the Public Service Board that other economic benefits it provided to the state — revenue sharing, tax payments and jobs for over 600 employees — should be enough for the certificate of public good it needed.

"They just for some reason could not negotiate a long-term deal with the Vermont utilities," recalled Tony Klein, the House Natural Resources and Energy Committee chair. "Didn't want to meet 'em halfway."

Finally, at the end of 2009, "Entergy came out with their 'best offer' – 6.1 cents per kilowatt hour," VPIRG noted in a statement. "That's 45 percent more than the rate they currently sell power to the utilities at, and barely less than the cost of clean, renewable energy.

"This is absurd," VPIRG charged. "Vermont Yankee has a sweetheart property tax deal, they provide fewer jobs than clean energy would, they produce dangerous, expensive radioactive waste and they have yet to fully fund their decommissioning. Vermont Yankee is a bad deal, period."

A mention of underground pipes

I n December 2008, a Tennessee nuclear engineering firm called Nuclear Safety Associates (NSA) reported that it had conducted a "comprehensive vertical audit" of Vermont Yankee's reliability, and had concluded that the plant was safe to run for another 20 years. In calling for the audit, the Legislature had asked NSA to find out if Yankee had any underground pipes that carried radionuclides, or unstable radioactive isotopes.

It did not, said the 415-page report NSA submitted to the state Department of Public Service.

"Despite this assurance, several independent observers remained unconvinced and kept asking questions," said Public Meltdown. "Chief among these was Arnie Gundersen," the veteran nuclear engineer.

Gundersen had become a special consultant on Yankee to the Legislature, which now hired him, together with Maggie Gundersen, to make an independent assessment of the consultant's report.

As part of his research, Arnie read through Entergy's 2008 annual report on effluent discharged by the plant. He "came across a mention of underground pipes that had leaked in the past," Watts wrote.

What followed was a dark comedy of confusion and contradiction, if not much worse. Gundersen pointedly asked the Department of Public Service if, in fact, Yankee had "underground piping that carries radioactivity."

DPS asked Entergy. Entergy said no. Asked again, Entergy said no again.

"We consider this issue closed," it declared.

But it was not.

֍

"The issue came up as Entergy Vice President Jay Thayer testified under oath last May [2009] at the Public Service Board," John Dillon reported that year on Vermont Public Radio. "With Thayer on the stand, lawyer John Cotter for the Department of Public Service asked:

"'Does Vermont Yankee have any underground piping that carries radionuclides?'

"Thayer paused for a full 12 seconds as he contemplated his answer. 'The reason I hesitate [Thayer said] is I don't believe there is active piping in service today carrying radionuclides underground.'

"Thayer went on to say that he was aware of an old underground piping system — but he said it was no longer in use," Dillon said.

During discovery for the Public Service Board hearing, a VPIRG attorney asked Entergy if it had *ever* had an underground piping system carrying radionuclides. Entergy said no, never.

Gov. Douglas made a statement urging state lawmakers to approve Entergy's relicensing. But on that same day, wrote Watts, "Entergy announced that a radioactive substance, tritium, had been discovered in one of the plant's monitoring wells."

֍

"The story continued to grow"

"The announcement ... flashed across headlines in Vermont's newspapers," said *Public Meltdown*. "... In the following days, the story continued to grow as radioactivity levels increased and Entergy scrambled to find the source. A few days later, officials announced that tritium had been found in a second monitoring well."

Gundersen told VPR that between autumn 2008 and autumn 2009, Entergy "had numerous opportunities to correct the record ... and they didn't. It was only when the pipes started to leak that they decided to correct the record."

"Gundersen said if the pipes are leaking, it could cost more to clean up the site and decommission the plant," added Dillon of VPR.

Entergy officials said they had taken the phrase "underground piping system" to mean only pipes buried in earth, not underground pipes encased in concrete. But semantics aside, the discovery of tritium in monitoring wells showed that pipes beneath ground level at the Yankee site *had* leaked radioactive fluid.

In early January, the Legislature convened for its 2010 session — and three days later, another tritium leak turned up in a monitoring well at the Yankee site. The radioactive isotope in this leak was measured at more than three times the federal limit for safety.

Entergy was by now receiving a torrent of bad publicity, and "every article that came out, I immediately made 180 copies and stuffed it in everybody's mailbox," said Bob Stannard, CAN's State House lobbyist. "I made goddamn sure they knew what was going on. It was a hard gig, but I have to hand a lot of credit to Entergy — they made my job so much easier by being such a bunch of incompetent boobs. It was unbelievable."

"Entergy made a ton of mistakes," agreed Duane Peterson, the VPIRG campaigner.

"At one point during this whole thing," said then-Rep. Tony Klein, "Entergy reaches out to me and says, We'd like to invite your whole committee down, we'd like you to tour the plant.' Great! Tell us when to come, you pick the date.

"They pick the date, we arrive. We go into the plant, and you have to go through all the security — and he says, 'Oh, the elevator's not working, so if you want to go see the wet pool storage and the top of the reactor, we're going to have to walk up seven flights.' You picked the date, and the elevator's not working? 'Oh, and by the way, walking up the stairs, don't use the bannister, because that's where the radiation collects, on the metal.'

"It's not like we had a surprise visit, here — you know how we feel about this place," Klein said, shaking his head. "And you can't even keep an elevator running?"

"We have to do it now"

Meanwhile, VPIRG's campaign coalition found itself having to execute a major last-minute shift in strategy.

Because of Act 160, a "no" vote in either the House or Senate on Entergy's bid to extend Yankee's license would block state approval. For some time, the campaigners had been focused on winning a vote in the House, which had voted unanimously for Act 160 and where organizers believed they had a better chance of winning.

"We had been organizing intensively for years with this whole coalition, all around the state, getting meetings in legislative districts, slowly moving the dial toward a vote for closure" in the House, said Ben Edgerly Walsh, who was then VPIRG's field director and now runs its Climate & Energy Program. "Then [Senate] President Pro Tem Peter Shumlin decided in late 2009 that we're going to do this in the Senate. And we're going to do it in 2010."

Shumlin represented Windham County, which included Vermont Yankee. He was eyeing the race for governor in 2010, which he would go on to win.

"So with a few months' notice," said Walsh, "we scrambled and tried to cram about three years of campaigning into six months in the Senate, and tried to get a similar level of in-district organizing happening all around the state. And that's of course also right around the time the tritium leaks started happening, in late December and early January."

"If we're going to do this, we have to do it now," said Duane Peterson. "So on little more than the back of a napkin, we put together the guts of what we thought could constitute a campaign. On December 29, we convened a group at Seventh Generation, their offices. Jeffrey Hollender, one of the founders of Seventh Generation, was on the board of VPIRG for a long time, and a fellow believer. So we convened a bunch of activists and some funders to propose this campaign. On the spot, we raised a couple hundred thousand dollars. And James said, 'Okay. We're doing this.'

"I went full-time [at VPIRG], and Jessica Edgerly Walsh managed the field effort," Peterson said. "She wove together 20 different organizations into a coalition." Walsh was working for the Toxics Action Center out of the VPIRG offices.

"We ran an adult, professional campaign," Peterson said. "We started with polling, to understand where people were at and what messaging worked and didn't work. We did professional advertising, targeting, and Jessica enforced messaging discipline — which is extraordinarily important, especially in a group of organizations that come to it with their own vantage points, their own histories.

"I think it was the quality of the campaign, and the message development and professional design and storytelling, that made it possible for these groups to throw in," Peterson summed up. Shumlin, he added, "was our champion. He was in our office weekly, and we worked hand-in-glove with him to map and perform

VPIRG staffers and volunteers on a phone bank before the crucial State Senate vote in 2010.

the campaign plan."

With the Legislature now in session, a room at VPIRG's headquarters on Main Street in Montpelier became the campaign's epicenter.

"We had on the big white board the 30 names [of senators], where they represent, and 15 other data points — how many VPIRG supporters we had there, what notable civic leaders do we have there, what's the local media landscape," Peterson said. "And then plotting a whole series of actions to garner the attention of that [senator]. It was quite targeted, quite focused, and that allowed the channeling of those resources in a very short period of time."

Within the State House, said CAN lobbyist Stannard, "I just kept the pressure on everybody.

"I worked on the Republicans, saying 'Listen, I know you love these guys, but they are not doing a good job down there!' First of all, it was an old plant, falling apart anyway. But they didn't do anything to fix any of that, because they didn't want to. They just wanted to suck money out of it, and then when they were done, walk away from the responsibility of cleaning up."

"We've made some mistakes"

"Levels of radioactive tritium have risen rapidly in recent weeks in the groundwater surrounding Vermont's sole nuclear power plant," the *New York Times* reported in late January 2010, "leading both long-time supporters and foes of the reactor to question whether it will be allowed to keep operating." Even though no tritium had yet shown up in drinking-water wells, the paper quoted Gov. Douglas, "a longtime supporter of the plant," saying that "recent events had 'raised dark clouds of doubt' about the plant's safety and management."

In early February, Entergy announced that the executive who had testified that Yankee had no underground pipes "has issued a public apology and made clear that he 'failed to provide full and complete information,'" said a report by *VTDigger*. Gov. Douglas had, the report said, "called for Entergy to make changes in management in order to restore the public's trust."

But events were now moving fast. On Feb. 16, Peter Shumlin said the State Senate would vote on Yankee's relicensing the following week.

Entergy quickly convened a press conference in the State House's ceremonial Cedar Creek Room. At the podium, Curtis Hebert, a poised and well-spoken executive vice president who had taken over the role of spokesperson, said the corporation was placing five senior employees on leave and reprimanding six others over the underground-piping confusion — even though, he maintained, there had been "no intention to mislead."

An in-depth investigation by Entergy had, Hebert said, found communication failures but no intentional falsehoods. He promised Entergy would do better.

"They said, 'We understand we've made some mistakes, we're going to turn over a new leaf. We're going to be ultra-transparent,' said Paul Burns of VPIRG. "And then they didn't take any questions from the media. At their press conference!"

Entergy also declined to make its own report public.

"They just didn't know how to operate in Vermont," VPIRG's Ben Walsh summed up.

"They got just about everybody"

n the final weeks before the Senate's planned vote, "the campaign was hitting full stride," said *Public Meltdown*. Emailing supporters around Vermont, VPIRG's James Moore stressed that Entergy officials had misled the public, even under oath. "We have to make sure legislators know that Vermonters won't stand for this kind of corporate behavior any longer," he wrote.

"By now more than five VPIRG staff were engaged full-time in the effort to close the plant," wrote Richard Watts. "Organizers from Greenpeace, League of Conservation Voters, VNRC, the Toxics Action Center, CAN and citizen activists with Safe Power Vermont joined the strategy sessions." Campaign volunteers sent out a flood of calls and emails to state senators. Several senators who had been undecided now said they would vote in favor of a motion to deny the license extension.

After months of advance work, some 200 activists organized by the nonprofit Safe and Green walked for 126 miles from Brattleboro to the State House, through the bitter January weather. They carried flags, signs, banners and a petition to the Legislature, signed by 1,656 residents of the three-state region around Yankee, calling for the plant to be retired on schedule.

The Senate vote was set for Wednesday, February 24. The day before, Entergy's Hebert held another press conference in the Cedar Creek Room. This time, he announced that the first 25 megawatts of Yankee's output would be sold to Vermonters at the discount rate of 4 cents per kilowatt hour.

In the exchange with reporters that followed his announcement,

Yannick Vedder bicycled Vermont byways as a VPIRG canvasser in summer 2018.

Hebert became dismissive and testy when asked if this offer was a bribe, if the leaking tritium should have surprised the public, and if Entergy should be more public with reports about incidents at the plant.

After the press conference ended, Shumlin and Senate Majority Leader John Campbell stepped to the same podium and said they were still planning to call the vote the next day, on whether Yankee should get its certificate of public good.

That evening a snowstorm hit central Vermont, with eight inches falling overnight. "Concerned that not enough activists would get in the next day, organizers arranged for people to come early and sleep on living room floors and couches," said *Public Meltdown*. The next day, the book added, some 600 calls came into the State House, "50 to 150 phone calls for each senator still considered to be on the fence."

"As usual, the alliance was working on many levels: in the Legislature, outreach to senators, organizing, leafletting, educating," recalled Cort Richardson, the Clamshell Alliance veteran who had been VPIRG's first anti-Yankee organizer back in the 1980s. "It was persistent and sustained. They got just about everybody."

Now an energy and utility policy consultant, Richardson and his wife Ginny Callan, another longtime anti-nuclear activist who was then working for the New England Grassroots Environmental Fund, were among those planning to be at the State House Wednesday morning. They wanted to witness the Senate's final debate and vote.

It was still snowing in the morning when the couple made it into the Senate gallery, a narrow space whose seats loom just above the Senate floor. "You're just about sitting in the laps of the senators," Richardson said.

The floor debate lasted two hours. A crowd of spectators who hadn't been able to fit in the gallery watched it on closed-circuit TV in Room 11, a large State House space often used for sizable gatherings.

Democratic senators kept counting votes almost continually throughout the morning's debate. The votes looked good, Richard Watts wrote, "but the margin of victory was uncertain."

"A multi-generational thing"

Senators and onlookers alike were startled when conservative Republican Randy Brock III of Franklin County, a longtime backer of nuclear power, stood up to say he would vote no.

"If the board of directors and management of Entergy were thoroughly infiltrated by anti-nuclear activists," Brock declared, "I do not think they could have done a better job of destroying their own case."

Peter Shumlin gave the final speech. He asked if it really mattered whether Yankee had been untruthful about the leaking underground pipes, or truly hadn't known they existed. "Neither is very comforting," he said.

The vote was 26-4 to to oppose relicensing. "Unless the chamber reverses itself, it will be the first time in more than 20 years that the public or its representatives has decided to close a reactor," the *New York Times* declared.

"It was a rout for the anti-nuclear side," Cort Richardson said. "The reasons are many: People were sick of the plant, and the parent company had really alienated people by its conduct. So the vote was about the plant, and about nuclear power and the safety concerns

Ginny Callan and Cort Richardson, longtime Vermont anti-nuclear activists. Richardson, a renewable-energy consultant, is a former executive director of VPIRG.

and all of that — but a lot of it had to do with a real disgust at the parent company."

When the vote total was announced, spectators erupted in cheers. For the long-time anti-nuclear activists, the moment was especially emotional. But there were also jobs at stake in Vernon, and some Yankee supporters were also in the chamber.

"And you know, the great thing about democracy in action in Vermont, and hopefully elsewhere too," said Richardson, "is that you can simultaneously manage to experience great emotion and strong feeling, while still maintaining the decorum and respect needed for a whole lot of people with opposing views to crowd into one tiny little space."

Afterward came the celebration.

Harsh winter weather continued all afternoon, yet "there was a lot of theater" outside the State House, Richardson said. Campaigners had inflated an outsized balloon fashioned after the devastating caricature of an ailing Vermont Yankee — a decrepit cooling tower with bandaids stuck on and a bandage-wrapped nose — that had been a feature of many drawings in the press by Vermont political cartoonist Tim Newcomb.

"There was a big party at Sarducci's [restaurant] that night," Ginny Callan said. "There was a huge mob of us."

"And then later at Julio's [tavern]," Richardson added. "It was very celebratory."

"Lots of champagne," Callan said. "John Warshow was there, a lot of the old-time anti-nukers."

"It was also a multi-generational thing," Richardson added. "There were a lot of young people, staffers from young environmental groups."

"Literally thousands of Vermonters contacted their legislators in the lead-up to this vote," VPIRG's Colleen Halley said in the group's statement on the Senate vote. "Vermonters spoke out in hundreds of letters to the editor in papers across the state. And on the day of the vote, braving one of the few snowstorms this winter,

more than 250 Vermonters crowded the State House to witness this historic moment.

"... This monumental effort would not have been successful without the dedication and support from key coalition partners," noted VPIRG. It thanked a long list of those partners: CAN, CLF, Credo Action, Democracy for America, Greenpeace, Nuclear Free Vermont, Safe and Green, Sierra Club of Vermont and New Hampshire, Toxics Action Center, True Majority, Vermont League of Conservation Voters, Vermont Natural Resources Council, and Vermont Yankee Decommissioning Alliance.

"Most of all," VPIRG concluded, "our thanks to the thousands of Vermonters who got involved and made the voices of Vermonters a loud roar that drowned out the corporate lobbyists, and in the end helped democracy work."

"The controversy in Vermont is viewed with deep apprehension and some anger by the nuclear industry," the *New York Times* reported the day after the vote. "The Nuclear Regulatory Commission in Washington, which normally makes the decisions on safety issues, is poised to give the plant 20 more years. Commission officials declined to comment on Vermont's actions."

Political chartoonist Tim Newcomb's caricature of an ailing and leaky Vermont Yankee nuclear plant became a familiar media presence in the debate about closing it – so much so that, on the day of the State Senate's historic vote in February 2010, anti-nuclear activists carried a replica of the image onto the snowy State House lawn.

"The industry is in rapid decline"

"Don't think this is over," VPIRG warned its allies and supporters after the State Senate vote. "We know that Entergy is not going to take defeat sitting down."

It didn't.

In 2011, Entergy appealed the Legislature's decision to block its certificate of public good — and it won. In January 2012, a U.S. District Court judge in Brattleboro "blocked Vermont from forcing the Vermont Yankee nuclear reactor to shut down when its license expires in March, saying that the state is trying to regulate nuclear safety, which only the federal government can do," the *Times* reported.

"The state mounted a very weak defense," said Duane Peterson, who attended the trial. "They sent well-meaning, earnest Vermont public trial attorneys up against the biggest law firms in the United States. I sat in front for the whole thing. We just got our heads handed to us."

Vermont appealed the decision, and the nonprofits cranked up their campaign yet again. VPIRG, CAN and the Vermont Yankee Decommissioning Alliance co-organized a November rally at the State House, and VPIRG and the Toxics Action Center offered training that month for "you activists interested in getting involved in the VY fight." VPIRG urged opponents of the plant's relicensing to "fill the rooms" at 13 Vermont Interactive Television studios, to participate in a Public Service Board hearing on whether the certificate of public good should be granted after all.

Then Entergy won again. In August 2013, the U.S. Court of Appeals for the Second Circuit in New York City upheld the District Court's decision that permitted Yankee to keep running.

And *then*, less than two weeks later, Entergy said it would shut down the nuclear power plant for good in 2014.

"The company ... said a long depression in natural gas prices had pushed the wholesale price of electricity so low that it was losing money on the reactor," the *Times* reported. "So far this year, owners have announced the retirements of five reactors, with the low price of gas being cited as a factor in all of the cases. ... The industry is in a period of rapid decline."

"I think the benefit of our campaign was, it toxified Vermont Yankee," Duane Peterson reflected. "During the campaign, all of the Vermont utilities abandoned Vermont Yankee, and refused to buy any more power from it. And interestingly, shortly thereafter it was Entergy itself that pulled the plug. "It died a quiet death, because I think no one wanted to play with it."

"Of course, all the pro-nuke people blamed the toxic environment that we created," said Tony Klein, who retired from the Legislature in 2015. "And did we create a toxic environment? Well, I guess we did, but it was only because they were so bad at running the plant, and the plant was just wrought with problems, and they were exposed."

And in the years from 2001 to 2014, the New England Coalition on Nuclear Pollution "kept up a constant stream of legal interventions opposing Entergy VY at the state and federal level, with sometimes as many as three legal actions concurrent," said Ray Shadis of the Coalition. "Based on NRC and PSB decisions ... we believe those actions were effective."

On December 29, 2014, Vermont Yankee's fission reactor was powered down for the final time. VPIRG's Ben Walsh issued a statement that began: "It's possible that no single issue has received more attention from VPIRG staff, activists and attorneys over the past 42 years than Vermont Yankee."

In all the years since the plant was commissioned and VPIRG came online in 1972, he said, "VPIRG has advocated for less costly and more sustainable ways to generate the power we need in Vermont. ... The answer to our energy needs, and ultimately the solution to global warming, will come with conservation, efficiency and renewable power. These are the areas in which Vermont can lead.

"Our thoughts today," Walsh concluded, "are with the workers at Vermont Yankee," including "those who may continue to play a vital role in securing the site and eventually decommissioning it. We wish them well. Our fight was never with them."

"It must be protected ... for 250,000 years"

Vermont Yankee's story has not ended. Essentially, it can't: The spent fuel from the reactor's core, now encased in 110-ton steel canisters that are sealed inside 200-ton concrete casks at the retired plant's riverside site, "is so radioactive that it must be protected from terrorism and/or destruction for 250,000 years," noted a publication by Fairewinds Energy Education, the nonprofit founded by Arnie and Maggie Gundersen.

Fairewinds developed a 41-page paper, funded by the Lintilhac Foundation, on Entergy's plans to dismantle the plant. Submitted in 2015 as a comment to the Nuclear Regulatory Commission, the paper charged that "weak NRC nuclear power plant decommissioning regulations have not created a solid financial and technical foundation to protect the public's health and welfare."

Having scrutinized the data in Entergy's own cost analysis, Fairewinds projected that "it will take at least 60 years for the underfunded [decommissioning] trust fund to finally accumulate adequate funds to address the excessive cost estimates of decommissioning." The paper cited a 2002 report by the research and consulting firm Synapse Energy Economics, which said: "Entergy has noted that the NRC has on several occasions said the burden of paying any such shortfalls would fall on taxpayers."

"Vermont Yankee is the *test case*," Fairewinds declared, "for the issue of who is responsible for the ultimate costs of decommissioning a nuclear power plant: the corporation that owned it and made all the profit or the taxpayers of a region."

The Fairewinds paper "was prescient yet ignored by the NRC," Arnie Gundersen said in a 2020 interview. "Our opinions have not changed."

In 2016, Entergy announced it was leaving the nuclear power business. It had agreed to sell Yankee to NorthStar Group Services, a large, New York City-based environmental-services firm that had expertise in large-scale demolition but had never taken apart a nuclear plant.

"The sale is the first of its kind in the nuclear power industry," said an Entergy news release — "a permanent ownership and license transfer to a company that is slated to perform timely and efficient decommissioning and site restoration."

The NRC and Vermont regulators approved the sale in 2018. When NorthStar took over the silent plant in early 2019, it said it would run a speeded-up dismantling that would be finished by 2030, if not sooner.

The NRC reviewed NorthStar's operations in early 2019. "Our observations have been that decommissioning activities at Vermont Yankee have been conducted safely and in accordance with NRC regulations," said commission spokesperson Neil Sheehan, quoted in *VTDigger*.

Arnie Gundersen was still very skeptical.

Maggie Gundersen, at lower left, and Arnie Gundersen, at upper right, with fellow members of the Fairewinds Energy Education team.

"My bottom-line comment is that the regulator is not regulating," he said. "There's no NRC inspector on site, like there was when it was running — so you're counting on a company that's never done it before. And even those companies that have done it before, and there's not that many, have never dismantled a contaminated boiling water reactor."

Those reactors tend to have higher levels of contamination, he said. "The systems inside the building are known to be more radioactive."

ᕦ

"They're going to leave a bunch of contamination behind"

Fairewinds conducted an in-depth inquiry into the environmental aftermath of the Fukushima Daichi meltdowns in Japan. In a 2017 press release, it said air sampling had found that "radioactively hot particles" being emitted by the site "were considerably more radioactive than current radiation models anticipated."

The dismantling of Yankee poses a similar danger, Gundersen warned. "These hot particles go airborne, and are incredibly small," he said. "It's almost like inhaling a howitzer.

"We could set up a continuous air monitor on the periphery of the plant — it's not like we need NorthStar's approval," he suggested. "I would put one at the grammar school. Run them continuously under 2026, and every three months, pull the filter and send them to a lab. Citizens could do that."

"They're going to leave a bunch of contamination behind," CAN's Deb Katz predicted of NorthStar. With no solution anywhere in site for permanent storage of high-level waste, the steel-and-concrete canisters are an interim solution that will have to remain on the Yankee site, Katz noted, just as the canisters have at Yankee Rowe.

The casks "are not meant to serve as storage units longer than 100 years, leaving our generation's waste problem for a future generation to solve," Crea Lintilhac wrote in a *Free Press* "My Turn" column back in 2005.

"They're going to have to come up with guarding the waste at $5 million a year," Katz said, "and it could be 50 years! They don't have that kind of money sitting around, to do that."

As the nuclear power industry continues to decline and more plants are retired, NorthStar "hopes to use its experience to bid on similar jobs around the country," Vermont Public Radio reported in 2019. "To do that, it's got to get the decommissioning process right in Vermont.

"Train cars roll slowly into, and out of, the Vermont Yankee property in Vernon," said VPR's Howard Weiss-Tisman. "The cars bring in massive machines, specialty tools and rigs that are used to cut up and transport the nuclear reactor, and all the machinery and buildings around it.

"And on their way out, the train cars haul away specially made boxes, packed with low-level radioactive waste."

One summer day in July 2019 at the Yankee site, two very large Northstar excavators began ripping into the cooling towers, the 462-foot-long louvred structures that became notorious when one sprang a water leak in 2007 and a plant employee snapped a few photos.

Among those who came to watch the demolition was Josh Unruh, chair of the Vernon Select Board.

"It's definitely bittersweet to see the end of an era," Unruh told *VTDigger*.

Sarah Dennison, a VPIRG field organizer, spreading the word on the resistance to the Addison County natural gas pipeline.

9

Toward a Clean Energy Future

A shared effort shows what can be done — and what more is needed

I n July 1987, a research report titled *Power to Spare* from a coalition of New England nonprofits set in motion a long, ongoing process of change in how Vermont and its neighbors look at, plan for, and regulate electrical energy. Subtitled "A Plan for Increasing New England's Competitiveness through Energy Efficiency," the report began:

> The production and distribution of electricity in New England has an enormous impact on the region's economy, competitiveness and quality of life. New England's electricity system also now stands at an historic crossroads. Robust economic and population growth suggests steadily increasing demand for electrical services. But attempting to meet this demand by building ever-larger baseload power plants has proven an unwise and uneconomic strategy: since the mid-1970s, New England has poured hundreds of millions of dollars into the construction of cancelled plants. And the completed plants have caused significant rate increases and a drain on precious capital resources. We have joined together to ensure that the region avoids repeating these costly mistakes.

The coalition called itself the New England Energy Policy Council, and among its 26 members were the Union of Concerned Scientists, Conservation Law Foundation, Vermont Natural Resources Council and Vermont Public Interest

Research Group. Their conclusion was straightforward, and it challenged the electric-power establishment: "A substantial portion of the growth of our future electrical needs can be met by increasing the efficiency of electrical use and not by new supply."

At that time it was the cost of generating power, not yet its impacts on climate change, that had become a front-burner issue. Anti-nuclear activists had, it's true, been warning for years about the enormous long-term costs, and frightening hazards, of using nuclear fission to make power. That built into the case *Power to Spare* made, that the region's utilities had too long relied on building and operating big, expensive power plants, whether fueled by fission, oil or coal.

"Building more multi-billion dollar power plants would be both expensive and risky," the report said. "New generating facilities face uncertain construction and fuel costs as well as unpredictable electric demand. New power plants would also damage the quality of New England's air, water and landscape."

Instead, the Energy Policy Council said its research had found that "New England could meet between 35% and 57% of its total electricity requirements in the next two decades through the efficiency improvements studied in the Council's report ... while maintaining or increasing the rate of economic growth projected by the utilities." Those improvements, by now familiar, included high-efficiency lighting, ventilation and cooling; more insulation in homes, with plugged air leaks; and increased efficiency in motor technology.

"It is striking to note that if only half of the Council's lower estimate of efficiency potential were realized," *Power to Spare* declared, "New England's total electric demand would be approximately 17% lower than predicted by the nation's utilities — enough difference to eliminate the need for several coal or nuclear plants."

Power to Spare had an impact. Over the next few years in Vermont, utility regulators, state lawmakers and a pioneering energy nonprofit began what has developed into a gradual and continuing transformation of the state's electricity system. In the 1990s, the work began with energy efficiency. Propelled since the early 2000s by the urgency of addressing climate change and reducing carbon emissions, it has built into a broad move away from big centralized plants, toward a different kind of power grid — one that draws more and more from renewable generation projects, such as solar, wind and biomass, that by nature are smaller and can be distributed across the landscape.

The story of Vermont's effort to move toward powering itself by clean, renewable energy is instructive and inspiring. It's also a reality check. It shows what can be accomplished when all the key players — nonprofits, government, business, academic experts — work together to find common ground for moving forward. And it highlights how very far there still is to go.

In recent years, the energy-transformation work in this state has begun to push beyond electric power, with the ambitious aim of shifting virtually all use of fossil fuels into the past. The contributions made by the nonprofits the foundation has supported — VPIRG, VNRC, the Conservation Law Foundation, the Vermont Energy Investment Corporation, the Energy Action Network, the Vermont Council on Rural Development, 350 Vermont and others — have been meaningful and significant, and they're best seen in the context of this larger, networked effort.

"A diverse set of stakeholders in this small state has developed and promoted the adoption of a comprehensive energy plan with a goal of achieving 90% renewables in all sectors (electricity, heating, and transportation) by 2050," noted a paper titled "Operationalizing Energy Democracy: Challenges and Opportunities in Vermont's Renewable Energy Transformation," published in 2018 in the open-access journal *Frontiers in Communication*.

"Given the culturally and politically embedded nature of fossil fuel-based energy systems," efforts like Vermont's "threaten the status quo so resistance is strong," wrote the authors, five academics at UVM and Northeastern and McGill universities. "Despite the powerful intensity of this resistance, facilitating the renewable energy transformation is becoming a political priority in jurisdictions throughout the world. ... Vermont was a first mover and a leader in embracing such an ambitious goal."

1.

The 1990s: A commitment to energy efficiency

In 1986, a year before *Power to Spare* came out, the late Blair Hamilton and his partner Beth Sachs started the nonprofit Vermont Energy Investment Corporation to deliver energy efficiency services to Vermont homeowners, small businesses and owners of multi-family housing. The two became a regular presence at the State House, making the case for investing in efficiency to the House and Senate committees where legislation might begin.

"Blair used to live in my committee," recalled Tony Klein, who was a renewable-energy lobbyist in the late '80s, and would later chair the House Natural Resources and Energy Committee. "He and Crea used to sit right next to each other. He was so smart, I couldn't understand him half the time. Very unassuming — but absolutely brilliant. And he started all this stuff."

On the Senate side, Scudder Parker of Caledonia County was serving on the Natural Resources Committee. "That's where I got to know Beth and Blair, and we formed a kind of mind-meld among the three of us," said Parker, a Democrat who later ran for governor. "What I did, often at their prompting, was to write into the law a whole series of things about how you have to consider efficiency in any decision you make about a new supply option."

At about the same time, Parker said, "*Power to Spare* led the Public Service Board to begin this massive investigation into efficiency." Chaired by Richard Cowart, who led the PSB from 1986 to 1999, Vermont's utility regulator issued a set of rules in 1990 that ordered electric utilities to put in place programs that would help customers reduce their power use through efficiency measures.

But the Board soon realized its action had put utilities in an awkward spot: They were now expected to work to reduce the volume of power sales on which their operating margins relied. Only two smaller utilities — the Burlington Electric Department, serving the city, and Washington Electric Cooperative in central Vermont — made serious efforts to promote and provide efficiency measures to their customers. The state's largest utilities, Green Mountain Power and Central Vermont Public Service, "did not, at the time," said Parker.

For their part, Hamilton and Sachs had been floating "the idea that energy efficiency should be a matter of state law, with a single energy efficiency administrator regulated like electric utilities," says the website of the Vermont Energy Investment Corporation (VEIC). In 1999, after a long and complex negotiation, the PSB made that possible. It accepted a settlement among utilities and the state that provided for a new kind of utility — one devoted to promoting and delivering efficiency services.

The Legislature approved, and in 2000 VEIC won the contract to create Efficiency Vermont, the country's first statewide, state-regulated "energy efficiency utility." Burlington Electric, at the same time, became the efficiency utility for that city's customers.

Scudder Parker had been in the midst of the negotiations that gave rise to the efficiency utility. Having left the Senate, since 1990 he had been directing the new Energy Efficiency and Renewable Energy Division at the Vermont Department of Public Service, which represents consumers in utility matters. Before the 1999 settlement, Parker's division sought through expensive, often-acrimonious litigation to force utilities to provide efficiency services. With the settlement, he said, "the deal we cut was, 'The efficiency utility will be counted as fulfilling your obligation under the law to do efficiency programs.'

"What we built with Efficiency Vermont was a whole different way of providing energy service," said Parker, who later became energy policy director at VEIC. "Utilities know how to build wires and poles. They're not that great at persuading customers, at introducing and marketing the new efficiency products."

The state's commitment to energy efficiency opened the way for the shift that was coming toward renewable, distributed generation. It all began, Parker said, with *Power to Spare.* "In my judgment, that was an example of a not-for-profit articulating an option that the regulatory and eventually the legal structure of a state builds into its law. And that's a wonderful pattern."

"We work on everything"

Efficiency Vermont has made a difference. It continues to, in gradually expanding ways.

"Efficiency Vermont helps electricity customers find ways to cut their consumption, often just by providing them with free technical advice ... but sometimes by subsidizing the purchase of energy-efficient products like lightbulbs or boilers," wrote Susan Arterian Chang in "The Rise of the Energy Efficiency Utility," a 2008 article in *IEEE Spectrum*, the journal of the Institute of Electrical and Electronics Engineers.

"The program ... is funded by a 4.5 percent fee attached to each customer's electricity bill," Chang explained. Having helped "close to 60 percent of the state's electricity customers in seven years, Efficiency Vermont ... saved the state 105,000 megawatt-hours of electricity in 2007 at a cost of just 2.6 cents per kilowatt-hour, versus the 10.7 cents per kWh it cost the state's utilities to supply electricity to taxpayers."

"We work on everything from small convenience stores and retailers to large manufacturers and ski areas," Blair Hamilton wrote in an article on the website EnergyStar.gov. "We have probably provided rebates as high as $50,000 to $70,000 for major projects because their savings are so great. And saving energy is a good thing for Vermont ratepayers, because it means the utilities won't have to go out and enter into expensive power supply contracts which are going to raise rates."

"Similarly structured service providers are now operating with positive results in a number of other states," noted the *IEEE Spectrum* article in 2008.

"We had a harder time than most of the other states as they got started, because they did combined gas and electricity, or they could do solar," said VEIC co-founder Beth Sachs. "In Vermont we were prohibited from doing solar or doing anything that wasn't electric, and there was very little electric heat. For us, the residential sector was appliances and lighting."

By 2008, enough customers had asked Efficiency Vermont for help in lowering their heating bills that the state gave it a new designation as an all-fuels utility, allowing it to expand into thermal efficiency. The utility now works with a network of contractors to provide homeowners with energy audits, insulation, air sealing and similar means of saving on heating fuel, with incentive payments to homeowners that reduce their cost.

Through a partnership with Capstone Community Action in Barre, Efficiency Vermont also delivers weatherization measures to low-income multi-family buildings around the state, and it helps businesses weatherize their facilities and save on fuels used in commercial processes. Funding for the utility's thermal services comes from a couple of sources, though not as steadily as the revenue from the fee on Vermonters' power bills that still funds its electrical work.

By 2017, Efficiency Vermont had "saved enough energy to power every home in the state for 5.3 years," said Karen Glitman, then the program's director. "In 2016, we helped Vermonters save over $18.9 million in energy costs, and avoid close to 900,000 tons of carbon dioxide, equal to removing over 190,000 cars from the road for one year."

2.

1996 to 2008: Energy action meets climate change

I n his 1989 book *The End of Nature*, environmentalist, journalist and Ripton, Vt. resident Bill McKibben put as plainly as he could a concern that would grow more urgently alarming in the years ahead. In his book, the first to describe climate change for general readers, McKibben linked the warming of the planet to the burning of fossil fuels:

> When we drill into an oil field, we tap into a vast reservoir of organic matter that has been in storage for millennia. We unbury it. When we burn that oil (or coal or natural gas) we release its carbon into the atmosphere in the form of carbon dioxide. ... We have increased the amount of carbon dioxide in the air by about 25 percent in the last century, and will almost certainly double it in the next; we have more than doubled the level of methane; we have added a soup of other gases.
> We have substantially altered the earth's atmosphere. ...
> The models that have been constructed agree that when, as has been predicted, the level of carbon dioxide or its equivalent in other green-house gases doubles from pre-Industrial Revolution concentrations, the global average temperature will increase, and that the increase will be 1.5 to 4.5 degrees Celsius, or 3 to 8 degrees Fahrenheit. ...
> There are an infinite number of possible effects of such a temperature change. For example, the seas may well rise seven feet or more as polar ice melts and warmer weather expands, while the interiors of the continents may dry up. ...
> We must act, and in every way possible, and immediately. ... The only thing we absolutely must do is cut back immediately on our use of fossil fuels. That is not an option; we need to do it in order to choose any other future.

McKibben continued to sound the alarm, and in time his warnings and his activism did help to motivate action. In April 2007, "the largest global warming demonstration in American history took place," said an article in *The Middlebury Campus*, the student newspaper of Middlebury College. "Thanks to an idea conceived by six recent graduates of the College and Scholar-in-Residence Bill McKibben," the *Campus* reported, "Step It Up 2007, a campaign of more than 1,400 coordinated demonstrations in all 50 states, called on Congress to pass comprehensive climate change legislation aimed at cutting carbon emissions by 80 percent before 2050."

"It's the beginning of a movement," McKibben said in an email to the student paper.

"Will you help me raise awareness?"

Having been closely involved in the campaign to retire Vermont Yankee, in 2006 the Lintilhac Foundation began supporting nonprofits' work on renewable energy and climate action. At that time in Vermont, "there was far less urgency around climate — there were far fewer players focused on energy issues and climate action," recalled Johanna Miller, director of the Energy & Climate Program at the Vermont Natural Resources Council (VNRC). "The number of groups that have grown out of concern around climate, and interest in developing jobs in the clean energy sector, has really increased in the last decade."

VNRC began doing energy work in 2005, "when we started the Vermont Energy & Climate Action Network, which is the network of town energy committees in Vermont," Miller said. The network today webs together and supports some 100 local energy committees, all over the state.

In 2006, Miller said, "our friend Bill McKibben knocked on our door and said, 'Will you help me raise awareness on climate? I'm going to get arrested on the stairs of the federal building in Burlington.' When he realized that they didn't care if he sat there day in and day out, he organized a five-day walk across Vermont. We helped him do that. That was the catalyst that triggered the Step It Up movement, which then became 350.org."

The nonprofit 350.org is named for the highest concentration of CO_2 in the atmosphere that scientists consider to be safe: 350 parts per million. The world passed that threshold in 1988, according to data from the Mauna Loa Observatory, the National Oceanic and Atmospheric Administration's atmospheric baseline observation station in Hawaii. In the summer of that year, a U.S. government scientist became the first to tell Congress what passing the 350 threshold meant.

"Global Warming Has Begun, Expert Tells Senate," said the page-one headline in the *New York Times* on June 24, 1988, as the paper recounted the previous day's testimony by Dr. James E. Hansen, of the National Aeronautics and Space Administration, to the U.S. Senate's Energy and Natural Resources Committee.

In the years to come, 350.org would go on, led by McKibben, to organize "global days of action that linked activists and organizations around the world, including the International Day of Climate Action in 2009, the Global Work Party in 2010,

Moving Planet in 2011," said the organization's website. "350 quickly became a planet-wide collaboration of organizers, community groups and regular people fighting for a fossil free future." The foundation has been a modest supporter of 350 Vermont, the collaboration's in-state nonprofit.

"The United States alone now pours nearly 15 percent more CO_2 into the atmosphere than it did when this book was first published," McKibben wrote in a new introduction to a 2006 edition of *The End of Nature*.

Also in 2006, atmospheric CO_2 levels, measured throughout the year at Mauna Loa, reached almost 382 parts per million.

"Just saying there's a better way"

"We've been working on energy issues for decades," said Ben Edgerly Walsh, Climate & Energy Program director at VPIRG. "This is something Crea brings to the board as well: It's not enough to say no. You have to figure out what you're saying yes to.

"If you're saying no to dirty power, if you're not providing an alternative that's cleaner and safer, then you are by default just going to be switching from one dirty power source to another. That has always been part of our DNA, just saying there's a better way."

In 2006, VPIRG's educational arm, the Vermont Public Interest Research and Educational Fund (VPIREF), released an influential publication that laid out the case for the better way.

"The electricity generated across New England is dominated by dirty, dangerous and expensive power sources ... from either the burning of fossil fuels, which contributes to global warming, or from aging nuclear power plants," declared *A Decade of Change: A Vision for Vermont's Renewable Energy Future*, written by James Moore, then director of VPIRG's energy work. "Thankfully, a future with clean, safe and affordable electricity is possible using current technologies."

James Moore joined VPIRG in 2006, and became director of its Clean Energy Program.

Highlighting his argument with four-color charts and graphs, Moore wrote: "The electricity that can be generated by Vermont's renewable resources, together with a portion of the electricity we currently get from Hydro-Québec, can provide for 80% of our electricity needs by 2015."

The coming decade offered a vital opportunity, *A Decade of Change* declared. The Vermont Yankee nuclear plant had been providing about a third of the state's power, as had Hydro-Québec, a massive generation complex in northern Canada; but over the next few years, both Yankee's operating license and Hydro-Québec's Vermont contracts would expire.

"Vermont can and should seize this moment in history," Moore urged in his report, "to build an electricity portfolio that is based on clean, safe, and affordable electricity generation ... that will be the envy of the nation and an example for other states to follow. ... We must start where all energy discussions should start — with a commitment to energy conservation and efficiency."

At this point in the national discussion on energy and climate, leading thinkers were even looking beyond efficiency and conservation, toward a growing array of increasingly practical ways to safely, sustainably power the world. In a 2007 web exchange, Amory Lovins, the influential chair and chief scientist at the Rocky Mountain Institute, drew a distinction between "negawatts," or saved electricity, and "micropower," or renewable generation projects — such as solar, wind and biomass — that by nature are smaller than centralized power plants, and so can be distributed widely across the landscape.

"In 2006, distributed renewable power sources worldwide got $56 billion of private risk capital; nuclear projects got zero," Lovins wrote. "Micropower — small-scale generation that emits little or no carbon dioxide — provided one-sixth of the world's electricity and one-third of its new electricity in 2005.

"... Micropower plus negawatts, which are probably about as big, now provide more than half of the world's new electrical services," Lovins summed up.

James Moore put this in a Vermont context, in the 2009 VPIREF report *Repowering Vermont: Replacing Vermont Yankee for a Clean Energy Future*:

> The way that electricity is being produced, distributed and even used is undergoing monumental change. Wind power and solar power, which were once fringe energy sources, are now being talked about as mainstays of our energy future. Massive coal and nuclear plants are increasingly seen as symbols of the past and not compatible with a smart energy grid. ...
>
> Energy goals committed to by the Legislature and Governor Douglas have echoed those of President Obama — including the need to bring our electricity system into the 21st century, create local green jobs, and push towards energy independence. The Legislature and

governor also have committed Vermont to reducing Vermont's global warming pollution to 25% below 1990 emissions by 2012, and to 75% below 1990 by 2050.

These aggressive goals will require Vermont to build the local renewable generators capable of meeting our future energy needs and successfully integrate those resources through a smart electricity grid. It is this work that, over the next two decades, will be the foundation for a thriving clean energy economy in Vermont.

3.

2009-2011: Laying new groundwork

By 2009, the governor and the Legislature had taken several steps that helped lay the groundwork for the renewable-energy future that Moore and others envisioned:

- The passage of Act 74 in 2005, as described in the previous chapter, created the Vermont Clean Energy Development Fund and gave it substantial startup funding from the corporation that owned Vermont Yankee. The fund continues to support efficiency and renewable energy projects, especially wood-pellet heating.

- Having been called by Gov. Madeleine Kunin in 1986 to review Vermont's energy use and look for ways that it might become more affordable, renewable and environmentally friendly, in 1991 the state government adopted a Comprehensive Energy Plan — then revised it in 1998, with the goals Moore cited for greenhouse gas reductions. "The Vermont Legislature further required public updates to the state energy plan," based in part on "an intense engaged public process," said the previously mentioned article "Operationalizing Energy Democracy." That public process would be key in the development of the more ambitious Comprehensive Energy Plan that the state would adopt in 2011.

- In 2009, the Legislature created Standard Offer, "the nation's first statewide, guaranteed price for renewable energy projects," said a VPIREF publication. The first year's pilot round offered guaranteed pricing for 50 total megawatts of power generated by in-state renewable projects. It "was wildly successful and was oversubscribed by 150 megawatts within three hours of its launch," VPIREF said. Of the 51 projects supported by Standard Offer in that first year, 19 generated power on dairy farms, using methane emitted by cow manure. Twelve were solar projects, nine used wind, six were small-scale hydro, three used biomass fuel from Vermont woodlands, and two turned methane from landfills into energy.

The Standard Offer program continues. In 2016 it entered into contracts with seven renewable-generation projects.

Another fresh commitment to innovation came at this time from Vermont's largest utility. As she prepared to become the president and CEO at Green Mountain Power, Mary Powell, who had been chief operating officer, announced in summer 2008 "a broad plan to drive the development of renewable energy sources, to combat climate change, to spur a green energy economy in Vermont, and to maintain our competitive electricity pricing advantage in the region," said a GMP news release.

"This is an exciting but very serious time to be discussing our customers' energy future," Powell said. "Vermont needs to build on the foundation laid by the Department of Public Service in the Vermont Comprehensive Energy Plan 2009, and the good information gleaned through the public engagement process" that helped form the plan.

The new CEO promised "aggressive development of renewable energy resources for the state," and pledged to communicate about GMP's efforts in that direction "with a broad coalition of energy industry leaders, regulators, renewable energy developers, environmental groups, legislators and educators."

The "explosion point"

The year 2011 brought two other important events in Vermont's push toward renewables. The first was a decision by the Legislature, early in the year, to place attractive incentive terms on the billing mechanism known as net metering.

When a homeowner or business produces electricity through a small-scale renewable installation, such as a solar array, net metering requires the utility serving the customer to help them use that power to lower their electricity bill. When customers produce more power than they use, net metering requires the utility to buy the excess energy at a set rate.

Net metering had been in state law since 1989, "but there wasn't enough incentive," said Tony Klein. In his House Natural Resources and Energy Committee, "We were looking to jumpstart an industry for Vermont, so we could develop our clean, green, renewable in-state generation — create jobs, create our own electricity. My first year as chair, Mary Powell comes to me and says, 'You know, solar is so valuable to us, because we're a summer-peaking utility.'

"She said, 'Even at peak demand, solar is so much cheaper for us than firing up some jet-engine generator that on our own we've been paying people a six-cent premium to build solar, and supply us through net metering,'" Klein said. "I looked at her and I said, 'Wow. We're going to require that every utility do that.' And that was the explosion point."

"Net metering, a system that pays corporations and individuals more for their renewable power than the retail cost, has triggered a burst of solar installations in Vermont, from almost nothing in the early 2000s to more than 300 megawatts today — enough to power roughly 60,000 homes," *VTDigger* reported in 2019. "The number of new net-metered solar installations has leveled off over the past two years, but Vermont has one of the highest amounts of small-scale power generation compared to electricity usage in the country."

"VPIRG was the leading organization, both inside and outside the State House, pushing for the creation of a strong net metering program, and the Standard Offer program," said James Moore. "I was in the State House every day, working with legislators, utilities and Renewable Energy Vermont to craft lasting clean energy legislation that would prove to be the foundation of Vermont's renewable energy industry."

The VPIREF publications *A Decade of Change* and *Repowering Vermont* had, Moore said, helped in "laying the groundwork for the legislative push," as had VPIRG's door-to-door summer canvassing and its efforts to help build Vermont's emerging renewable energy coalition.

The other major climate-related event of 2011 was a disaster.

On the morning of Sunday, August 28, weather forecasters predicted that Tropical Storm Irene would continue moving north along the Atlantic coast — but instead it veered up the Hudson River basin and blasted Vermont in a day of devastating fury. "Before Irene's rains receded, six Vermonters had lost their lives and some $733 million in damages had been inflicted in southern, central, western, and eastern regions of the state," said a 2014 report on the recovery effort that followed. [See Chapter 6 for more on the impacts of the storm.]

Gov. Peter Shumlin led a fast-paced, successful effort to rebuild most of the damaged public infrastructure before winter set in. A new multi-partner nonprofit, the Vermont Long-Term Disaster Recovery Group, raised some $6.8 million, including more than half a million dollars from sales of "I Am Vermont Strong" license plates, to help individual Vermonters rebuild their homes, relocate when needed, and otherwise recover from the storm.

But the core lesson was clear. As climate change brought storm activity with new levels of intensity to the U.S., the Caribbean and elsewhere around the world, Vermont was not going to be spared.

"If anyone thought they could hole up in bucolic Vermont and avoid the woes of a warming earth, Irene was the final proof that was folly," Bill McKibben wrote in an afterword to Elizabeth Courtney and Eric Zencey's 2012 book *Greening Vermont: The Search for a Sustainable State*:

Vermont has to help take the lead in getting the whole planet off the fossil fuels that cause climate change and toward some kind of reasonably soft landing.

Given Vermont's tiny size, that seems laughable. Except that the biggest grassroots climate change movement began in the state in 2008, when a small team of Middlebury students and faculty launched 350.org, taking its name from what scientists said was the most carbon we could safely have in the atmosphere. (We're currently at 393 parts per million and rising two parts per year.)

"Vermont is not now a sustainable state, but in the effort to achieve that goal, it has a head start," wrote authors Courtney, then executive director of VNRC, and Zencey, an ecological economist. "We have work to do, but we have a relatively solid foundation on which to build."

"A community organizing model of clean energy"

Early in 2010, VPIRG board chair Duane Peterson was busily organizing the campaign to retire Vermont Yankee. Then that spring came the State Senate's historic vote to oppose the nuclear plant's relicensing.

"So the campaign's over," he said. "What's next? I'm on my seventh career, and I'm versed at imaging what's next. And I start things."

Peterson had worked with James Moore on the Yankee campaign, and he'd been impressed with *A Decade of Change* and *Repowering Vermont*, Moore's publications calling for the move to renewables. "He was there for VPIRG in the State House for seven years — so the policy at the time was adept, and we thought there were robust technologies," Peterson said. "What was lacking was the concept of adoption. So we had a look at the landscape, and the solar providers at the time."

They learned, he said, that most solar power enterprises had been "founded by male engineers who were just in love with the gizmos, and the parts per million and the BTUs: 'This crap is so cool, I love it and everyone should want it.' Well, that's kind of not how it works. The way most people view electricity is, you write your utility a monthly check and you get to turn your lights on. There you go. So expecting people to do something radically different, I thought, required a whole campaign — marketing, communications, a whole effort. Gosh, that's what we know how to do. Maybe we should try that.

"So we talked the board of VPIRG into launching essentially a business inside the nonprofit," Peterson said. "We called it VPIRG Energy, and it was a marketing effort. Starting with the VPIRG membership, let's do all the legwork and package up this thing so it's really easy for people to do what they've always wanted to do, but couldn't wrap their heads around — because nobody had helped them."

"We wanted to prove the concept of what we called turnkey solar," said Paul Burns, VPIRG's executive director. "We wanted to show that we believe in the solutions — and if there's a good idea, go ahead and incubate. These guys figured out how we could do it, here in Vermont, and then proved the concept."

"We created essentially a community organizing model of clean energy," said Peterson. As the startup's first and only full-time employee, he said, "I was out there in the rain at the farmers' markets with the clipboard, communicating.

"Essentially, we were lead generators. Because we didn't know anything about actually building solar, we would hand the leads off to a fulfillment partner, a solar installer. They would close the sale, design the system, pull the permit, procure the equipment, build the thing, and pay us a little commission for having gotten the ball rolling."

VPIRG Energy launched in September 2010. "In the course of a year, the program … installed 130 electric solar systems and 170 solar hot water systems," said a 2012 report in *Seven Days*. "According to VPIRG Executive Director Paul Burns, the program generated $4 million to $5 million in sales, raising $275,000 for VPIRG. … Peterson and Moore spent the second half of 2011 establishing a new company."

The two registered the firm with the state as a "benefit corporation," or B Corp — a new designation, created that year by the Legislature to recognize companies whose decision-making embraced social, community and environmental concerns.

The new business needed a new name. As they set out to raise investor funds, Peterson and Moore decided on SunCommon. Their business's core approach is straightforward: the customer — whether a homeowner, business, farm or community group going in on a project — typically pays nothing up front.

If SunCommon finds that an installation of photovoltaic panels will be cost-effective, when financing is needed it facilitates a low-interest loan. The solar array it installs is designed to produce enough power that, over the time the customer is repaying the loan (usually 12 years, sometimes 20), those loan payments plus the customer's total spending on home or building energy (electricity, heating oil, etc.) roughly equal what the customer paid for energy before installing the solar array. Once the loan is paid off, the customer owns the system.

Between 2012 and 2018, SunCommon installed 3,618 residential solar arrays, 40 commercial solar projects and 27 community solar projects, all of which have a generating capacity of just over 35 megawatts. By 2018 the business had expanded into New York State, and was offering its Vermont customers air-source heat pumps and Tesla Powerwall home storage batteries. By 2019, SunCommon had won almost 80 percent of the Vermont market share in residential solar.

"Arguably," said Peterson, "we've moved the needle."

4.

2012-2015: Networking for change

I n 2012, a coalition of Vermont stakeholders involved in the energy sector — nonprofits, businesses, utilities and others — came together to create the Energy Action Network, a new convener nonprofit. Andrea Colnes, the network's first executive director, had been leading the four-state Northern Forest Initiative.

In that latter project, Colnes said, "we took an incredibly complex situation of land conservation, forest management practice, and local communities and economies, and put them together into an integrated effort to secure the forestlands of the region and address sustainable forestry and local economies. It was this whole approach of building collaboration to drive change."

The Forest Initiative was an example of what the organizers of the Energy Action Network (EAN) hoped it would be: a means of achieving collective impact.

The concept of collective impact had been winning interest around the country since it had been the focus of a much-discussed 2011 article in *Stanford Social Innovation Review*. The article defined the term as "the commitment of a group

of important actors from different sectors to solving a specific social problem." Unlike a coalition of groups with a common interest — say, nonprofits pushing for renewable energy — a collective-impact network brings people together from all aspects of the issue.

At EAN, Colnes said, "we had utilities, environmentalists, banks, businesses; all kinds of players. It was a gathering of folks who profoundly disagreed — Associated Industries of Vermont, VNRC, VPIRG — in the same room to say, 'Despite all the places that we differ, what do we hold in common? Can we find common cause,' which we did, 'and can we work

Talia Crowley, a **VPIRG** summer canvasser and student member of the nonprofit's Board of Trustees, at a 2019 march on climate change and clean energy.

together to understand how to advance it?'"

EAN structured its work around four leverage points that its founding circle had defined. "On each of these," Colnes said, "we would try to identify what we could do that could drive Vermont forward toward energy action, without getting in the way of our members."

For each leverage point, the strategies were these:

- Public engagement: "We developed some consistent messaging tools and approaches that could be used in different ways by members of the network," Colnes said.

- Technology innovation: "We created the Vermont Community Energy Platform, a very complex platform that enables every single community to see baseline information about where they are, where they need to go, and how different strategies could help them do their part toward 90 percent by 2050. It's a highly interactive tool that integrates data, community outreach, and communications toward driving innovation."

- Clean-energy finance: "Understanding how we get investment to flow into the clean-energy space. What are the barriers to that in Vermont; how might we address those, and better allow private investment to flow?"

- Regulatory reform: "We couldn't step right into the arena and advance any particular policy, because our network was far too diverse for that," Colnes said. "But we could convene conversations, and strategic efforts to identify what are the opportunities to enable people to discuss their differences and maybe find their way through."

"I think the only way we can make durable social change happen is by building from an understanding of mutual interests and mutual concern," said Colnes, who's now director of global green bank development for the Coalition for Green Capital. "So it's not one group dominating, but rather solutions that are born from collaborative thinking across different perspectives.

"It's everything the country can't do right now. And it's really consistent with Vermont's way of doing public policy. We don't typically ride roughshod over each other; we seek to understand each other, and to build common solutions. So EAN is really well-suited to Vermont."

"They don't lobby," noted VNRC's Johanna Miller. "They're a really important partner for us, though — they do the number-crunching and the ground-truthing, and we take their base of factual information and frame out how much work we have to do, and what kind of policies are are going to be required to get us where we need to go."

"It is affecting Vermont today"

The 2018 article "Operationalizing Energy Democracy" outlined the next steps that state government took:

> The 2011 Comprehensive Energy Plan led to a two-year Total Energy Study ... completed by the Department of Public Service in December of 2014. ... A concluding claim of this study was that the state could achieve its GHG [greenhouse gas] emission reduction goals and its renewable energy goals while maintaining or increasing the state's economic prosperity.
>
> Another important policy innovation focused on net metering. Act 125 of 2012 doubled the size of solar PV systems eligible for the simple registration process to systems up to 10 kW from 5 kW, and allowed customers with demand or time-of-use rates to take greater advantage of the ability to net meter. Act 99 of 2014 raised the program capacity to 15% of utilities' peak demand, from 4%.

In 2014, UVM's Gund Institute for Ecological Economics (now the Gund Institute for the Environment) released *Vermont's Climate Assessment: Considering Vermont's Future in a Changing Climate*, the nation's first statewide climate assessment. Said the report:

> Climate change is no longer a thing of the future; it is affecting Vermont today. Extreme weather events, such as heavy downpours, have become more frequent and/or intense. Across the state, there have been significant changes in the length of the frost-free growing season. ... The state's average temperature has increased by 1.3°F since 1960; 45% of this increase has occurred since 1990. The most recent decade was Vermont's hottest on record. ... Adaptation through the use of renewable, local energy sources will be critically important as extreme weather events increase and threaten fossil fuel-based energy supplies.

Meanwhile, the worldwide clamor for a carbon-free future continued to grow.

"It isn't about data and science, it's about power," Bill McKibben told *The New Yorker* in a September 2014 interview. "The most powerful industry is fossil fuel, because it's the richest. At a certain point it became clear that our only hope of matching that money was with the currencies of movement: passion, spirit, creativity — and warm bodies." On September 21 of that year, the magazine reported, "tens of thousands of demonstrators are expected to join the People's Climate March in midtown Manhattan. Its website describes it as the 'largest climate march in history.'"

"The economy itself is changing and everyone can see it," McKibben observed in the interview. "The price of a solar panel is dropping like a rock — you can go to Home Depot and buy a set of solar panels for not that much. So people are becoming more optimistic, and as Mother Nature continues to educate us about the follies of our ways ... we'll be making more progress."

New standards, new technologies

In 2014, VPIRG launched Energy Independent Vermont, a statewide campaign that pushed for a tax or price on carbon pollution. Two years later, "over 43,000 Vermonters have signed our petitions," VPIRG said in a 2016 report to the Lintilhac Foundation. "Our effort has grown to include two colleges, organizations representing healthcare professionals, outdoor enthusiasts, the local chapter of the Citizen Climate Lobby, national student groups, and over 500 local businesses."

The Vermont Natural Resources Council had been lobbying since 2011 for state legislation that would require Vermont's electric utilities to meet specific goals for renewable energy. In June 2015, VNRC's work bore fruit: Vermont became the first state to enact an integrated standard that says utilities must buy a gradually

Representing VPIRG at a Burlington march that was part of the 2019 global climate strike: from left, Zach Tomanelli, communications and engagement director; Liz Edsell, associate director, with her daughter Ida; Paul Burns, executive director, with his son Braeden; and Lily Seward and Anna Marchessault, both of whom were summer canvassers and student members of the VPIRG Board of Trustees.

rising portion of their power from renewable sources.

The Renewable Energy Standard required utilities, by 2017, to buy 55 percent of the electricity they sell to customers "from any source of renewable energy." That portion must grow steadily, until it hits 75 percent in 2032.

Utilities must also buy a portion of their power from "new distributed renewable generation," facilities that can generate up to 5 megawatts. That portion rises to 10 percent in 2032. And utilities must buy some of their power, rising to 12 percent by 2032, from either distributed renewables or projects that reduce their customers' fossil fuel use and carbon emissions.

"For average Americans ... the biggest source of carbon emissions is their home, so utilities' help is crucial in making the transition," McKibben observed in writing "Power to the People," a June 2015 *New Yorker* article. The electric-utility business is traditionally conservative, he wrote — but "disruptive new technologies" were presenting utilities with "a combination of threat and opportunity."

Solar panels, the most important of these technologies, now produced power almost as cheaply as oil and gas. And McKibben noted another newly advanced technology that would soon be at work in a fast-growing number of Vermont homes: the air-source heat pump.

"These devices have made it practical for electricity to be used for tasks traditionally performed by oil and gas," he wrote. "Smart thermostats ... allow you to make your home far more energy-efficient — and can even, when connected to the 'smart meters' that are now appearing on many houses, permit the utility to turn your demand down for a few seconds in response to fluctuations in the supply of sun and wind."

Some utilities were resisting residential solar power, but Vermont's largest utility was continuing to cut a different path. Green Mountain Power became the nation's first utility to offer its customers the new Tesla Powerwall home storage battery. GMP leader Mary Powell had, McKibben wrote, "become fixated on new technologies: everything from electric-vehicle charging stations to utility-scale storage batteries. 'If we move in this direction very rapidly, we can, hopefully, keep rates flat forever,'" he quoted Powell saying — "and, in fact, G.M.P. cut its electric rates by two percent last year."

Also in 2015, the CO_2 levels measured at Mauna Loa passed 400 parts per million.

5.

2016-2019: Progress and predicament

The Progress

"Over the four years since the publication of the last Comprehensive Energy Plan [CEP], Vermonters have built a foundation of infrastructure, policies, and programs on which to construct an increasingly renewable energy economy," began the 2016 revision of the CEP. "...Vermont is well-positioned to thrive in the transition to distributed energy resources."

To reach its aim of 25 percent renewables by 2025, the 2016 Comprehensive Energy Plan set goals by sector of energy use. It said electric power should be 67 percent renewable by 2025, buildings 30 percent, transportation 10 percent.

"Since the last CEP was published in 2011, Vermont has added more than 100 MW of in-state wind and solar photovoltaic electric generation," the plan said, and noted that the state's 2015 Renewable Energy Standard would further drive progress. "We are doing all this while keeping electric rates stable and low. Electric rates in Vermont have increased only 3.7% since 2011 ... while New England average rates rose 12.3% and U.S. average rates have increased 5.6%."

In 2017, an analysis by the Union of Concerned Scientists led it to rank Vermont second in the nation for overall progress in moving toward clean energy. The group said Vermont "leads the nation in clean energy jobs per capita and for its carbon reduction target and has top-five scores in energy savings, electric vehicle adoption, and energy efficiency policy. The Green Mountain State earns 10 top-10 appearances, the most of any state."

"In total," reported the Energy Action Network in 2018, "Vermont has reached almost 20% renewable across transportation, thermal and electric energy. Electricity is the most renewable, at 63%."

That year, Vermont had over 338 megawatts in total solar installed, enough to power 63,666 homes, and 47 companies were doing solar installation and development in the state, said a report by the Solar Energy Industries Association. Also in 2018, Vermont had 10,600 jobs in clean energy, amounting to 6 percent of total jobs statewide — the highest share in the nation, said EAN. Most of those jobs, 7,800 of them, were in weatherization and thermal efficiency.

Johanna Miller directs the energy and climate work of the Vermont Natural Resources Council.

By 2019, Vermont's efficiency efforts had ranked it in the top five nationally in 11 of the 12 years since 2007, Efficiency Vermont reported.

"The city of Burlington has recently received international fame for becoming one of the first cities to achieve 100% renewable electricity," said the 2018 article "Operationalizing Energy Democracy." "This was achieved by the municipal utility, Burlington Electric Department, by prioritizing local renewables including a biomass power plant, the McNeil Generating

Station. Also, conservation and efficiency have been prioritized in Burlington."

By this time, more than 100 Vermont communities had organized local energy committees, all of them connected and supported by the Vermont Climate & Energy Action Network (VECAN), a project of VNRC in partnership with the Energy Action Network, Efficiency Vermont, the "people-centered downtown" nonprofit Net Zero Vermont, the New England Grassroots Environmental Fund, and Vital Communities, a nonprofit serving the Upper Connecticut River Valley.

And in 2017, the nonprofit Vermont Council on Rural Development (VCRD) started its Climate Economy Model Communities Program, to support selected towns in setting and achieving goals for strengthening the local economy while reducing energy use and carbon emissions. "For two years, VCRD has been convening a statewide conversation about the climate change economy and how the inevitable transition from carbon-based fuels represents a huge economic opportunity for Vermont," the nonprofit said. "The program provides concentrated services ... to model effective change at a rapid rate."

Thanks to net metering, the state had seen the creation of a variety of community solar projects, in which groups of neighbors or community members invest together in a solar-generation facility. "Genuine community energy projects, such as the Boardman Hill Solar Farm, the Randolph Community Solar Farm, and White River Community Solar, take an approach that prioritizes full community ownership," said "Operationalizing Energy Democracy."

Air-source heat pumps were now being installed in homes and other buildings all over the state, surprising many with how well they worked. Even in winter, "the heat delivered to buildings by an air-source heat pump is extracted from the ambient air," the Comprehensive Energy Plan explained. It estimated that a typical Vermont family heating its home with a heat pump, with an oil furnace for backup, would spend about $1,700 per year on heating, about a quarter of that to fuel the backup furnace. In contrast, the same family would spend $1,800-$2,200 per year to run a full-time oil furnace.

The number of air-source heat pumps at work in Vermont was now more than doubling each year, said the state's 2016 energy plan. It projected that by 2025, some 35,000 heat pumps will be at work in homes, businesses and other buildings around the state.

The 2016 CEP also addressed the region's electric grid, which by now was connecting both centralized and distributed sources of power. The grid, it said, "is in the midst of a transformation, away from a centralized, one-way electric grid to an integrated grid where both demand and supply adjust moment to moment to maintain balance. ... Electricity is expected to play a major role in the clean energy transformation of both heating and transportation — and the hardware, software and regulation of the grid need to be ready."

"Today," noted the Conservation Law Foundation on its website, "clean, renewable energy can be harnessed right where we live, so electricity doesn't have to come from polluting power plants miles away. But we have to modernize our grid to take advantage of it. ...

"We're pushing to update old pole-and-wire systems to better incorporate local solar and wind energy," CLF said. "We're urging incentives for utilities to add smart meters to improve communication between the electric system and homes and businesses. And we're working with the state agencies that oversee our public utilities ... to change energy policies to better reflect 21st century technology and needs."

The Predicament

But at the same time, "while all that great work was happening, fossil fuel use and costs were increasing in the transportation and thermal sectors," noted Jared Duval, who had become executive director of the Energy Action Network. And even though the state had achieved almost 20 percent renewables by 2018, most of that progress came in the smallest of the energy sectors.

"Electricity is the most renewable, at 63%," EAN reported in 2018 — "however, the electric sector only makes up 14% of Vermont's energy use. Transportation and thermal combined make up 87% of our energy use and are only 5% and 19% renewable, respectively." What's more, "we've only reduced our greenhouse gas emissions by 2% below 2005 levels — and our emissions are up 16% since 1990."

"Eighty percent of our emissions result from energy use," said the 2016 Comprehensive Energy Plan. "Here transportation dominates, with 47% of all GHG emissions." Meeting the state's goal of 10 percent renewable energy in transportation by 2025, "on the way to at least 80% by 2050," the CEP said, will depend on promoting "smart land use," with "compact centers surrounded by rural countryside"; shifting Vermonters "away from single-occupancy vehicles"; and powering a more efficient fleet of light- and heavy-duty trucks and buses with electricity or renewable fuel.

"We've got 10 years to reduce our fossil fuel consumption by half," said Johanna Miller of VNRC. After years of "incremental action," she said, "people are fed up. We've done a lot in the electric sector — we regulate the electric sector in Vermont, and we've required our utilities to clean up. And oh by the way, it's grown jobs.

"We've not done the same in the liquid fuels sector. And when you import 100 percent of those fossil fuels, it's a massive strain on the economy. Eighty percent of those dollars on average go out of state, and we don't have the same levers to pull to require reductions of energy usage and fossil fuels in the thermal and transportation sectors."

The rapid advance of solar power in Vermont took a hit in 2018, when the Public Utilities Commission, revising the state's net-metering rules, reduced the rate at which utilities were required to buy power from new small-scale renewable systems. The 2011 net-metering law had set the rate at 19 to 20 cents per kilowatt hour, "depending on the size of the system," *VTDigger* reported in 2019. "After a few subsequent reductions, net metering compensation for new systems dropped to around 14 cents to 18 cents this July."

"Despite the drive to have more renewably sourced energy and reduce fossil fuel use," *VTDigger* said, "the state Department of Public Service thinks the payment Vermonters can now receive for installing residential solar should be cut ... largely to prevent cost shifting to other ratepayers."

"Our view is that they have hit the breaks too hard," said Ben Walsh of VPIRG. SunCommon's Duane Peterson said the reductions in net-metering compensation had cost some 800 jobs in the state's solar industry — and "net metering 2.0," as it became known, also made it more complex and costly to develop new community solar projects.

"We need to be in a position where every Vermonter can go solar, if that is something that they want to do, to be part of this transition toward renewable energy," said Ben Walsh. "We're just not there right now."

On the national level, Donald Trump's inauguration in 2017 kicked off a hard reversal of the Obama administration's support for renewable energy. Trump promoted fossil fuels, ridiculed renewables, repealed measures aimed at cutting carbon emissions from power plants, opened up federal lands in Alaska to oil and gas drilling, spent heavily on a failed effort to revive the U.S. coal industry, placed new tariffs in the way of solar development, and pulled the United States out of the 2015 Paris Agreement, the international treaty on climate change.

U.S. oil production soared, thanks to oil and gas production in North Dakota and Texas that depended on hydraulic fracturing, or fracking, of shale deposits. Fracking is a controversial process that often involves high-volume leakage of methane, a greenhouse gas "which pound for pound can warm the planet more than 80 times as much as carbon dioxide over a 20-year period," said the *New York Times*.

In Vermont, meanwhile, the broad, multi-year coalition effort that VPIRG put together to promote a carbon-pollution tax was not succeeding. "Carbon pricing can grow the economy, promote equity and help reduce carbon pollution," the nonprofit continued to argue — but Gov. Phil Scott, a Republican, opposed it.

"There will be no carbon tax in Vermont. Not this year, not next year, possibly not ever," *VTDigger* political columnist Jon Margolis declared in 2019. "No carbon tax bill has been introduced." Even the latest climate action plan by the nonprofit coalition, he noted, "does not talk about taxes and calls instead for seeking 'ways to cut carbon pollution across our economy.'"

At the same time, though, "more people came to the State House in 2019 in support of climate action than any other issue," VPIRG's educational arm VPIREF reported. "From small groups of CEOs, or physicians meeting with individual legislators, to grassroots groups and Olympians addressing the Climate Solutions Caucus, to hundreds of students striking and rallying for action — no other issue mobilized as many Vermonters as the climate crisis."

Having so far worked closely with the Vermont business community, and with low-income Vermonters and their advocates, in 2018 VPIRG's Energy Independent Vermont (EIV) Campaign added "a third pillar community: students. Inspired by leaders like Greta Thunberg and organizations like the Sunrise Movement, youth engagement in the climate movement is surging," VPIRG said, and "EIV has worked in close collaboration with the Vermont Youth Lobby."

"Most importantly," the nonprofit added, "there is an undeniable shift among policymakers as a whole toward VPIREF's longstanding position that Vermont must do far more on climate. ... Montpelier is moving inexorably toward climate action. The outstanding question is: will we move fast enough to achieve our goals?"

In 2019, CO_2 measurements at Mauna Loa topped 411 parts per million.

6.

2020: A possible pivot

When 2020 began, energy campaigners aimed to make it a pivotal year. Strong momentum had been building for major state action on climate and energy: Some 30 nonprofits had joined the climate-solutions coalition that VPIRG, VNRC and others had developed, and allies in the State House were prepared to introduce several significant bills.

The most far-reaching of those, the Global Warming Solutions Act, had been presented the year before at the yearly gathering of the Energy Action Network. "The annual summit is an opportunity for folks to think strategically, to pitch the rest of the network on a big opportunity or a strategic idea — and the proposal for the Global Warming Solutions Act was our most popular pitch last year," EAN's Duval said in 2020.

EAN had grown by now to include some 100 members: 50 businesses, 38 nonprofits, nine utilities, 11 higher education providers, 14 state agencies, four cities and three regional organizations, along with legislators and town energy committees from across Vermont. A number of its members "have worked incredibly hard" on the global warming bill, Duval said.

"Yes, collective impact takes more time," he reflected. "It takes a lot of work on relationships and communication. But when you get it right, you can create the collective will to move transformative change much more quickly and durably."

If it passed, the Global Warming Solutions Act would require that the state meet its own timeline for achieving net-zero carbon emissions by 2050. When the

Legislature convened in January, the 30 nonprofits in the climate-solutions coalition — not just environmental and energy groups but also business, anti-poverty and public-health organizations — announced their support for the bill, which VPIRG's Ben Walsh called "the bold, just climate legislation that this moment calls for."

"We have seen vocal support from a wide range of Vermont politicians about the need to meet our pollution reduction targets — and now it's time to act on those pledges," said Lauren Hierl of Vermont Conservation Voters.

There was more. The coalition also backed a bill that would require all Vermont electric utilities to purchase 100 percent renewable power by 2030, and another that would experiment with allowing Efficiency Vermont to work on curbing fossil fuel use and emissions in the transportation and heating sectors.

"We can get more electric vehicles on the road, maximize energy efficiency, and use far more clean, renewable power," said Sandra Levine of the Conservation Law Foundation.

Among climate and energy advocates around the world, the sense of urgency had grown intense. "The extra heat that we trap near the planet because of the carbon dioxide we've spewed is equivalent to the heat from 400,000 Hiroshima-sized bombs every day, or four each second," Bill McKibben wrote in his 2020 book on the climate crisis, *Falter: Has the Human Game Begun to Play Itself Out?*, which bookended his 1986 *The End of Nature*.

"This extraordinary amount of heat is wreaking enormous changes," McKibben wrote. "In the 30 years I've been working on this crisis, we've seen all 20 of the

A 2019 "Rally for the Planet" at the Vermont State House.

Demonstrating inside the State House.

hottest years ever recorded. So far, we have warmed the earth by roughly two degrees Fahrenheit. ... Since 2000, more than a dozen U.S. states have reported the largest wildfires in their recorded histories."

Citing recent firestorms in Australia, Canada, Greece and Siberia, plus record-setting fires that had raged in California after years of drought, McKibben also noted that hurricanes were setting new records for rainfall, and were now reaching such unlikely locales as Ireland. "In the Northeast United States, where I live in landlocked Vermont," he wrote, "we've watched extreme precipitation (two inches or more of rain in 24 hours) grow 53 percent more common since 1996. Much of the sea ice that filled the Arctic in the early pictures from space is gone now. ... Climate change is currently costing the U.S. economy about $240 billion a year, the world $1.2 trillion annually."

In the face of all this, the global climate action campaign that McKibben and a clutch of Middlebury students kicked off in 2006 "has become the largest of its kind in history," he wrote. "Endowments and portfolios worth nearly $8 trillion have joined in it — and it has clearly stung. Recent academic studies have proved that it has helped move the climate issue to the fore and reduced the capital the fossil fuel companies can mobilize for new exploration."

"It's not that renewable energy is our only task," said *Falter*. "We also need to eat lower on the food chain, build public transit networks, densify cities, and start farming in ways that restore carbon to soils. But renewable energy may be the easiest of those tasks, especially since it's suddenly so cheap."

"The only energy sources that grow"

Some remarkable things did seem to be happening. As the Covid-19 pandemic spread around the globe in early to mid-2020, news accounts reported signs that the world's energy economy could be entering a time of deep change:

- "Clean energy investment in the United States surged to a fresh record of $55.5 billion last year, despite the government's attempts to roll back supportive policies," Reuters reported in January, citing a report by Bloomberg New Energy Finance. "President Donald Trump's withdrawal of federal support for Obama-era climate goals indirectly helped the industry here by inspiring a backlash among U.S. cities, states and corporations, which have grown more ambitious about installing cleaner forms of energy."

- "Oil companies are collapsing, but wind and solar energy keep growing," announced a New York Times headline in April. "Renewable energy sources are set to account for nearly 21% of the electricity the United States uses for the first time this year, up from about 18% last year and 10% in 2010, according to one forecast published last week. And while work on some solar and wind projects has been delayed by the [coronavirus] outbreak, industry executives and analysts expect the renewable business to continue growing in 2020 and next year even as oil, gas and coal companies struggle financially or seek bankruptcy protection."

- "The United States is on track to produce more electricity this year from renewable power than from coal for the first time on record, new government projections show," the Times said in May. "It is a milestone that seemed all but unthinkable a decade ago, when coal was so dominant that it provided nearly half the nation's electricity."

- "Oil and gas companies in the United States are hurtling toward bankruptcy at a pace not seen in years, driven under by a global price war and a pandemic that has slashed demand," the Times reported in July. "... Analysts now expect oil demand will begin falling permanently by decade's end as renewable energy costs decline, energy efficiency improves, and efforts to fight climate change diminish an industry that has spent the past decade drilling thousands of wells."

A big bill passes, yet "the work is just beginning"

Vermont's Global Warming Solutions Act aimed to create a new structure and new accountability for the state's efforts to curb carbon emissions from the burning of fossil fuels. In a February 2020 *Seven Days* article, Kevin McCallum wrote:

> The bill would require the state to hit its climate-related emission-reduction targets or face lawsuits from citizens, much like the federal Clean Water Act allows Americans to sue those who pollute waterways.

The state would have to reduce its emission to 26 percent below 2005 levels by 2025; 40 percent below 1990 levels by 2030; and 80 percent below 1990 levels by 2050.

The state has already committed to those goals, but they don't have the force of law. ... The bill would create a 22-member Climate Council that would be responsible for ensuring target goals are met. Some legislators were hesitant to turn that responsibility over to a new body.

Proponents of the bill noted that the Legislature could still object to any new rules, and that it retained the power to decide whether to fund new climate action.

The Vermont House approved the bill by a 105-37 vote in February; then the pandemic struck. As legislators struggled to do essential business via technology from remote locations, some measures fell by the wayside. The bill that would have required utilities to purchase 100 percent renewable power by 2030 failed to make it out of committee. But in June, the Senate approved the Global Warming Solutions Act (GWSA), 23-5.

Then, in an August-September session tacked onto the Legislature's calendar to make up for the pandemic's disruption, the House approved changes the Senate had made to the GWSA. But Gov. Scott vetoed the act, citing concerns that it would "lead to inefficient spending and long, costly court battles." He did sign a separate bill that created a three-year pilot program allowing Efficiency Vermont to do more on reducing fossil fuel use and carbon emissions in the transportation and building sectors. Scott had called the electrification of transportation "a key transformation we must achieve."

Two days later, the House voted 103-47 to override Scott's veto of the GWSA. The Senate concurred, 22-8. Both votes met the two-thirds majority needed to reverse a gubernatorial veto, and the Global Warming Solutions Act became law.

"While the legislation sets up new emissions reduction requirements, it does not spell out how the state will meet them," *VTDigger* explained. Instead, the new Climate Council, chaired by the governor's secretary of administration and including citizen experts and representatives from state government and the manufacturing sector, is directed to develop a plan for reducing emissions, with the Agency of Natural Resources responsible for adopting any new rules. Citizen lawsuits, while permitted, could not seek monetary damages, and would essentially be limited to pushing the state to achieve its goals.

"Vermont currently lacks the kind of strategic planning process and implementation framework this bill offers," VPIRG said in welcoming the new law. "Next year, VPIRG and our allies will be working hard to ensure that the plan that is developed is as robust as possible. ... The work is just beginning."

"We need to do a lot more"

"One of the things that's next for us is a very deep engagement with the processes and planning that this bill is creating," said VPIRG's Ben Walsh, "so that it really does put us on a path toward net-zero carbon pollution and renewable energy. That's number one.

"As we're moving toward net zero, we need to do that in a way that makes Vermont and Vermont communities more resilient," he said, "so rural communities that are struggling right now, for reasons that are related to climate change and a whole lot that aren't, can be lifted up as we're moving toward a cleaner energy system."

Walsh had been working on energy issues for VPIRG since 2011. Early in the decade, Vermont was one of the states leading the move toward renewables; but over the last few years, he believes, that leadership faded.

"When we're talking about the climate crisis, if you move in the right direction too slowly, you're still moving backwards. And that is where we are right now, as a state," Walsh said. "I am both frustrated by how little has happened in the last

At a wind farm in Lowell in 2016: VPIRG Climate & Energy Program Director Ben Edgerly Walsh, center, with then-VPIRG clean energy advocate Sarah Wolfe, at left, and clean energy legal intern Natalia Teekah.

decade, and very optimistic about what could happen in the coming decade. We have an enormous opportunity, and a long way to go."

"How do we transition from a carbon economy to a non-carbon economy?" asked Tony Klein, the former House energy chair, who continues to work on the energy transformation. "In order to get Vermonters to want to transition, you have to have the products that work for them. Those products have to be affordable to them, and the fuel that drives those products has to be affordable, or at least competitive, with fossil fuels. How do we do that? And how do we do that without there being a mandate or tax?"

What's more, he added, "we have to flip people's minds from efficiency. We want you to use more [electricity], not less now. That's a hard thing to change."

In the movement's early years, "anything you did to reduce electricity was good," agreed Beth Sachs, co-founder of Efficiency Vermont. "Now, with air-source heat pumps and electric vehicles, that's all changed."

That is a change — and it's a challenge.

"Continued acceleration of electric vehicle adoption in the transportation sector could dramatically increase total electricity demand," wrote the authors of *Electrification Futures Study: Scenarios of Electric Technology Adoption and Power Consumption for the United States*, a 2018 report by the National Renewable Energy Laboratory for the U.S. Department of Energy. "Impacts in this sector could be especially magnified because transportation currently accounts for less than 1% of U.S. electricity demand but accounts for nearly 30% of primary energy consumption."

Ben Walsh put that in a larger context. "If we're getting to all our cars and all our buildings using electricity as our primary [energy source], yeah, we're going to need a lot more electricity," he said. "But the increase in electric usage is not going to be nearly as significant as the decrease in fossil fuel usage, because of how efficient electric cars and heat pumps are."

"It's the start of a new change"

On his first day in office in 2021, President Joe Biden brought the United States back into the Paris climate accord, and began preparing for negotiations to boost the energy efficiency of cars, pickup trucks and SUVs and extend tax credits for wind and solar power. By the end of his first 100 days in office, Biden had announced a new climate goal: cutting the country's carbon emissions to at least 50 percent below 2005 levels by 2050. His administration began to seek passage of a national clean energy standard — one that would, Reuters reported, "require 80% of retail power sales to come from sources that produce little or no carbon emissions by 2030, rising to 100% by 2035."

In August, Biden "announced a multistep strategy," the *Times* reported, "aimed at rapidly shifting Americans from gasoline-powered cars and trucks toward electric vehicles," with newly strict emission standards intended to "prevent the burning of about 200 billion gallons of gasoline over the lifetime of the cars." The president said he envisioned "a future of the automobile industry that is electric — battery electric, plug-in hybrid electric, fuel cell electric."

To reach Biden's climate goals, the *Times* said recent studies suggested that more than half of new cars would need to be electric-powered, "nearly all coal-fired power plants would need to be shut down," and the number of wind turbines and solar panels "could quadruple."

At the state level, the 2021 Legislature committed some $250 million in federal pandemic stimulus funding to climate and clean energy programs. The money will support weatherization for low- and moderate-income homeowners, programs making renewable energy affordable for low-income Vermonters, incentives for adopting electric and high- efficiency gas vehicles, and funding for electric-vehicle charging stations, electric bikes and cost-free public transit.

"We are in a historic moment," said Brian Shupe, VNRC's executive director. Lauren Hierl, executive director of Vermont Conservation Voters, called the funding allocation "a huge day for Vermont, as we meet the climate crisis head-on and work to build a healthier, more resilient, more equitable economy together."

For more power to be provided in sustainable ways, electric utilities need to complete a pivot — away from generating revenue by investing in major assets like power plants, and toward providing the clean power that people want and the energy services and technologies they need, as Green Mountain Power has done with storage batteries. That was the case made in a 2016 paper, *The Old Order Changeth: Rewarding Utilities for Performance, Not Capital Investment*, published by the American Council for an Energy-Efficient Economy and written by Scudder Parker with Jim Lazar of the Regulatory Assistance Project, a Vermont nonprofit that advises utility regulators around the world.

State utility regulators can and should be guiding that shift, the authors argue. "Although evolving public policy has given the utility sector new missions, and changes in technology have given the utility sector (and customers) new tools, the basic framework of regulation remains largely unchanged," they wrote. Regulators, they explained, generally allow utilities to draw their revenue through an allowed rate of return on capital investment, along with recovery of "prudently incurred operating expenses" — and that structure "produces an incentive to invest."

Linking utility earnings to performance, instead of investment, "will help utilities move to cleaner energy, energy efficiency, and their corollaries: customer-friendly and environmentally responsible service," wrote Parker and Lazar.

Under Mary Powell's leadership, Green Mountain Power made big strides toward that orientation. Powell left GMP at the end of 2019, having led it to become the nation's first utility certified as a social-benefit B Corp. Before she left, she said, "we did a lot of modeling that showed we could transform massive parts of the transportation system, and the home heating system, and not create '90s-era thinking about load growth. Because you can manage it in a way that you couldn't before.

"If I could wave a magic wand, every home in Vermont would have some sort of storage device," Powell said. "Those would allow us to completely flatten the load curve — and there would be no peaks any more that would have dirty carbon tied to them in the summer." The larger power producers, such as Hydro-Québec, she predicted, will play more of a backup role, "which is why we need them to be as green as possible.

"I think the opportunities are only going to grow, as technology and innovation are accelerating in this space," Powell summed up. "As we move to this decentralized opportunity — which will be more resilient, which will be better from a climate perspective — we just need to do it in a way that is very Vermont-y: to share our energy, so it can benefit all the Vermonters that are serviced from the grid."

David Blittersdorf, CEO of the Vermont firm AllEarth Solar, has long been an influential voice in the statewide conversation on energy. "I think the way we're going, by 2030 we may decrease carbon by 20 percent to 30 percent, if we go all out," he said. "But we need to do a lot more.

"If you go out to 2050, you have to reduce carbon about 7 percent a year. It takes a long time to get down to close to zero. What we just saw in the Covid pandemic is, we've decreased abruptly, in the world, about 7 percent to 8 percent carbon. Look what it took to do that! It took shutting down the aircraft industry, shutting down transportation. We did all those things. Okay, now we have to do this for the next 30 years, same thing every year?

"We have over 600,000 cars in the state," he said. "Until we get the cars down to about 100,000, you have no chance. If you switch to electric [cars], you get some of that carbon out — but you have an infrastructure based on carbon emissions. So you have to decrease the car. We need to get to a transit system that works."

In the wake of the pandemic, Blittersdorf predicted, "We're going to have a lot more people working from home, and that reduces energy use. I think we'll never go back to that normal consumption of fuels and carbon. It's the start of a new change.

"We're in a transforming time," he summed up. "There have been other turnings in the United States — the Revolutionary War, the Civil War, the Great Depression and World War II. During a turning, the old thing dies off and we have a rebirth of our society. I think we're right in the middle of it, and we're going to see some dramatic change — because we have to. Otherwise we're not going to survive."

FIGHTING "GOLIATH":
THE BATTLE OVER THE ADDISON PIPELINE

Nate and Jane Palmer have a small bottomland farm in a valley in Monkton. They grow hay and vegetables, they have a few animals and an orchard, and they've put in a stand of fast-growing willows for wood pellets to heat their home.

"I really didn't want to have anything more to do with fossil fuels," said Nate, who used to run Palmer's Garage, which his father started in 1951 over in North Ferrisburgh. "I wanted to be a little more environmentally sensitive, and get away from that stuff."

So when the Palmers heard in 2013 that a natural-gas pipeline might be coming through their area, "we started researching natural gas a little bit," Nate said. But they didn't feel too concerned, even when neighbors started saying the pipeline might come straight through town. They meant to attend a couple of local meetings about the project, but didn't make it. Then another landowner said the pipeline was being rerouted to go right through their farm.

"A few days after that we got a call from a local guy, who was actually a customer of my garage," Nate said. "Turns out he wants to come look at our property, to see if it's feasible to put the pipeline through. When he came and talked to us, he would not admit that he worked for the gas company — he said he was working for a surveyor who was working for another company that was working for the gas company. We ran into this many times, where people were working for the gas company but didn't want to admit they were."

What began at that time was a years-long struggle that ultimately involved not just the Palmers but hundreds of other Vermonters who became alarmed at the bid by Vermont Gas Systems, which already served northwest Vermont with gas piped down from Canada, to install a 41-mile underground gas pipeline from Colchester south through Addison County to Middlebury.

"It was coming," Jane said, "and the attitude was that it's a done deal, basically — you can't fight this project, just deal with it. Our first reaction was wait a minute, let's find out more."

The Palmers spent evening after evening digging and researching. They learned that much of the gas the pipeline would transport would be the product of hydraulic fracturing, or fracking, a controversial process that uses large volumes of highly pressurized water to release petroleum deposits from shale, sandstone and limestone far underground. Along with various damaging local impacts, fracking — the source of the recent years' boom in North American oil and gas production — releases methane, among the most destructive of greenhouse gases.

Beyond Middlebury, Vermont Gas planned to extend its pipeline in two followup projects: Phase II beneath Lake Champlain to the International Paper plant in Ticonderoga, New York, then Phase III south to Rutland.

Over the next few years, the Palmers would become veteran activists who found out firsthand what can happen when ordinary citizens oppose the expansion of fossil fuel infrastructure — even in a state that has committed itself to phasing out almost all fossil fuels.

The Palmers figure that by December 2013, when the Vermont Public Service Board issued its ruling on the certificate of public good that Vermont Gas needed for the pipeline, they had put a thousand hours into building and presenting their case. They had no money for lawyers or experts; a UVM agronomist testified without charge, and Nate traded a transmission job for testimony from a hydrogeologist.

Vermont Gas's plan called for the pipeline to cut a 75-foot swath "right through every-thing that was important to us," said Nate: their orchard, fields, willows and pond. Afterward, no plantings would be allowed on the swath except for grass or shallow-rooted bushes.

The PSB approved the pipeline proposal. But in 2015 it agreed to reconsider, because the project's estimated cost had risen from $86.6 million to $154 million. "Vermont Gas is relying on the 54,000 ratepayers in Franklin, Addison and Chittenden to pick up $134 million of the tab," *VTDigger* reported.

Meanwhile, "frustration with Vermont Gas has been bubbling up in homes and commu-nities all along the proposed pipeline," *Seven Days* reported in mid-2014. "... Critics allege a pattern of bad behavior: Surveyors who trespassed, or misrepresented their affiliation with Vermont Gas; land agents who portrayed themselves as 'mediators' or brokers rather than employees of the company; company officials who left questions unanswered for months; a corporation that pushed for an aggressive schedule in Public Service Board meetings, leaving landowners and some town officials feeling frantic, rushed and overwhelmed."

The paper quoted Kevin Ellis, a Montpelier public affairs consultant: "'You know something is wrong when a couple of days before Town Meeting, they send out a letter to various landowners threatening to take their land by eminent domain.'"

The PSB again gave the pipeline the go-ahead. But Vermont Gas also needed easements or agreements from landowners of 222 parcels along the route, and some 60 landowners declined to cooperate. With financial support from the Lintilhac Foundation, opponents of the project hired an attorney, James Dumont of Bristol, who fought the project vigorously in PSB proceedings. Yet one by one, Vermont Gas secured the land it needed, either through negotiation or by eminent-domain seizure.

At the same time, between 2014 and 2016, protesters who ranged in age from their twenties to their late seventies shut down an eminent-domain hearing in Monkton, rallied outside the Montpelier offices of the Vermont Department of Public Service, blockaded a construction staging area in Williston, refused to leave a construction site in New Haven, and perched in platforms high in trees to stop construction in Monkton. In 2016, opponents lay down to stage a "die-in" outside the PSB's hearing on Vermont Gas's bid to seize the very last of the 222 parcels, Geprags Community Park in Hinesburg.

During that series of protests, some opponents were arrested. One was Jane Palmer.

"I have tried everything"

It was July 2014, and Jane was outraged that Vermont Gas had pressed charges against several young people who had staged a protest at the company's headquarters. "And I had friends, three other landowners who were being bullied into taking this pipeline, and they were outraged," she said. "We decided to go talk to Don Gilbert," then Vermont Gas's CEO. "We took our knitting, in case we had to wait for him. We went into the office and sat down."

Gilbert wouldn't see them. Company staffers tried to persuade them to leave. But the four held firm to demands that Vermont Gas drop charges against the protesters and stop using eminent domain, or use it only as a last resort.

"They would not even talk to us," Jane said. "Eventually they called the police, and my

Jane Palmer being arrested at the Vermont Gas corporate offices in 2014. *Photo by Taylor Dobbs.*

friends decided they didn't want to get arrested. I just said, 'I'm staying.' And they arrested me."

A Vermont Public Radio reporter shot a photo of Jane in handcuffs, "with five police cruisers and I don't know how many cops," she said, "arresting this little old lady in a sundress who's accused of knitting in the office. It went viral on the internet."

Eventually Vermont Gas dropped the charges. But "I don't know how many times I went to Burlington, to the courthouse," said Jane, who couldn't afford a lawyer and represented herself. In "Why I Protest," a December 2016 essay posted by *VTDigger*, she wrote:

> I pushed the envelope on that occasion because I had tried to argue against the viability of this project in lengthy proceedings before the Vermont Public Service Board. To no avail. I, along with many others, was familiar with the arguments for and against the pipeline — from the exorbitant costs, the climate impacts, the destruction of farmland, wetlands and waterways, and the corporate abuse of the eminent domain process against my neighbors. ...
>
> I have tried reasoning. I have tried standing up to the army of lawyers that were being paid to get this pipeline approved. I have tried everything I can think of to do.

The nonprofits VPIRG, Toxics Action and the Conservation Law Foundation joined the battle. Labeling the project "the fracked gas pipeline" in every communication it put out, VPIRG argued that the pipeline "is outdated and out of touch with current economic and environmental realities," said Ben Walsh of the group.

"New technologies like cold climate heat pumps, which have fewer greenhouse gas emissions than gas," VPIRG said in a statement, "have become readily available and more cost-effective in the four years since Phase I of the pipeline was conceived."

Jane and Nate Palmer. *Photo by Caleb Kenna.*

In January 2016, just before the Public Service Board was to make yet another ruling on the project, VPIRG joined 1,400 Vermont businesses, organizations, community leaders and individuals in signing a letter to Gov. Peter Shumlin, who had supported the pipeline. The letter asked him to "close this painful chapter in our state's history and turn our positive energies toward a prosperous and sustainable future."

But the PSB again approved the pipeline. It ruled in January 2016 that "even though it has gone up dramatically in price," the project "will still benefit ratepayers," *VTDigger* reported. "The order says the Public Service Board will not reopen proceedings for the pipeline, which effectively means the project can go ahead."

"You have to keep keep *keep* going"

The pipeline began transporting natural gas in 2017. But Vermont Gas has so far tabled the plans for its second and third phases, and opponents continue working to shut the conduit down in Addison County. They have raised and documented multiple safety-related issues, documenting concerns over the quality of welding and of protective coatings, over whether the pipeline was buried deeply enough — even whether construction crews followed correct procedures.

"We did a bunch of public record requests, and we became more and more aware of all the shortcomings in the construction process," said Rachel Smolker of Hinesburg, who has helped lead the ongoing fight. "We realized, this is just a ticking time bomb in people's yards."

In early 2018, the state Department of Public Service asked the Public Utility Commission, successor to the PSB, to fine Vermont Gas $25,000 for failing to bury the pipeline deeply enough in a section in New Haven. The proposed fine "was in response to violations [attorney] Dumont's clients brought to the attention of state and federal authorities, Dumont has said," *VTDigger* reported.

"It's a David-and-Goliath kind of thing," said Smolker, who is co-director of the nonprofit Biofuelwatch and an organizer with the Energy Justice Network. "A lot of people came in thinking that if they chained themselves to a piece of work equipment, that would be the thing to do. And of course those helped — but all those strategies have to work together, and people have to be willing to really slog it out over the long term.

"When you get involved in a long-range ongoing struggle like this has been, it's really nice to have funders who step in and say, 'Yes, we get it, you have to keep keep *keep* going.'"

Meanwhile, the fracking industry has entered a time of serious difficulty. The price of oil having dropped dramatically in the five years ending in April, "there were 215 bankruptcies for oil and gas companies," the *New York Times* reported in spring 2020. And after suffering years of damaging publicity over the Addison pipeline, Vermont Gas announced in late 2019 that it would seek to reduce greenhouse gas emissions in customers' homes and businesses by 30 percent by 2030, then altogether by 2050.

"Vermont Gas Systems, to its credit, is among the most progressive gas companies in the country, if not the most progressive," said Paul Burns, VPIRG's executive director. "But it's still a gas company. That's part of their challenge.

"I would never say the fracked gas industry is done," he added. "It would be foolish to believe that, because there are billions of dollars at stake."

Underscoring that reality, in late 2019 the Public Utility Commission denied a petition by a group of Vermont ratepayers to block the sale of a public company that owned both Vermont Gas and Green Mountain Power to Noverco, a Canadian investment holding company.

"The intervenors, many of whom fought Vermont Gas's Addison County pipeline, opposed the deal because one of the primary owners of Noverco is Enbridge, a Canadian multinational that has come under scrutiny from environmental advocates for its massive network of oil and natural gas pipelines," *VTDigger* reported.

Opponents of the Vermont pipeline have long feared that, if it were eventually extended to link up with a growing network of gas pipelines in New York State, Vermont could become a pass-through — a fossil-fuel "superhighway."

"We have legislation that would ban new fossil-fuel infrastructure, in particular an emphasis on these large pipelines," Paul Burns said. "It would be a mistake to move forward with more large pipelines in the state, if we are at all serious about meeting our climate commitments.

"All sorts of economic issues arise if you say, 'We're turning off the pipeline entirely' — but a big step would be saying, 'No more.' Let's not build any more of this stuff, and make sure that people have enough time to transition away from gas, so that when you're thinking about what's next for your home, you can be thinking about air-source heat pumps and so forth, instead of fossil fuel and an oil tank or a gas pipeline.

"It gets right down to the individual homeowner who says, 'I see the availability of heat pumps; I think they're cost-competitive and way better for the climate and future generations," Burns added. "Sometimes it's the fight against the bad stuff that gives a tremendous boost to the good solutions that we need. And I think people deserve credit for that, as part of this fight."

As for the Palmers, they got a reprieve. Vermont Gas decided to reroute its pipeline to go around their farm. The whole pipeline saga, Nate said, "was a terrible experience to go through — but we've met the most amazing people that we never would have met, if it hadn't been for this thing."

"The one thing I have taken away from this: I am not afraid any more," Jane Palmer said. "I am not afraid of going before a judge, I am not afraid of speaking up to the CEOs of these companies. I am not afraid of anybody. And that has really changed my life."

From left: Will, Louise and Paul Lintilhac.

10

The Next Generation

Staying engaged with Vermont's landscape
and communities

Louise, Will and Paul Lintilhac, Crea and Phil's adult children, are serving on the foundation's board as its third generation of family leadership. Each also has their own work. Louise is currently a brand manager for the Vermont firm Press Forward PR, and co-owner of her local gym, Waterbury Functional Fitness; Will serves on the board of the Vermont Natural Resources Council and works at Bicycle Express, a mountain biking hub in Waterbury; and Paul is a PhD student at Dartmouth College's Thayer School of Engineering. He's also chief information officer at Trace, a software company that uses cutting-edge technology to increase transparency and trust in regulated agricultural industries.

In a conversation with the author, the three shared their thoughts about the future of the Lintilhac Foundation.

How do you anticipate the foundation's priorities evolving?

LOUISE: I think that while we stay within the framework our mission gives us, the landscape here in Vermont is evolving — so from a landscape standpoint, from a community standpoint, the needs evolve, too. We have far fewer working farms in the state; that affects how the landscape looks. We have different rules and regulations for water quality; that affects what we do. So we keep our ears to the ground, and try to stay in tune with how we might need to adjust where and why we give.

WILL: The world of conservation is changing, as are conservationists. There's a dramatic shift toward thinking about it in terms of people, and the impact that our actions are having on people. Just as we're coming to realize that a lot of environmental measures are good business, conservationists are starting to realize that good social justice policy is good conservation, and vice versa. A lot of organizations are thinking about water quality, energy use, access to the outdoors, or any other issue from a human perspective, realizing that each of these issues is fundamentally a social justice issue.

PAUL: I think about food security and the way that our food supply chains work, especially with the Covid-19 pandemic. Food security, not just organic but organic regenerative, and energy as well — they're environmental issues, but they're social justice issues. Advocating for policies that support renewable energy is something I would like to see more and more of. So in my eyes, those are two themes that have been growing recently for the foundation: energy and food supply chains in Vermont.

Has the pandemic changed your thinking, in terms of what you want to focus on?

LOUISE: We've always given to local news media, but the pandemic, and this past election cycle, made it very clear that we need good investigative journalism to help citizens educate themselves about the issues at hand. *VTDigger* has been nationally acknowledged for how amazing they are at investigative journalism, and the work that we do with VPR is ongoing. It's become clear that we're doing the right thing in giving to these organizations that do such an incredible job of fact-finding, making sure that they're hunting down the science behind the claims, and making sure the public is aware of what's going on, from water quality to politics and whatever else is on the table.

PAUL: We're also looking to support small-town organizations that support food security in places that are economically getting hit pretty hard. Some don't have a good hub to purchase affordable, accessible, healthy, local food. We're looking for communities and ways to help affect change in this area as well.

This has been an unusually activist family foundation. You don't just write checks; under Crea's leadership it's been an engaged relationship with nonprofits, sitting on boards, being present in the State House. Do you see that changing as you bring your own personalities and styles to the way the foundation works?

LOUISE: We think about that a lot — and realistically, it's going to be a hybrid. We know the importance of having Mom be in the State House, listening to these conversations on a regular basis and interacting with people on the ground. She just listens; she wants to be informed. That's invaluable, and we know that. So we look to the future and ask, "How do we continue to keep a finger on the pulse like she does, but accommodate the fact that there are three of us, and we all have different jobs and different goals in life?"

We all care deeply about where the foundation is going and what we're doing. So that's something we're going to have to figure out.

PAUL: It will evolve over time. It's the early stages of what will probably be a similar level of activism in 10, 20 years. There was a time when Mom was the new person on the scene.

WILL: I honestly don't think any one of us, or all three of us combined, are going to do what Mom does — but that doesn't mean we can't garner all types of really good relationships and connections with policy experts, scientists working in the field, legislators. We can cover all the bases. It's just going to look different.

Honestly, if we stay involved in things like water quality, food systems, energy, we can't just write checks and hope the people receiving the money and doing the work are informed, know the experts, have good connections and relationships. We have to be informed. We're going to have to go about it in our own way, but we're going to have to go about it. We can't be removed from it. Other families do, but that seems cheesy. It seems floppy and flimsy.

PAUL: That's the point of being a Vermont foundation. We can know every single grantee.

The Lintilhac family, from left: Will's wife, Rosy Metcalfe; Paul, Will, Crea, Louise, Phil, and Louise's husband, Dana Allen.

Is there one way in which each of you sees the foundation as distinctive?

WILL: One thing that comes to mind is simply our ability to be fleet of foot. If we need something done quickly, we can make that happen. Opportunities to fund conservation, push vital policy through, and help partners bring legal cases can arise suddenly, and the window to act can disappear just as fast.

Every year, we understand a little bit more about what our real skill set is as a family and a foundation. Every year we get better at asking questions of partner organizations, pushing their work to be better, and creating accountability. We don't just fund things and then disappear back into the woodwork. There are plenty of opportunities to fund new things and learn from the experts, but we are always interested in being engaged in active conversation with any partner.

PAUL: Some other things that are special about the foundation — first of all, Mom. It's her full-time job, and she puts in the effort to become an expert on every single thing she's involved in. That's pretty rare, and that's going to be hard to replace.

The other thing is that Vermont is a special place. We all genuinely love Vermont, and the influence that Vermont has, relative to its economic and population size, makes it kind of unique in the country. So having a foundation in this state gives you more leverage, more influence, than in any other state.

LOUISE: For me, that's the real power of the Lintilhac Foundation: the community connections we've been able to both foster and help to thrive in Vermont. We're a small family foundation, but the power is in the fact that we have chosen to stay within the Vermont community, to do good where we live.

We try to stay local, not to spread ourselves too thin. And because of that, it allows us to see the intricate social connections, environmental connections, that other foundations might overlook. That's our wheelhouse.

BEHIND THE SCENES, A SINGLE-PERSON STAFF

For more than 30 years, Nancy Brink has been the office manager and one-person staff of the Lintilhac Foundation. She has handled tasks and duties of all sorts, while fielding queries and providing guidance and information to a wealth of Vermont nonprofits — all from an extremely well-organized office in Crea and Phil Lintilhac's home.

"They've been a second family to me," Nancy said. "For half my life I've driven up there and been in their home. It has just been a joy to work for an organization that has goodness at its core.

"It has been Crea and me, working together. She's been the pilot — and I guess," she added with a laugh, "you could say I've driven the boat."

"Nancy has always given us thoughtful and discreet advice and guidance," Crea reflected. "When people called the foundation office, she was the person at the other end of the line, fielding questions and offering advice about the logistics of applying for grants. Our family has always been thankful for Nancy's professionalism and faithful friendship and appreciative of her helpful assistance. Her tactful and speedy work made the foundation run smoothly."

It all started in the mid-1980s. Nancy was working as a legal secretary for Stowe attorney Tom Amidon, who was handling the new foundation's affairs while serving on its first board. Nancy had attended a couple of the board meetings at Claire's home in Stowe, and after Claire's passing in 1984, Crea and Phil came to see her.

"I'll never forget it," Nancy said. "They said, 'We're thinking of moving the foundation out of the law office, would you like to come?' I said, 'Absolutely.'

"I liked what the foundation stood for," she said. "It has always been about the

Nancy Brink

betterment of the community, the whole state, and their interests are everything that a Vermonter regards highly: education, clean water, the environment, health care, the arts, and now recreation, with the kids coming on board."

The "kids" are Phil and Crea's adult children, Louise, Will and Paul. Nancy has watched them grow from childhood into serving on the foundation's board and now gradually stepping into leadership roles.

"Crea is still very much involved, but the torch is passing," Nancy observed. "The kids have their own ideas of what they would like to see the foundation do. They're very active and involved, and they have the same heart that Crea and Phil do, the same mindset. They want to do it for the betterment of Vermont."

Over these years, Nancy has developed working relationships with a wide range of Vermonters at the nonprofit organizations the foundation has helped to fund — yet she has rarely met those folks face to face. "It's been phone calls, correspondence, emails, whatever. Crea would talk about their projects, just using me as a sounding board. I learned a lot just from listening."

An ordained minister who led a church women's ministry in Moretown for a dozen years, Nancy pared back her foundation work to part-time in 2019. She and husband Michael, who retired after three decades as chief packaging engineer for Ben & Jerry's, have two grown children, and now two grandchildren.

"How I could sum it all up," Nancy said of her years with the foundation, "would be honored. And full of gratitude."

Postscript: After the Pandemic

by Crea Lintilhac

The world has changed since the start of the pandemic. But while it has been difficult for everyone to be confined, Vermont has proven to be a great place to get outside close to home. Having nearby forest trails where people can safely and responsibly get fresh air and exercise has never been more important. Our foundation's longstanding mission to ensure that our shared public lands are protected and accessible may have especially shown its worth in this time.

Meanwhile, Covid-19 food insecurity has hit record levels in Vermont. NOFA and Hunger Free Vermont have been working with our state agencies and with Vermont's Congressional delegation. New connections across Vermont communities have improved access to food for low-income families in times of stress. The USDA authorized waivers that have allowed schools to provide free meals to all children ages 18 and under for the entire 2020-21 school year. NOFA and Hunger Free Vermont made it possible for Vermont schools to take advantage of this option, ensuring that students could get nourishing meals no matter where they were learning.

As we look to rebuild from Covid-19, Vermont's Global Warming Solutions Act will help accelerate our economic recovery. The Solutions Act provides the framework to reduce our greenhouse gas emissions to net-zero by 2050, while creating an economy and communities that are stronger, self-reliant and more equitable. The bill advances solutions that are guided by science and grow the economy while protecting public health and the environment.

The economic and health impacts of coronavirus have been devastating for Vermonters. It will take a suite of strategies to rebound from this unprecedented crisis, and one that should not be overlooked is the cleanup effort of our iconic Lake Champlain and other impaired waters of the state. While our lakes, ponds and streams are a significant driver of our economy year-round, the work to clean up our water bodies can help fuel Vermont's recovery from the pandemic — creating a win-win for our environment and economy, both in the short-term and in the future.

Civic engagement: a shift that may continue

As the Covid-19 pandemic made social distancing the norm across the country, much of civic life — from our schools to political campaigning to voter registration drives to our work activities — has shifted to virtual environments.

Young people are increasingly turning to online social media platforms to learn about, engage with, and share information about Covid-19, politics, and social movements like Black Lives Matter. This can provide entry points into civic engagement that may not be limited to the online sphere: Research has found that online activism among young people is associated with offline forms of civic and political activism, giving youth multiple pathways to engage with issues they care about and build a political identity.

This shift toward online engagement will hopefully continue, as it better reaches those who cannot travel to legislative committee meetings or town meetings, for instance — but can, with internet access, view testimony and conversations in real time, or at any time of the day. The virtual environment, despite its shortcomings for personal interaction, has made it easier by far for people to collaborate and share and participate in meetings without the usual long drives required in our rural environment (not to mention the search for a place to park in Montpelier).

We've reshaped the way we communicate and amplified local civic behavior, and this has been a good bridge to helping us find better connections with people and providing more avenues for participation. Online engagement has its limitations, of course; but even so, it's a powerful tool for people to be engaged.

Since the start of the Covid-19 pandemic in 2020, "kids have been getting free school meals, regardless of their family's income," the nonprofit Hunger Free Vermont has reported. The organization is leading a campaign to make school meals for all Vermont students, at no extra charge to their families, a permanent program.

Sources

Lintilhac Foundation. *Annual Reports.* Vermont: 1985–86, 1987, 1988, 1989–1990, 1991–1992, 1993–1994, 1995–1996, 1997–1998, 1999–2000, 2001, 2002–2003, 2004–2005, 2006–2007, 2008–2009, 2010–2012, 2013–2015, 2016.

Chapter 1

Interviewed by Author

Eleanor Capeless, Kathy Keleher, Audrey Linn, Crea Lintilhac and Mary Gibson.

Interviewed by Kathy Keleher, 1994

Barbara Blauvelt, Alice Blodgett, Steve Blodgett, and Doris Maeck.

Publications

Churchill, Martha, CNM. "40th Anniversary Speech." Delivered at the Claire M. Lintilhac Birthing Center, Fletcher Allen Health Care (formerly Medical Center Hospital of Vermont, now the University of Vermont Medical Center), 2008.

"Claire Lintilhac: A Dedication to Mothers and Babies." *Hall A*, a publication of the University of Vermont College of Medicine (Autumn 1981).

"Claire Lintilhac Dies at Age 85." *Stowe Reporter*, August 16, 1984.

Keleher, Kathleen Carrigan, CNM, MPH, and Leon I. Mann, MD. "Nurse-Midwifery Care in an Academic Health Center." *Journal of Obstetric, Gynecologic & Neonatal Nursing* 15, no. 5 (September 1986): 369–372.

Keleher, Kathy, CNM, MPH, and Eleanor Capeless, MD. *Lintilhac Foundation Nurse-Midwife Report.* Burlington: 1985, 1986, 1987.

Lintilhac, Claire M. *China in Another Time: A Personal Story.* Montpelier: Rootstock Publishing, 2019.

———. Letter to leaders of the Medical Center Hospital of Vermont, October 1979.

———. Personal journals.

Lintilhac Foundation Board of Trustees. "Reported Meeting Minutes." Stowe, Vt.: June 1975–February 1989.

Maeck, John Van S., MD, FACOG. "Obstetrician-Midwife Partnership in Obstetric Care." *Obstetrics & Gynecology* 37, no. 2 (February 1971): 314–319.

Mann, Leon, MD. Letter to the Lintilhac Foundation, 1980.

Nurse-Midwifery Program. *Annual Report to the Lintilhac Foundation.* Burlington: Medical Center Hospital of Vermont, 1979.

———. *Annual Report to the Lintilhac Foundation.* Burlington: Medical Center Hospital of Vermont, 1983.

———. "Five Year Program." Burlington: The University Associates in Obstetrics and Gynecology, 1981.

———. "Nurse-Midwifery History (Brief Summary)." Burlington: Medical Center Hospital of Vermont, 1978.

———. "Progress Report on Development of Nurse-Midwifery Program for January 1–December 31, 1979." Burlington: Medical Center Hospital of Vermont, 1979.

Rooks, Judith Pence. *Midwifery & Childbirth in America.* Philadelphia: Temple University Press, 1997.

Chapter 2

Interviewed by Author

Philip and Crea Lintilhac.

Publications

Conservation and Research Foundation. *Annual Reports.* 1953, 1963, 1973, 1978, 1983, 1988, 1993, 1998, 2003.

Goodwin, Richard H. *A Botanist's Window on the Twentieth Century.* Petersham: Harvard Forest, Harvard University, 2002.

Chapter 3

Interviewed by Author

Eleanor Capeless, Martha Churchill, Eugene DeClercq, Nathalie Feldman, Kathy Keleher, Crea Lintilhac, Kelly McLean, Laura Pentenrieder, Sandra Wood and Gail Zatz.

"A Mom's Story" interviews: Vanessa Melamede Berman, Susan Sheckler Leff, Carina McCauley, Maureen McGrath, Julia Melloni, Ashley Olinger, Doma Sherpa, Lisa Simon, Cory Simon-Nobles, and Susan Wargo.

Publications

"America's Best Cities for Women." *Ladies Home Journal*, November 1997.

American College of Nurse-Midwives. *Midwifery: Evidence-Based Practice. A Summary of Research on Midwifery Practice in the United States.* Silver Spring, Md.: April 2012.

————. *"Normal, Healthy Childbirth for Women & Families: What You Need to Know."* Silver Spring, Md.: 2014.

Belluz, Julia. "California Decided It Was Tired of Women Bleeding to Death in Childbirth." *Vox*, June 29, 2017.

Centers for Disease Control & Prevention. "Total Cesarean Delivery and Low-Risk Cesarean Delivery, by Race and Hispanic Origin of Mother: United States, Each State and Territory, 2014." *National Vital Statistics Reports.* U.S. Department of Health and Human Services, December 23, 2015.

Certified Nurse-Midwifery Service. "Core Principles to Our Midwifery Practice." Burlington: Medical Center Hospital of Vermont, n.d.

Champlain OB/GYN. "We Are Excited to Announce that Champlain OB/GYN Has Added Certified Nurse Midwifery to the Practice." Announcement, Essex Junction, Vt., July 9, 2014.

Committee on Obstetric Practice. "Approaches to Limit Intervention During Labor and Birth." Committee Opinion no. 687. The American College of Obstetricians and Gynecologists, February 2017.

Copley Hospital. "Copley Birthing Center Plans Open House." News release, *News & Citizen* (Morrisville, Vt.), May 8, 1986.

DeClercq, Eugene. "Midwife-Attended Births in the United States, 1990–2012: Results from Revised Birth Certificate Data." *Journal of Midwifery & Women's Health* 60, no. 1 (Jan–Feb 2015): 10–5.

————. "The Transformation of American Midwifery: 1975 to 1988." *American Journal of Public Health* 82, no. 5 (May 1992): 680–684.

Fletcher Allen Health Care. "Fletcher Allen Names New Birthing Center in Honor of Claire M. Lintilhac." News release, Burlington, Vt., May 10, 2004.

Health Resources and Services Administration. "Screening and Treatment for Maternal Depression and Related Behavioral Disorders Program (MDRBD)." *HRSA Maternal & Child Health.* U.S. Department of Health and Human Services. Accessed October 1, 2020. https://mchb.hrsa.gov/maternal-child-health-initiatives/mental-behavioral-health/mdrbd.

Hollenberger, Leah. "This Month Marks 20 Years of Midwifery Services at Copley Hospital." Morrisville: Copley Hospital, September 23, 2016.

Keleher, Kathy. "Obstetrical Care in Vermont: The Place of Nurse-Midwives." Unpublished paper, July 1991.

MacDorman, Marian F., PhD, Eugene Declercq, PhD, Howard Cabral, PhD, and Christine Morton, PhD. "Recent Increases in the U.S. Maternal Mortality Rate: Disentangling Trends From Measurement Issues." *Obstetrics & Gynecology* 128, no. 3 (September 2016): 447–455.

Martin, Nina. "A Larger Role for Midwives Could Improve Deficient U.S. Care for Mothers and Babies." *ProPublica*, February 22, 2018. https://www.propublica.org/article/midwives-study-maternal-neonatal-care.

McLean, Kelley, MD. "Obstetric Care in the U.S.: *Less* Appears to be *More*." Presentation by the medical director for the Certified Nurse-Midwifery Service and assistant professor of maternal fetal medicine. Burlington: University of Vermont Medical Center, 2016.

Park, Regina, Lori Tarrant, and Emily Watkins. Letters to the *Burlington Free Press*, September 2007.

Picard, Ken. "Fletcher Allen Downsizes Nurse-Midwife Program to Dismay of Supporters." *Seven Days* (Burlington, Vt.), September 19, 2007.

Ripley, Patrick. "Fletcher Allen Restores 24-Hour Midwife Service." *Seven Days* (Burlington, Vt.), December 26, 2007.

Rosenstein, Melissa G., MD, MAS, Malini Nijagal, MD, Sanae Nakagawa, MS, Steven E. Gregorich, PhD, and Miriam Kuppermann, PhD, MPH. "The Association of Expanded Access to a Collaborative Midwifery and Laborist Model With Cesarean Delivery Rates." *Obstetrics & Gynecology* 126, no. 4 (October 2015): 716–723.

University of Vermont Medical Center. "Lintilhac Grant Expands Midwifery Program." News release, Burlington, Vt., December 30, 2014.

Vedam, Saraswathi, Kathrin Stoll, Eugene DeClercq, Renee Cramer, Melissa Cheyney, Timothy Fisher, Emma Butt, Y. Tony Yang, and Holly Powell Kennedy. "Mapping Integration of Midwives Across the United States: Impact on Access, Equity, and Outcomes." *PLOS ONE* 13, no. 2 (February 21, 2018).

Chapter 4

Interviewed by Author

Anne Galloway, Jon Erickson, Jeff Kauffman, Bob Kinzel, Jane Lindholm, Crea Lintilhac, Sunny Nagpaul, M.J. Reale, Beth Robinson, Jay Rosen, Lisa Scagliotti and Richard Watts.

Publications

"Foundation Partnerships Meeting Local Information Needs." Recorded discussion at 2018 Knight Media Forum, Knight Foundation, February 2018.

Gaining Ground: How Nonprofit News Ventures Seek Sustainability. Knight Foundation, April 2015.

Mitchell, Amy, Jeffrey Gottfried, Michael Barthel, and Elisa Shearer. "The Modern News Consumer: New Attitudes and Practices in the Digital Era." *Pew Research Center.* July 7, 2016. https://www.pewresearch.org/journalism/2016/07/07/the-modern-news-consumer/.

Mitchell, Amy, Mark Jurkowitz, Jesse Holcomb, and Monica Anderson. "Nonprofit Journalism: A Growing but Fragile Part of the U.S. News System." *Pew Research Center.* June 10, 2013. https://www.pewresearch.org/journalism/2013/06/10/nonprofit-journalism/.

"Newspapers Fact Sheet." *Pew Research Center.* 2017.

Parks, Dan. "With $46 Million Raised, New Journalism Effort Seeks to Spark Revival of Local News." *The Chronicle of Philanthropy*, April 16, 2020.

Thompson, Derek. "The Print Apocalypse and How to Survive It." *The Atlantic*, November 3, 2016.

Thornton, John. "This Is the Future of Vermont Journalism." *VTDigger*, May 4, 2020.

Thys, Fred. "Newly Merged VPR and Vermont PBS Aim for New Audiences." *VTDigger*, July 8, 2021.

Vermont Freedom to Marry Task Force. Grant request to the Lintilhac Foundation, December 2006.

———. Letter to Crea Lintilhac, April 22, 2009.

———. Reports to the Lintilhac Foundation: March 2006, January 2008, January 2009.

Chapter 5

Interviewed by Author

Bob Beach, Art Cohn, Ashley Eaton, Erin Eggleston, Burch Fisher, Richard Furbush, Kathleen Kelleher, Elizabeth Lee, Kat Lewis, Crea Lintilhac, Pat Manley, Tom Manley, Ellen Marsden, Al McIntosh, Laura Pergolizzi, David Praasma, Angela Shambaugh, Kris Stepenuck, Jason Stockwell, Charlie Wanzer, Mary Watzin and Angus Warren.

Publications

Cohn, Art. "Zebra Mussels and Their Impact on Historic Shipwrecks." Prepared by the Lake Champlain Maritime Museum. Presented at the Lake Champlain Management Conference, Vermont, January 1996.

Eggleston, Erin. *Adventures in Molecular Microbial Ecology* (blog). Eggleston Lab, Middlebury College. 2018. https://sites.middlebury.edu/eggleston/blog/.

Hill, Ralph Nading. *Lake Champlain: Key to Liberty.* Taftsville: Countryman Press, 1976.

"Inside the New Nautical Archeology Center." *Lake Champlain Maritime Museum News*, 1995.

"Jeffords Joins Growing List of LEED Gold Buildings on Campus." News release, University of Vermont, February 14, 2012.

Kane, Adam I., A. Peter Barranco, Joanne M. DellaSalla, Sarah E. Lyman, and Christopher R. Sabick. *Lake Champlain Underwater Cultural Resources Survey, Volume VIII: 2003 Results and Volume IX: 2004 Results.* Lake Champlain Maritime Museum, February 2007.

Kane, Adam I., and Christopher Sabick. *Lake Champlain Underwater Cultural Resources Survey, Volume IV: 1999 Results and Volume V: 2000 Results.* Lake Champlain Maritime Museum, April 2002.

Kane, Adam I., Christopher R. Sabick, and Sara Brigadier. *Lake Champlain Underwater Cultural Resources Survey, Volume VI: 2001 Results and Volume VII: 2002 Results.* Lake Champlain Maritime Museum, December 2002.

Lake Champlain: An Illustrated History. Jay: Adirondack Life, 2009.

Lake Champlain Maritime Museum 2017 Impact Report. Vergennes: Lake Champlain Maritime Museum, 2017.

Lundeberg, Philip K., Arthur B. Cohn, and Jennifer L. Jones. *A Tale of Three Gunboats: Lake Champlain's Revolutionary War Heritage.* Vergennes: Lake Champlain Maritime Museum and Washington, D.C.: Smithsonian Institution National Museum of American History, 2017.

Manley, Thomas O., and Patricia L. Manley, eds. *Lake Champlain in Transition: From Research Toward Restoration.* Washington, D.C.: American Geophysical Union, 1999.

McLaughlin, Scott A., and Anne W. Lessmann. *Lake Champlain Underwater Cultural Resources Survey, Volume I: Lake Survey Background and 1996 Results.* Lake Champlain Maritime Museum, December 1998.

"Reborn Aiken Center an Energy Star; Serves as National Model for Green Renovations." News release, University of Vermont, January 13, 2012.

Sabick, Christopher R., Anne W. Lessmann, and Scott A. McLaughlin. *Lake Champlain Underwater Cultural Resources Survey, Volume II: 1997 Results and Volume III: 1998 Results.* Lake Champlain Maritime Museum, May 2000.

"Sen. Patrick Leahy and Middlebury College President Ronald D. Liebowitz Unveil a New Map of the Underwater Landscape of Lake Champlain." News release, Middlebury College, July 7, 2005.

State of the Lake and Ecosystems Indicators Report. Grand Isle, Vt.: Lake Champlain Steering Committee and Lake Champlain Basin Program staff, 2018.

Chapter 6

Interviewed by Author

Roger Allbee, Dana Bishop, Megan Camp, Jared Carpenter, Dave Chapman, Guy Choiniere, Mathieu Choiniere, Ross Conrad, David Deen, Laura DiPietro, Sam Dixon, Jen Duggan, James Ehlers, Jon Erickson, Kanika Gandhi, Chase Goodrich, David Grayck, Jon Groveman, Hisashi Kominami, Lauren Hierl, Chris Kilian, Steve Langevin, Crea Lintilhac, Will Lintilhac, James Maroney, Trey Martin, Don Meals, Elena Mihaly, Davey Miskell, Taylor Ricketts, Angela Shambaugh, Eric Smeltzer, Mary Watzin, Alec Webb, Eric Wolinsky and Michael Wironen.

Publications

Allbee, Roger. "Conventional Dairy Farmers Need a New Business Model." *VTDigger*, September 1, 2016.

Allbee, Roger, and Dan Smith, Esq. *Re-establishing a Viable Vermont Dairy Industry and Agricultural Economy: Call for BOLD State Action*. Report submitted to Governor Phil Scott, December 2019.

Allington, Adam. "EPA Proposes Continued Use of 'Bee-Killing' Insecticides." *Bloomberg Law Environment & Energy Report*. January 30, 2020. https://news.bloomberglaw.com/environment-and-energy/epa-proposes-continued-use-of-bee-killing-insecticides.

Barth, Brian. "CLF Calls for Cleanup of Industrial Farm Pollution: New Report Says Lack of Required Federal Permits Leaves Farmers, Waterways Vulnerable." News release, Conservation Law Foundation, June 30, 2008.

"*Bloom W*ins New England Emmy Award." News release, Bright Blue EcoMedia, May 17, 2011.

Bowden, William B. "Background Facts: Role of Phosphorus in Lake Champlain Pollution." The Lake Champlain Issue. *Vermont Journal of Environmental Law* 17, no 4 (Spring 2016): 501–515.

Chapman, Dave. "The Hydroponic Threat to Organic Food." *Independent Science News*, June 24, 2019.

Chapman, Matt, and Jen Duggan. "The Transition Towards the 2016 Lake Champlain TMDL: A Survey of Select Water Quality Litigation in Vermont from 2003–2015." The Lake Champlain Issue. *Vermont Journal of Environmental Law* 17, no. 4 (Spring 2016): 629–650.

Conrad, Ross. "Neonicotinoid Pesticides: A Major Problem For Bees." *Bee Culture*, six-part series, October 2017.

Conservation Law Foundation. "Clean Water in Crisis: CLF Pushes EPA to Control Devastating Nutrient Pollution." *Conservation Matters* (Autumn 2010).

Conservation Law Foundation. "CLF, PEER Call for Immediate Pause on Use of PFAS-Laden Pesticides." News release, May 17, 2021.

———. "Closing the Clean Water Gap: Protecting our Waterways by Making All Polluters Pay." White paper, February 2015.

———. "Interview with Crea Lintilhac." *Conservation Matters* (Spring 2010).

———. "Making A Splash in New England Water Management." *Conservation Matters* (Autumn 2006).

———. "Sprawl & Water Pollution: What You May Not Know About How Development Patterns Are Threatening Our Lakes and Rivers." *Conservation Matters* (Autumn 2004).

———. "Troubled Waters: CLF's Lake Champlain Lakekeeper Keeps a Close Watch on a Persistent Threat." *Conservation Matters* (Autumn 2007).

Craven, Jasper. "Is the USDA the Latest Site of Corporate Takeover in the Trump Administration?" *The Nation*, March 13, 2018.

Dillon, John. "'We Don't Want To Contaminate The Water': Tough Finances Add To Farmer's Pollution Problems." Vermont Public Radio, February 7, 2020.

———. "Who Regulates Vermont's Water? Records Show Confusion, Delayed Enforcement By Two Agencies." Vermont Public Radio, February 7, 2020.

Douglas, James H. *The Vermont Way: A Republican Governor Leads America's Most Liberal State*. New Haven, Vt.: Common Ground Communications, 2014.

Edgar, Chelsea. "Who Wants to Work on a Vermont Dairy Farm? A Reporter Spent a Week Finding Out." *Seven Days* (Burlington, Vt.), March 23, 2019.

Editorial Board. "Calamity for Our Most Beneficent Insect." *New York Times*, April 6, 2013.

———. "Risking Another Silent Spring." *New York Times*, June 30, 2014.

"EPA Grant: Investigating Blue Green Algae and Its Impact on Health & Well-being of People and Wildlife." *SAAWA*, newsletter of the St. Albans Area Watershed Association, March 2018.

"Good Health from the Soil Up. For the Choiniere Family, Switching to Organic Pastures Was a Lifesaver." *Organic Valley*. Organic Valley Cooperative. 2021. www.organicvalley.coop/our-farmers/11074/.

Goodman, Jasper. "Vermont Falls Short in EPA Plan for Lake Champlain Cleanup." *VTDigger*, July 14, 2020.

"Governor Scott Signs First-in-Nation Restrictions on Toxic PFAS Chemicals." *Vermont Business Magazine*, May 20, 2021.

Greenberg, Peter. *Don't Go There! The Travel Detective's Essential Guide to the Must-Miss Places of the World*. New York: Rodale, 2008.

Gribkoff, Elizabeth. "House Approves Long-Term Water Clean Water Funding Plan." *VTDigger*, May 22, 2019.

———. "How Healthy is Vermont's 'Crown Jewel'? Report on the State of Lake Champlain." *VTDigger*, June 15, 2018.

———. "Senate Scraps Clean Water 'Cloud Tax,' Looks to Increase Rooms and Meals Tax." *VTDigger*, May 16, 2019.

———. "Senate's Skepticism Over Clean Water Bill Gives Way to Unanimous Approval." *VTDigger*, April 2, 2019.

———. "Treasurer Warns Lawmakers Against Punting on Clean Water Funding." *VTDigger*, May 15, 2019.

Gribkoff, Elizabeth, and Xander Landen. "Halfway through Session, Clean Water Funding Source still Elusive." *VTDigger*, March 19, 2019.

Groveman, Jon. "LaPlatte River Natural Area Deserves Protection." *VTDigger*, August 10, 2017.

Guadagno, Victor, producer and director. *Bloom: The Plight of Lake Champlain*. Bright Blue EcoMedia, 2010.

Hallenbeck, Terri. "Vermont Panel Recommends No New Fees for Water Cleanup." *Seven Days* (Burlington, Vt.), October 19, 2017.

Hauser, Christine. "Beekeepers Confront the E.P.A. Over Pesticides." *New York Times*, September 12, 2019.

Hoffer, Douglas R., Vermont State Auditor, and Fran Hodgins, Principal Investigator. *Examining Vermont State Spending on the Dairy Industry from 2010 to 2019: A Report from the Vermont State Auditor's Office*. May 10, 2021.

Kilgannon, Corey. "When the Death of a Family Farm Leads to Suicide." *New York Times*, March 19, 2018.

Kominami, Hisashi, and Sarah Taylor Lovell. "An Adaptive Management Approach to Improve Water Quality at a Model Dairy Farm in Vermont, USA." *Ecological Engineering* 40 (March 2012): 131–143.

Johnson, Mark, and Anne Galloway. "Vermont Legislative Leaders Want Lake Champlain Cleanup Plan." *VTDigger*, December 15, 2017.

Landen, Xander. "House Approves Clean Water Funding Plan with $6 Million 'Cloud Software' Tax." *VTDigger*, May 9, 2019.

———. "House Budget Aims $650 Million in Federal Funds at Broadband, IT Upgrades, Clean Water." *VTDigger*, March 22, 2021.

———. "Senate Decides Against Raising New Revenue for Clean Water Fund." *VTDigger*, May 20, 2019.

Lazor, Jack. "Changing Paradigms in Food and Farming." *VTDigger*, January 14, 2018.

———. "A New Direction for Vermont Agriculture." *VTDigger*, September 14, 2016.

Lemelin, Annie. "Beelieve It! Maryland and Connecticut Pass Landmark Legislation to Protect Pollinators." Conservation Law Foundation. June 24, 2016. www.clf.org/

blog/beelieve-maryland-connecticut-pass-landmark-legislation-protect-pollinators/.

Lewis, Iris. "EPA Endorses Vermont's New Clean Water Funding Law." *VTDigger,* July 21, 2019.

Mandel, Kyla. "The Climate Crisis Is Threatening Bees. Here's What's Helping to Save Them." *Huffington Post,* February 12, 2020.

Manley, Thomas, Patricia Manley, and Timothy Muhuc, eds. *Lake Champlain: Partnerships and Research in the New Millenium.* New York: Kluwer Academic/Plenum Publishers, 2004.

Maroney, James. "Vermont Dairy Needs Complete Overhaul." *VTDigger,* February 6, 2020.

Martin, Trey. "The Vermont Clean Water Act: Water Quality Protection, Land Use, and the Legacy of Tropical Storm Irene." The Lake Champlain Issue. *Vermont Journal of Environmental Law* 17, no. 4 (Spring 2016): 688–709.

McCallum, Kevin. "After House Approval, Clean Water Funding Plan Heads to Scott's Desk." *Seven Days* (Burlington, Vt.), May 22, 2019.

McAvoy, Seamus. "Toxic 'forever chemicals' may be contaminating pesticides." *VTDigger,* May 26, 2021.

Mears, David. "Birds Need Clean Water, Not Politics." *VTDigger,* April 3, 2019.

Mears, David, and Trey Martin. Introduction to the "Lake Champlain Issue." *Vermont Journal of Environmental Law* 17, no. 4 (Spring 2016).

Meyn, Colin. "Clean Water Plan Increases Fiscal Risk, but Still Gets Treasurer's OK." *VTDigger,* May 21, 2019.

Moore, Julie. "Stormwater Runoff from Developed Lands." The Lake Champlain Issue. *Vermont Journal of Environmental Law* 17, no. 4 (Spring 2016): 766–784.

———. "Vermont Is not Wavering on Clean Water." *VTDigger,* October 5, 2017.

Morse, Kathryn, and Diane Munroe. "Phosphorus Loading in Lake Champlain: A Geographic, Environmental, Civic and Economic Investigation into Its Causes, Effects, and Prospects for the Future." Middlebury: A presentation for the Middlebury College Environmental Studies Senior Seminar, Spring 2011.

National Agricultural Statistics Service. "2020 State Agriculture Overview: Vermont." U.S. Department of Agriculture. Last updated August 23, 2021. https://www.nass.usda.gov/Quick_Stats/Ag_Overview/stateOverview.php?state=VERMONT.

Page, Candace. "Lake Champlain Movie to Debut." *Burlington Free Press,* November 29, 2010.

Parsons, Bob, PhD. "Vermont's Dairy Sector: Is There a Sustainable Future for the 800 lb. Gorilla?" Food System Research Collaborative at the University of Vermont Center for Rural Studies. *Opportunities for Agriculture Working Paper Series* 1, no. 4 (2010).

Pearson, Christopher. "Farmers, Money, Cows and Water Quality." *VTDigger*, December 25, 2017.

Polhamus, Mike. "Lake Champlain Beaches Close." *VTDigger*, September 26, 2017.

"Re: Vermont's Phase 1 Implementation of the 2016 Lake Champlain TMDL." Letter by Dennis Deziel, regional administrator, U.S. Environmental Protection Agency, to Peter Walke, commissioner of the Vermont Department of Environmental Conservation, June 25, 2020.

Report and Recommendations of the Vermont Milk Commission. Montpelier: Vermont Agency of Agriculture, Food & Markets, January 2019.

Report on Agricultural Clean Water Investment. Montpelier: Water Quality Division, Vermont Agency of Agriculture, Food & Markets, March 26, 2018.

Scagliotti, Lisa. "Shelburne Ends Legal Fight over Salt Storage Sheds." *Shelburne (Vt.) News*, April 1, 2019.

Shambaugh, Angela. "Cyanobacteria and Human Health Concerns on Lake Champlain." The Lake Champlain Issue. *Vermont Journal of Environmental Law* 17, no. 4 (Spring 2016): 516–532.

Slayton, Tom. "Choiniere Farm: Generations on the Land." *News & Stories*. Vermont Land Trust. Last updated 2021. vlt.org/land-management/choiniere-farm.

State of the Lake and Ecosystems Indicators Report. Grand Isle, Vt.: Lake Champlain Steering Committee and Lake Champlain Basin Program staff, 2018.

Stein, Andrew. "Film Draws Attention to Lake Pollution Problem." *Addison Independent* (Middlebury, Vt.), May 16, 2011.

Strom, Stephanie. "What's Organic? A Debate Over Dirt May Boil Down to Turf." *New York Times*, November 15, 2016.

Tharp, Rebecca and Dana Allen. "Assessment of Deicing Salt Storage and Distribution as a Salinization Point Source: The Influence of Permitting Standards on Water Quality." *Environmental Systems Research* 9, no. 21 (September 2020).

A 2018 Exploration of the Future of Vermont Agriculture: Ideas to Seed a Conversation and a Call to Action. University of Vermont Extension Service and Vermont Housing & Conservation Board, October 2018.

"VCV and Vermont Natural Resources Council (VNRC) Celebrate Historic Investments in Climate Action and Clean Water." News release, Vermont Conservation Voters and VNRC, May 21, 2021.

Vermont Agriculture and Food Systems Plan: 2020. Montpelier: Vermont Agency of Agriculture, Food & Markets, January 2020.

Vermont Dairy Marketing Assessment: Final Report. Vermont: Karen Karp & Partners, 2019.

Vermont Dairy and Water Collaborative. *A Call to Action*. Vermont: VDWC, March 15, 2019.

Walsh, Molly. "Lake Carmi Pollution Triggers Call for Stricter Regulation of Dairy Farms." *Seven Days* (Burlington, Vt.), November 8, 2017.

———. "Plans for a Railroad's Freight Facility Outrage Shelburne." *Seven Days* (Burlington, Vt.), February 3, 2016.

Walters, John. "State Panel Provides Few Answers for Water Cleanup." *Seven Days* (Burlington, Vt.), November 15, 2017.

———. "Water Wariness: Concerns Rise Over Scott's Commitment to Cleanup." *Seven Days* (Burlington, Vt.), October 4, 2017.

"What Does USDA Organic Mean Today?" Why We Exist/About. *Real Organic Project*. Accessed February 2020. https://www.realorganicproject.org/.

Wironen, Michael B. "Governing Environmental and Economic Flows in Regional Food Systems." Thesis, Rubenstein School of Environment and Natural Resources, University of Vermont, May 2018.

———. Thesis presentation. Rubenstein School of Environment and Natural Resources, University of Vermont, March 2019.

Wironen, Michael B., Elena M. Bennett, and Jon D. Erickson. "Phosphorus Flows and Legacy Accumulation in an Animal-Dominated Agricultural Region from 1925 to 2012." *Global Environmental Change* 50 (May 2018): 88–99.

Zimmer, Carl. "2 Studies Point to Common Pesticide as a Culprit in Declining Bee Colonies." *New York Times*, March 29, 2012.

Chapter 7

Interviewed by Author

Hope Alswang, Marcy Christian, Pierre Couture, Allison Harig, Peter Kopsco, Louise Lintilhac, Phil Lintilhac, Anne Lusk, Shelly Lutz, Angus McCusker, Kim Quinlan, Carl Rogers, Glenn Seward, Kristen Sharpless, R.J. Thompson, Kate Wanner and Matthew Williams.

Publications

Averill, Graham. "Rock Steady: Tapping Millstone Trails' Secret Ingredient." *Bike Magazine*, November 2016.

Brown, Joshua. "A Milestone for Millstone." *Land & People*, the magazine of The Trust for Public Land, Spring/Summer 2012.

"Brownsville-Story Ridge Forest." *Stowe Land Trust*. Last updated 2021. https://www.stowelandtrust.org/conserved/properties/brownsville/.

"Catamount Community Forest." *The Trust for Public Land*. 2018. https://www.tpl.org/our-work/catamount-community-forest.

Hauser, Christine. "Algae Can Poison Your Dog." *New York Times*, August 12, 2019.

"Huntington Community Forest." A publication of The Trust for Public Land, Montpelier, Vt.

Lintilhac Foundation. *Partnerships at Work: Supporting Multi-Use Outdoor Recreation for Vermont Communities*. Vermont: 2018.

Mingle, Jonathan. "Take Your Marks." *Land & People*, the magazine of The Trust for Public Land, Fall/Winter 2019.

Newbeck, Phyl. "Millstone Trails: A Gem Hidden in Plain Sight." *Best of Central Vermont Magazine*, Summer 2018.

"News: 750-Acre Brownsville Tract in Stowe Becomes State Forest." *Stowe Land Trust.* August 7, 2019. https://www.stowelandtrust.org/news/post/news-750-acre-brownsville-tract-in-stowe-becomes-state-forest.

Pogge, Drew. "The Second Coming of Millstone Hill." *Vermont Magazine*, September/October 2009.

"Rockfire: The Elemental Experience." *RockFire*. Last updated 2021. http://www.rockfirevt.com/.

"Stowe Recreation Path." *Stowe Parks & Recreation.* Town of Stowe, Vt. 2021. https://www.stowerec.org/parks-facilities/rec-paths/stowe-recreation-path/.

Vermont Fish & Wildlife Department. *Birdseye Wildlife Management Area*. Accessed October 2019. https://vtfishandwildlife.com/sites/fishandwildlife/files/documents/Where%20to%20Hunt/Rutland%20District/Birdseye%20WMA.pdf.

Vermont's Return on Investment in Land Conservation. The Trust for Public Land, September 2018.

Chapter 8

Interviewed by Author

Paul Burns, Arnie Gundersen, Maggie Gundersen, Deb Katz, Tony Klein, Crea Lintilhac, James Moore, Tim Newcomb, Duane Peterson, Cort Richardson, Bob Stannard, Ben Walsh and Richard Watts.

Publications

"About Us: Mission and History." *Citizens Awareness Network*. Accessed March 2020. http://www.nukebusters.org/about.shtml.

Bidgood, Jess. "Vermont Yankee Nuclear Plant Begins Slow Process of Closing." *New York Times*, January 4, 2015.

Broncaccio, Diane. "Yankee Rowe Closing Took 15 Years, $608M" *Greenfield (M.A.) Recorder*, September 1, 2013.

Conservation Law Foundation. "Vermont Yankee: The Costs of Nuclear." *Conservation Matters*

(Summer 2009).

———. "Vermont Yankee Redux." *Conservation Matters* (Spring 2002).

Cronin, Brian P.J. "People Power: What Role Should Residents Play in Decommissioning Nuclear Plants?" *The Highlands Current*, August 6, 2017.

de Seife, Ethan, Alicia Freese, and Ken Picard. "Gone Fission: Assessing a Future Without Vermont Yankee." *Seven Days* (Burlington, Vt.), December 10, 2014.

Edsell, Liz. "News and Updates: Retire Vermont Yankee: March, Rally, Trainings & Hearings." *VPIRG*. Vermont Public Interest Research Group. November 12, 2012. https://www.vpirg.org/news/vermont-yankee-march-rally-training-hearings/.

"Entergy Completes Sale of Vermont Yankee to NorthStar." News release, Entergy Corporation, January 11, 2019.

Faher, Mike. "NRC Says Vermont Yankee Cask Maker Violated Safety Regulations." *VTDigger*, April 28, 2019.

———. "Regulators Ramp Up Oversight as Vermont Yankee Dismantling Begins." *VTDigger*, May 9, 2019.

Fretwell, Sammy. "Barnwell Leaks Worse than Feared." *The State* (Columbia, S.C.), August 19, 2007.

———. "Why Did Nuclear Waste Leak at SC Dump? Supreme Court Rebukes Landfill Operator, DHEC." *The State* (Columbia, S.C.), March 27, 2019.

Gilbert, Steve. "Closed Yankee Rowe Nuclear Plant Fades into History." *Keene (N.H.) Sentinel*, August 30, 2013.

Gram, David. "Nuclear Waste: Meltdown of Vermont Harmony." Associated Press, May 24, 1987.

Gribkoff, Elizabeth. "Vermont Yankee Cooling Towers Coming Down, Marking 'End of an Era.'" *VTDigger*, July 11, 2019.

Gundersen, Arnold, Peter Bradford, and C. Frederick Sears. *Report of the Public Oversight Panel Regarding the Comprehensive Reliability Assessment of the Vermont Yankee Nuclear Power Plant*. Report to the Vermont General Assembly, March 17, 2009.

Halley, Colleen. "Radioactive Leak Found in Well Water at VT Yankee." Statement by Vermont Public Interest Research Group, January 7, 2010.

———. "Senate Votes to Retire VT Yankee." Statement by Vermont Public Interest Research Group, February 23, 2010.

"Lightning Strikes Nuclear Plant's Transformer." United Press International, June 16, 1991.

Lintilhac, Crea. "Insurmountable Problems of Storing Nuclear Waste." *Burlington Free Press*, March 1, 2005.

———."Is Vermont Yankee's Review Process Adequate?" *Burlington Free Press*, February 4, 2006.

———. "Transparency Is Needed in Yankee Debate." *Burlington Free Press*, March 22, 2009.

———. "Waste Storage Is Dark Cloud Over Nuclear Power Industry." *Burlington Free Press*, July 20, 2009.

Lintilhac, Philip. "Nuclear Not the Best Solution." *Burlington Free Press*, 2010.

Lovins, Amory, Steve Berry, and Peter Bradford. *Nuclear Power and Climate Change*. 2007 web exchange originally posted on the Bulletin of the Atomic Scientists website. Rocky Mountain Institute. 2007. https://library.uniteddiversity.coop/Climate_Change/Nuclear_Power_and_Climate_Change.pdf.

O'Connor, Kevin. "Vermont Yankee Sale to NorthStar Generates New Questions." *VTDigger*, February 1, 2019.

Picard, Kevin. "The Insiders: Nuclear Industry Experts Arnie and Maggie Gundersen Predicted the Problems at Vermont Yankee." *Seven Days* (Burlington, Vt.), February 17, 2010.

Ruyter, Elena. "U.S. Citizens Campaign to Close Nuclear Power Plant in Rowe, Massachusetts, 1991." *Global Nonviolent Action Database*. Swarthmore College. September 17, 2011. nvdatabase.swarthmore.edu.

Sidebotham, Sylvia, and Diana Sidebotham. *A Brief History: Twenty-Five Years with the New England Coalition on Nuclear Pollution*. The New England Coalition, 1995.

Tomanelli, Zach. "VPIRG Opposes Permit Extension for Vermont Yankee: Calls for Increased State Role in Decommissioning Process." *VPIRG: News and Updates*. Vermont Public Interest Research Group. October 5, 2013. https://www.vpirg.org/news/vpirg-opposes-permit-extension-for-vermont-yankee-calls-for-increased-state-role-in-decommissioning-process/.

Vermont Yankee Nuclear Power Commission. Letter and report to U.S. Nuclear Regulatory Commission on impacts of lightning strike at Vermont Yankee nuclear power plant, July 11, 1991.

"Vermont Yankee Owner Cites Cause of Fire." Associated Press, July 4, 2004.

Vermont Yankee's Decommissioning as an Example of Nationwide Failures of Decommissioning Regulation. Comments submitted by Fairewinds Energy Education Corp. to the Nuclear Regulatory Commission, March 23, 2015.

"VPIRG Wants Plan for Closing Yankee." *Brattleboro Reformer*, March 5, 1979.

Wald, Matthew. "Appeals Court Blocks Attempt by Vermont to Close a Nuclear Plant." *New York Times*, August 14, 2013.

———. "Doubts Raised on License Renewal for Oldest Nuclear Plant in Nation." *New York Times*, July 9, 1991.

————. "A Gamble for Vermont Yankee." *New York Times*, July 19, 2011.

————. "A Judge Rules Vermont Can't Shut Nuclear Plant." *New York Times*, January 19, 2012.

————. "Radiation Levels Cloud Vermont Reactor's Fate." *New York Times*, January 27, 2010.

————. "Vermont Nuclear Reactor Is Purchased by Entergy." *New York Times*, August 6, 2001.

————. "Vermont Senate Votes to Close Nuclear Plant." *New York Times*, February 10, 2010.

————. "Vermont Yankee Plant to Close Next Year as the Nuclear Industry Retrenches." *New York Times*, August 27, 2013.

————. "Vermont Yankee Reactor Restarts." *New York Times*, November 11, 2010.

Walsh, Ben. "VPIRG Statement on the Closing of Vermont Yankee." *VPIRG: News and Updates*. Vermont Public Interest Research Group. December 29, 2014. https://www.vpirg.org/news/vpirg-statement-on-the-closing-of-vermont-yankee/.

Watts, Richard A. *Public Meltdown: The Story of the Vermont Yankee Nuclear Power Plant*. Amherst: White River Press, 2012.

Watts, Richard, Katie Gallagher, and Ben Johnson. "History Space: 30 Years of VPIRG Canvassing." *Burlington Free Press*, July 30, 2018.

Weiss-Tisman, Howard. "Decommissioning Test: NorthStar Uses Vermont Yankee as Launch Pad for Other Power Plant Jobs." Vermont Public Radio News, October 26, 2019.

"What Is Decommissioning?" *Fairewinds Energy Education*. Last updated 2021. www.fairewinds.org/decommissioning-and-rubbilization.

Chapter 9

Interviewed by Author

David Blittersdorf, Paul Burns, Andrea Colnes, James Dumont, Jared Duval, Kevin Ellis, Lauren Hierl, Tony Klein, Johanna Miller, James Moore, Jane Palmer, Nate Palmer, Duane Peterson, Scudder Parker, Mary Powell, Beth Sachs, Leigh Seddon, Rachel Smolker and Ben Walsh.

Publications

Act 62: Preliminary Report on All-Fuels Energy Efficiency. Report by the Vermont Public Utility Commission to the House Committee on Energy and Technology and the Senate Committee on Natural Resources and Energy, January 15, 2020.

Annual Benefit Report 2018: The Change We Seek. Vermont: SunCommon, 2018.

"Atmospheric CO2 at Mauna Loa Observatory, Atmospheric Baseline Observation Station on Hawaii Island, 1959–2019." *Global Monitoring Laboratory*. Earth System Research Laboratories, National Oceanic & Atmospheric Administration. Accessed July 2020. https://gml.noaa.gov/ccgg/trends/.

Brown, Alex. "Electric Cars Will Challenge State Power Grids." *Washington Post*, January 27, 2020.

Chang, Susan Arterian. "The Rise of the Energy Efficiency Utility: Vermont's Efforts to Curb Electricity Demand Are Working, and Delaware Is Starting the Most Ambitious Plan Yet." *IEEE Spectrum*, May 1, 2008.

"Clean Energy and Climate Action." *VNRC*. Vermont Natural Resources Council. Last update 2021. vnrc.org/climate-action/.

Clean Heat: Comfortable Homes, Affordable Future – A Vision for Vermont's Heating Future. Montpelier: Vermont Public Interest Research and Education Fund, Spring 2011.

"Climate & Transportation Advocates React to State's MOU for Transportation & Climate Initiative (TCI)." Vermont Natural Resources Council, et al., December 17, 2019.

Cohen, Armond. *Power to Spare: A Plan for Increasing New England's Competitiveness Through Energy Efficiency.* New England Energy Policy Council, July 1987.

Comprehensive Energy Plan 2011. Vol. 1: Vermont's Energy Future. Montpelier: Department of Public Service, with other state agencies, 2011.

Comprehensive Energy Plan 2016. Montpelier: Department of Public Service, with other state agencies, 2016.

Conservation Law Foundation. "Going Low-Carb: Transforming New England's Energy System." *Conservation Matters* (Fall 2016).

———. "In Memoriam: Scott Skinner." *Conservation Matters* (Fall 2019).

Copans, Jon. "Modelling a Local and Vibrant Climate Economy." *VTDigger*, March 6, 2017.

Courtney, Elizabeth, and Eric Zencey. *Greening Vermont: The Search for a Sustainable State.* North Pomfret: Thistle Hill Publications, 2012.

Davenport, Coral. "Biden, in a Push to Phase Out Gas Cars, Tightens Pollution Rules." *New York Times*, August 5, 2021."

———. Biden Pledges Ambitious Climate Action. Here's What He Could Actually Do." *New York Times*, October 25, 2020.

Dennis, Brady, and Juliet Eilperin. "In Confronting Climate Change, Biden Won't Have a Day to Waste." *Washington Post*, December 22, 2020.

Dickinson, Tim. "Trump's War on Solar." *Rolling Stone*, April 3, 2020.

Dobbs, Taylor. "Protestors Stage 'Knit-in' at Vermont Gas Offices." Vermont Public Radio, July 2, 2014.

Doing Our Part: 2020 Plan for Climate Action in Vermont. Audubon Vermont and 29 other nonprofit organizations, January 2020.

Dostis, Robert. *Energy Transformation — The Story*. Green Mountain Power, January 19, 2017.

Edsell, Liz. "Heating Report Lays Out Job Creation, Energy Savings, and Environmental Benefits for Vermonters." News release, VPIRG, January 15, 2013.

Eilperin, Juliet, and Brady Dennis. "As Biden Vows Monumental Action on Climate Change, a Fight with the Fossil Fuel Industry Has Only Begun." *Washington Post*, January 27, 2021.

"Energy Action Network: Finding the Path to Renewable Energy in Vermont." *Rockefeller Foundation*. 2014. https://engage.rockefellerfoundation.org/story-sketch/energy-action-network-of-vermont/.

Fischer, Ethan. "Quick Facts on Vermont Solar Energy." *SunCommon*. December 4, 2015. https://suncommon.com/vermont-solar-energy-policy/.

Gillis, Justin. "Short Answers to Hard Questions About Climate Change." *New York Times*, July 6, 2017.

"Green Mountain Power Outlines Energy Future for Customers." News release, Green Mountain Power, July 28, 2008.

Gribkoff, Elizabeth. "Regulators Approve Groundbreaking Home Energy Storage Programs." *VTDigger*, June 2, 2020.

Gribkoff, Elizabeth, and Anne Wallace Allen. "In Net Metering Talks, State Ideals Clash with Ratepayer Realities." *VTDigger*, November 13, 2019.

Gund Institute for Ecological Economics. *Vermont Climate Assessment: Considering Vermont's Future in a Changing Climate*. Burlington: University of Vermont, 2014.

Hamilton, Blair, John Plunkett, and Michael Wickenden. *Gauging Success of the Nation's First Efficiency Utility: Efficiency Vermont's First Two Years*. Panel 5, Utility Issues. European Council for an Energy Efficient Economy, 2003.

Heintz, Paul. "SunCommon Conflict? How VPIRG's Solar Spinoff Company Went from Org to Inc." *Seven Days* (Burlington, Vt.), March 14, 2012.

Independent Audit of the Reported Energy and Capacity Savings and Cost-Effectiveness of Vermont Energy Efficiency Utility Programs. Report to the Vermont Legislature by the Public Utility Commission, December 5, 2019.

Kania, John, and Mark Kramer. "Collective Impact." *Stanford Social Innovation Review* (Winter 2011).

Kaufman, Alexander. "Tesla's New Home Battery Could Be the iPad of Energy Storage." *Huffington Post*, May 1, 2015.

Kwoka, Bethany. "Why (and How) We Must Update Our Electricity Grid." *Conservation Law Foundation* (blog). January 27, 2020. https://www.clf.org/blog/update-our-electricity-grid-to-get-off-gas/.

Lenihan, Justin. *Home Energy Reports: Bringing Low-Cost Savings to More Vermonters.* Efficiency Vermont, July 22, 2015.

Lintilhac, Crea. "Using Efficiency Vermont's Potential." *Burlington Free Press*, 2007.

Margolis, Jon. "Relax, Everybody — There Will Be No Carbon Tax in Vermont." *VTDigger*, February 10, 2019.

McCallum, Kevin. "Vermont House Approves a Key Climate Bill." *Seven Days* (Burlington, Vt.), February 20, 2020.

McKibben, Bill. *The End of Nature.* New York: Random House, 2006.

———. *Falter: Has the Human Game Begun to Play Itself Out?* New York: Henry Holt, 2020.

———. Interview by Steve Curwood. "Step It Up 2007." *Living on Earth, Public Radio's Environmental News Magazine*, March 2, 2007.

———. "Power to the People: Why the Rise of Green Energy Makes Utilities Nervous." *The New Yorker*, June 22, 2015.

Moore, James. *A Decade of Change: A Vision for Vermont's Renewable Future.* Montpelier: Vermont Public Interest Research and Education Fund, Summer 2006.

———. *Repowering Vermont: Replacing Vermont Yankee for a Clean Energy Future.* Montpelier: Vermont Public Interest Research and Education Fund, Summer 2009.

Nadworny, Rich. "Disrupting the Business of Energy Delivery." *Huffington Post*, December 6, 2017.

Neme, Chris. *Comparative Analysis of Fuel-Switching from Oil or Propane to Gas or Advanced Electric Heat Pumps in Vermont Homes.* Hinesburg: Energy Futures Group, conducted for Vermont Public Interest Research Group and Kristin Lyons, May 6, 2015.

Norton, Kit. "Scott Vetoes Global Warming Solutions Act." *VTDigger*, September 15, 2020.

Panebaker, Alan. "VPIRG Spins Off Solar Company." *VTDigger*, March 8, 2012.

Parker, Scudder, and Jim Lazar. *The Old Order Changeth: Rewarding Utilities for Performance, Not Capital Investment.* American Council for an Energy-Efficient Economy, Summer Study on Energy Efficiency in Buildings, September 1, 2016.

Penn, Ivan. "The Next Energy Battle: Renewables vs. Natural Gas." *New York Times*, July 6, 2020.

———. "Oil Companies Are Collapsing, but Wind and Solar Energy Keep Growing." *New York Times*, April 7, 2020.

Plumer, Brad. "In a First, Renewable Energy Is Poised to Eclipse Coal in U.S." *New York Times*, May 13, 2020.

Plumer, Brad, and Henry Fountain. "A Hotter Future Is Certain, Climate Panel Warns.

But How Hot Is Up to Us." *New York Times*, August 9, 2021.

Power, Maeve. "Climate & Energy: Legislature Overrides Veto; Enacts Global Warming Solutions Act!" *VPIRG*. Vermont Public Interest Research Group. September 22, 2020. https://www.vpirg.org/news/veto-of-global-warming-solutions-act-overridden-in-house-and-senate-to-become-law/.

Reed, Stanley. "Europe's Big Oil Companies Are Turning Electric." *New York Times*, August 17, 2020.

———. "With Much of the World's Economy Slowed Down, Green Energy Powers On." *New York Times*, October 26, 2020.

"Renewable Energy Standard." *State of Vermont Public Utility Commission*. Last update 2021. puc.vermont.gov/electric/renewable-energy-standard.

"The Role of the Global Warming Solutions Act in a Resilient Recovery." *VNRC: News & Stories*. Vermont Natural Resources Council. May 19, 2020. https://vnrc.org/the-role-of-the-global-warming-solutions-act-in-a-resilient-recovery/.

Saylor, Lauren. "Vermont Senate Considering the Global Warming Solutions Act." News release, Audubon Vermont, June 22, 2020.

Schlickeisen, Derek. "Step It Up Campaign Leads National Demonstration." *Middlebury Campus*, April 18, 2007.

Sears, Justine. *Geographic Patterns in Vermonters' Thermal, Electric, and Transportation Energy Use*. Report by Transportation Efficiency Group and Vermont Energy Investment Corporation, for Efficiency Vermont, July 2016.

Shupe, Brian. "The Two Pillars of Resilience." *Vermont Environmental Report*. Vermont Natural Resources Council, Winter/Spring 2020.

Silverman, Adam. "Vermont Ranks No. 2 in U.S. for Renewable Energy." *Burlington Free Press*, April 30, 2017.

Solar Spotlight – Vermont. Solar Energy Industries Association, December 11, 2019.

Springer, Darren, and Rebecca Towne. "Renewable Energy Standard Is Driving Emissions Reductions." *VTDigger*, December 26, 2019.

Stachowiak, Sarah, and Lauren Gase. "Does Collective Impact Really Make an Impact?" *Stanford Social Innovation Review* (August 9, 2018).

Stephens, Jennie C., Matthew J. Burke, Brock Gibian, Elie Jordi, and Richard Watts. "Operationalizing Energy Democracy: Challenges and Opportunities in Vermont's Renewable Energy Transformation." *Frontiers in Communication* (October 3, 2018).

Tabuchi, Hiroko. "Fracking Firms Fail, Rewarding Executives and Raising Climate Fears." *New York Times*, July 12, 2020.

Tener, Beth. "Collaborating from the Place of Common Ground: Case Study of the Energy Action Network of Vermont." *New Directions Collaborative.* January 8, 2014. https://www.ndcollaborative.com/collaborating-from-the-place-of-common-ground/.

Threlkeld, Kathryn, and Steven Pappas. "Net-Metering Takes Its Toll on Vermont." *Rutland (Vt.) Herald,* March 3, 2018.

"2018 Annual Progress Report." *Energy Action Network.* Last updated 2019. https://www.eanvt.org/2018-progress-report/.

"2019 Annual Progress Report." *Energy Action Network.* 2019. https://www.eanvt.org/tracking-progress/annual-progress-report/2019-progress-report/.

2020 Annual Energy Report: A Summary of Progress Made Toward the Goals of Vermont's Comprehensive Energy Plan. Montpelier: Vermont Department of Public Service, January 15, 2020.

"U.S. Clean Energy Investment Hits New Record Despite Trump Administration Views." Reuters, January 16, 2020.

"Vermont Legislators Take Up Landmark Climate Bill." *VNRC: News & Stories.* Vermont Natural Resources Council. January 10, 2020. https://vnrc.org/vermont-legislators-take-up-landmark-climate-bill/.

Vermont Public Interest Research & Education Fund. *2016 Grant Report to the Lintilhac Foundation.* Montpelier: VPIREF, 2016.

———. *2019 VPIREF Climate & Clean Energy: Energy Independent Vermont Report to the Lintilhac Foundation.* Montpelier: VPIREF, 2019.

"Vermont State Energy Profile." *U.S. Energy Information Administration.* 2020. www.eia.gov.

———. *Vermont's Standard Offer: Providing Clean Energy and Rebuilding Vermont's Economy.* Montpelier: VPIREF, 2012.

Chapter 10

Interviewed by Author

Nancy Brink, Louise Lintilhac, Paul Lintilhac and Will Lintilhac.

Acknowledgements

————— ⭒ —————

The Sources section lists all the people we interviewed for this book, and we thank each and every one of them for their time, their expertise, and their helpfulness in answering questions and providing information.

We are especially grateful to the staff members and leaders, present and past, who told us their stories and shared their experiences at the Certified Nurse-Midwifery Service of the University of Vermont (UVM) Medical Center; at *VTDigger* and Vermont Public Radio; at the Lake Champlain Maritime Museum and UVM's Rubenstein School of Natural Resources and Rubenstein Ecosystem Science Laboratory; and at the Conservation Law Foundation, Trust for Public Lands, Vermont Public Interest Research Group, Vermont Natural Resources Council, Fairewinds Energy Education, and Citizens Awareness Network.

For their contributions to the making of *Catalysts for Change*, we thank Kim Quinlan at KO Designs, who created the interior page layout; Terri Parent at Stride Creative Group, who provided creative and art direction; and Mason Singer at Laughing Bear Associates, who designed the front and back covers. We're grateful also to Caleb Kenna for his photography, and to everyone else who kindly supplied photographs for the book. And we couldn't have done this without all the help generously provided by Nancy Brink, the Lintilhac Foundation's longtime single-person staff.

I would like to thank the Lintilhac Foundation for making this book possible, and Crea, Phil, Louise, Will and Paul Lintilhac for their generosity, kindness, and support all along the way.

Doug Wilhelm

We are particularly grateful to Doug Wilhelm, a writer and editor in Weybridge, Vermont who brought these stories to life from his interviews of many nonprofit leaders. They and their staff are the the ones who execute and develop strategies that accelerate positive social and environmental change. The stories and examples of their organization's work are the stories we wanted to tell. It is because of their efforts and encouragement — and I might add, their ability to guide, advise, challenge and push us — that the Lintilhac Foundation has a legacy to pass on and a relationship for effective philanthropy.

Crea Lintilhac